C0-ATN-607

EXCHANGE IN THE SOCIAL STRUCTURE OF THE OROKAIVA

EXCHANGE
IN THE
SOCIAL
STRUCTURE
OF THE
OROKAIVA

Traditional and Emergent Ideologies
in the Northern District of Papua

by

ERIK SCHWIMMER

ST. MARTIN'S PRESS · NEW YORK

73015

0748338

Copyright © 1973 by Erik Schwimmer
All rights reserved. For information, write:
St. Martin's Press, Inc., 175 Fifth Avenue, New York, N.Y. 10010
Printed in Great Britain
Library of Congress Catalog Card Number: 73—87566
First published in the United States of America in 1973

AFFILIATED PUBLISHERS: Macmillan Limited, London
— also at Bombay, Calcutta, Madras and Melbourne

CONTENTS

0748338

TABLES

MAPS AND FIGURES

ACKNOWLEDGEMENTS

This research was made possible through my appointment as an assistant to the Department of Anthropology at the University of Oregon. I was commissioned to write a report for a project directed by Professor H. G. Barnett, entitled 'A Comparative Study of Culture Change and Stability in Displaced Communities in the Pacific'. This commission enabled my wife and myself to visit the Northern District of Papua for one year. I also received help from the Canada Council and the Killam Foundation.

I should acknowledge here the contribution made to this research by my wife, Mrs. Ziska Schwimmer, who not only bore with it but made many valuable observations which have been incorporated in this work. Among others who were helpful, kind, encouraging and inspiring in the field I should mention: Dr. R. Crocombe, executive officer of the New Guinea Research Unit of the A.N.U.; Miss Nancy White, a missionary and collector of valuable Orokaiva texts; Mr. M. Lean, head teacher of the Sasembata mission school; Dr. A. Radford, director of the Saiho hospital; Mr. C. Searle, a planter of Awala; their wives; and many other individuals attached to the mission and the administration.

My Papuan interpreters, research assistants and chief informants were the following: Mr. Stephen Oriri of Inonda; Messrs. Harold Heru, John Douglas and Brian Orua of Hohorita; Messrs. Robert Nanisi and Leon Bhagi and Miss Patricia Jove, of Sivepe; the Rev. Albert McLaren of Sasembata mission station, and Mr. Walter Waki of Popondetta. I owe a very special debt to Mr. Cromwell Burau who stayed with me for three weeks and communicated to me some of his deep insight into Orokaiva culture: and to Samuel Jovareka, our Orokaiva father, of Sivepe.

I should like to thank also some of the scholars who, for better or for worse, have helped in the development of this work by their encouragement, criticism and information; in alphabetical order: Dr. Homer G. Barnett, Dr. Cyril S. Belshaw, Dr. Kenelm O. L. Burridge, Dr. A. Capell, Dr. Peter Carstens, Dr. Jan Pouwer and Mr. Adrian Tanner. Finally I would thank the Social Sciences Division, Scarborough College, University of Toronto, for excellent secretarial services.

PART I
THE OROKAIVA EXCHANGE SYSTEM

CHAPTER I

INTRODUCTION

I

A great deal of social behaviour may be explained, and traditionally has been explained by social anthropologists, with reference to rights and obligations arising out of membership in corporate groups. Such analysis was especially successful in societies where corporate groups are large and of wide scope. In a great many simpler societies these corporate groups define their members' rights and obligations with reference to the principle of descent, which accordingly offered an excellent analytical and comparative framework for anthropologists studying these societies.

It often happens that the participants in a social action do not behave as members of the same corporate group but rather as representatives of different and – for the purpose of the action – opposed social groups. The regularities found in this type of interaction have been the subject of exchange theory, as developed notably by Mauss, Lévi-Strauss, Homans, Blau, Barth and certain authorities in political, economic and religious anthropology. Although this theory has attained a high degree of sophistication, field anthropologists generally have preferred to organise their analysis around corporate groups and the principle of descent, as this seemed to provide explanations for many interesting institutional phenomena. When the workings of the 'principle of reciprocity' have been inquired into by ethnographers, these inquiries have tended to be in specialised areas of the culture, and only rarely have been based on the assumption that the explanatory value of the 'principle of reciprocity' might equal that of the 'principle of descent'.

Most ethnographers working in Melanesia, while following the traditional descent-based method of analysis of social structure, have been keenly aware of the paucity of corporate groups in that area, their extremely limited scope and, in contrast, the strong emphasis placed upon the principle of reciprocity. One reaction to this situation has been the 'configurational approach' advocated by Pouwer, which would place the principles of descent, reciprocity, residence, siblingship and some others not specified, on the same level, and the comparison of societies on the basis of the relative weight given to each principle. More recently some excellent ethnographies have appeared in which the importance of the principle of exchange is well recognised (e.g. Wagner 1967, Strathern 1971, Young 1971). But even when this approach is accepted as a basis of ethnographic operations, it is still not clear on what methods we may rely for the analysis of the working of the principle of reciprocity in primitive societies.

Exchange may be viewed from two opposite yet complementary starting

3

points. First let us consider exchange partners as though they are strangers, with distinct destinies and personal interests, who decide to seek an alliance with one another for reasons which may range from psychological attraction to economic expediency. From this viewpoint the establishment and maintenance of a social relationship is always problematical and incomplete. The problem of how social exchange can ever get started has been a subject of speculation not only for social scientists but also for the Melanesians themselves.[1] In the Orokaiva folk-system the starting mechanism of an exchange system is presented in the form of a myth recounting a unique free gift made by a demi-god whereby the exchange cycle was set in motion. Historical change is represented by the emergence of a new demi-god setting up new exchange cycles. Once the relationship is started, it is composed of a perpetual cycle of exchanges between the two partners.

We may call this view of exchange phenomenological because it starts from *ego's* experience of a social relationship. *Ego* experiences *alter's* world as transcendant. As Husserl and Schutz have pointed out, social relations are necessarily based on an idealisation of the 'interchangeability of standpoints' (Schutz 1967: 126, 312–29). For that reason they are always to some extent precarious and incomplete. If our method of ethnography is to go beyond pure phenomenology, we also need to view exchange from a second viewpoint which I shall call analytical. From this viewpoint, it is impossible to conceive of the making, receiving and reciprocating of gifts by individuals in any culture unless that culture has conceptualised in some way the complementarity of donor and receiver. This notion of complementarity is inseparable from all our discourse about giving and receiving. For instance, in the present work I shall write a good deal about the exchange relationships between mother's brother and sister's son, husband and wife, son-in-law and father-in-law, friend and friend, creditor and debtor, victor and vanquished. Not only have the patterns of relationship linking these dyads been laid down by Orokaiva custom, but the complementary nature of these relationships is already implicit in the words I have used to describe them.

Although one might, with Nadel (1957), describe these dyads as logically related *roles,* this could give the impression that I am concerned merely with a set of rights and obligations that the role partners have *vis-à-vis* each other. The present work, however, deals with economic and psychological as well as normative aspects of dyadic relations. In a study of corporate groups, one must assume that exchanges between a dyad (*Ego* and *Alter*) are determined by corporate obligations. In a study of exchange systems, however, one must assume that the exchanges are in principle voluntary, and that normative rules specify no more than a code of behaviour by means of which it is commonly believed that *Alter* may be induced to do what *Ego* wants. (This desired object is often no more than the establishment or maintenance of a social relationship.) There are often no positive rules obliging A to fit in with E's wishes if E performs some specific act of liberality. For reasons shown in detail in later chapters, I prefer to think of acts of giving as magical rather than as obligating devices. I do not thereby question the importance of norms in explaining social regularities. Magic certainly contains norms: acts which are regularly performed to bring about certain ends because such acts are thought to be especially effective in eliciting a generous response.

There is nothing very new in the above view of exchange analysis, which may be found in Malinowski and also in Mauss, provided that one reads the *Essai sur le don* in the French original rather than in the English translation.[2] The question considered by both these authors — and also by sociologists such as Homans and Blau — is how persons who have no prior obligations to one another can set up and maintain viable social relationships. In the simplest cases, and it was these that engaged the attention of Malinowski and Mauss, such transactions can be set in train by the proffering of one or more objects of exchange for which the donor later receives in exchange an object belonging to the same 'sphere'. Firth, Steiner, Bohannan, Salisbury and others have distinguished between transactions of this type and more complex ones called 'translations' (Steiner) or 'conversions' (Bohannan). Lévi-Straussian theory tended to follow the same tradition, as it dealt in great detail with transactions where women were exchanged for women while touching briefly upon marriage 'by purchase' which might be classified as a conversion.

II

For the task I have undertaken it is necessary to widen the range of objects of exchange in two directions; this will also greatly increase the importance that has to be accorded to 'conversions'. First, we should include as 'objects of exchange' the various types of social behaviour analysed by Homans and Blau: influence, prestige, power, authority, compliance, and so on. Now if these are treated as objects of exchange, it will be seen that asymmetry (or as Blau puts it, in a term not available to anthropologists, 'unilaterality') is characteristic of most transactions involving such objects of exchange. A person who gives a service receives influence, but the person who 'gives' the influence cannot 'receive' influence in return; he receives only service. Being inferior in status, any service he gives will gain him, not influence, but perhaps material goods, or perhaps a service of a different kind. Conversions are a normal phenomenon in social exchange.

We may further widen the concept of exchange if we include phenomena which are explained by people such as the Orokaiva as being similar in nature to social exchange. The Orokaiva view man and pig, pig and taro, coconut and betelnut, man and spirit, etc. as similar to exchange partners, a similarity which they express in mythology, philosophy, ritual and custom. In the course of this book we shall see exchange-oriented folk-models of explanation applied by the Orokaiva not only on the social, but also on religious, ecological, ritual, physiological, botanical, economic, technological, and philosophical levels. Exchange thus appears as pervasively as an *explicans* in Orokaiva culture as descent appears in some of the African societies analysed by anthropologists of the Radcliffe-Brownian school. Perhaps it appears even more pervasively, for on these levels, too, conversions are extremely frequent occurrences. Clearly, in transactions between partners such as man/spirit, man/pig, the prestations offered by each of the partners would be of a different order.

Such conversions, at any level, tend to be problematical. The exchange partners face each other as opponents; they have widely different objects of exchange to offer each other. Whether a social relationship between these opposites will actually be established in any given case depends on contingencies.

I shall take as a simple example a relationship between an offender and his victim. The former has suffered some misfortune which has been put down to sorcery inflicted by the person he has offended. The objects of exchange are: reparation by the offender (e.g. by payment of a pig) and forgiveness to be offered by the offended party. This is a highly problematical transaction. There is an intervening ritual that must take place before the transaction can be completed. This ritual includes a common meal. Even then it is not certain whether the misfortune really will be removed.

Here we may speak of a cycle of exchanges which may be interrupted at any point. If the cycle is not closed, it follows that the social relationship between the opponents has failed somewhere along the line. They will remain enemies. More is involved here than a mere exchange between a reparation payment and a willingness to forgive. Because of the magical implications and the unpredictability of success, the transaction is far closer in essence to a sacrifice which may or may not be accepted by a deity. The 'gift' of a pig, the common meal and all the other ritual may be compared to a sacrifice. We may thus speak of mediating links that are often inserted in a transaction to ensure its efficacy. Lévi-Strauss has used the concept of mediation in his treatment of primitive philosophic systems.[3] I think it is also useful in the discussion of exchange and sacrifice as long as it is remembered that in a classificatory system a 'mediator' is an actual intermediary between two real existents, whereas in a sacrificial or transactional scheme it is a magical device for establishing an illusory union between self and other.

In summary, an 'exchange cycle' in the sense intended here contains three pairs of elements: (*a*) the basic elements placed in opposition; (*b*) the objects of exchange entering the transaction on each side; (*c*) the mediating objects or acts that may be interposed as a prestation moves from A to B and as a prestation of a different kind moves from B to A. Such models of exchange cycles, developed by the investigator on the basis of his understanding of indigenous thought patterns, will be useful in the explanation of institutions, as Orokaiva institutions tend to appear at some point in such cycles. The models will reveal their relationship to other elements in the cycles and their conceptualisation in the context of exchange.

An interesting consequence of these models is that they place elements of the material culture on the same level as social institutions. While this similarity should not be pushed too far, it is still inevitable that in this type of ethnographical analysis material culture and technology should be given a far greater place than is customary in social anthropology. Let us take, as the most obvious example, the relationship between son-in-law and father-in-law, in the field of marriage exchange, the prospective son-in-law having abducted or eloped with his prospective bride. Here the essential exchange is characterised by what Sahlins might call 'negative reciprocity': the son-in-law's act of abduction is paid back by a number of hostile acts on the part of the father-in-law, varying according to the power of the latter's anger. A number of ritual acts, services and gifts of specified types act as mediating links, failing which the father-in-law would not even recognise the relationship as an affinal one. Thus objects such as pig, taro and feather ornaments appear as mediating links in the hazardous process of establishing an exchange cycle.

Now, if we regard such objects as analogous to sacrifices, as I have suggested, and adopt Lévi-Strauss' theory of sacrifice, (developing the theory of Hubert and Mauss) we need to demonstrate, in the case of all these mediating links, that each gift object can be identified, from one viewpoint, with the giver and, from another viewpoint, with the receiver. Our understanding of the institution of marriage thus depends vitally on our understanding of taro-symbolism, pig-symbolism, etc.

In our analysis, the marriage institution is represented by a set of elements in exchange cycles. The latter cannot be understood unless we know precisely how the exchanges are mediated. We must thus know what various material objects symbolise in given contexts, in exchanges between persons standing in specified relationships. But these symbolisations in turn arise out of a body of myths, ethnoscientific notions, rituals and technological practices related to the objects in question. In the present book the analysis of these symbolisations precedes the systematic discussion of social relationships, as it is found that these relationships are almost invariably mediated by the transfer of material objects so that we have to be clear about the former before we can understand much about the latter. If the method set out here finds favour, it may lead to an increased interest in material culture on the part of social anthropologists.

III

In the study of symbolism, we need to combine a synchronic and diachronic perspective. Thus, a person making a gift is usually involved in an ongoing (diachronic) relationship, but if the gift is made in a ritual context, there is likely to be some religious belief in its efficacy. In New Guinea such belief tends to be validated by a myth in which the gift in question is made by a primordial donor whose action has since, both in form and substance, been imitated by man. Such imitation might well be called a form of magic, in as much as it calls forth from the recipient a desired response not otherwise obtainable. F. E. Williams, who first noted this New Guinean technique of imitating actions of culture-heroes for magical purposes, gave it the term 'magic of impersonation' (1932–3; 1940: 135–7, 341–3; 1940–2: 82–3, 115–21).

The method we follow thus requires a detailed study of myths. One may say that a person making a ritual gift uses a myth as a charter for his behaviour. Malinowski, noting this correspondence, suggested that such myths are invented to account for previously existing behaviour. Such a view can never be wholly rejected; we may well argue that one cannot imitate a god unless one has previously, to some extent, invented him and thus imbued him with one's own action patterns. On the other hand, such invented patterns are not intelligible in themselves so that we need a structural analysis to make sense of them. Hence, the present work makes some limited use of Lévi-Straussian methods of myth analysis.

Nonetheless, the present work is basically an ethnography. No theory of exchange has been offered here, only an analysis of ethnographic data, indicating how Orokaiva conceive of the exchange of certain objects in which they have a special interest. In the course of analysis, I have drawn on a few theoretical sources in rather eclectic fashion. I believe that the method of description I have followed is especially appropriate for making sense of Melanesian societies, and perhaps other societies also. For the method to be consolidated, a second field study will be necessary, explicitly and systematically oriented towards communication systems, boundary systems, proxemics and the like, covering the communication of women, material objects and messages, and including at least some comparative perspective and some myth analysis. The present work, however, seems a necessary first step in plotting such new approaches to ethnography.

My work was much facilitated by a wealth of previous studies of the Orokaiva,[4] of which the most valuable is still F. E. Williams' *Orokaiva Society* (1930). Re-study proved it to be a highly accurate work, focusing on the most challenging problems posed by the social system. Among these are the bilateral tendencies in the kinship system classified as patrilineal; the plant emblem groups; the relation of 'homicidal emblems' to initiation rituals and especially the subtleties of the value system, brilliantly handled in the chapter on 'Morality'.

A successor can fulfil various useful offices, some minor, some major. First, Williams' work can be used as a basis for a study of culture change. I have done this to some extent in an earlier work (Schwimmer 1969) and in the present work where the argument demanded it. Secondly, *Orokaiva Society* provides a composite picture of a number of closely related, yet by no means identical systems (Mountain Orokaiva, Aika, Yega, Binandere, etc.) In this re-study, I confined myself to Mountain Orokaiva, reserving for another occasion a survey of the diversities in degree of patrilineality, kinship terminology, ritual forms, leadership patterns and the like, all related to the ecological base and settlement history.

Thirdly, Williams' study of the Orokaiva was made early in his career. When reading his later works, we note analyses (on sex affiliation, 1932; on dual division, 1924, Ch. VIII, 1936 Chs. VI–IX, 1940: 32–5; on 'disease and its treatment 1940–2: 90–105; and on totemic groups, e.g. 1940) that would apply with minor variations to the Orokaiva, but are not developed in Williams' writings on that tribe. We need not suppose that in the Northern District Williams failed to observe what he saw and described in relation to Kerari or Elema. It is more likely that he was progressing steadily along a highly individual analytical path, leading him only gradually to perceptions which were theoretically far ahead of his times. In any case, in my analysis of Orokaiva plant emblem groups (Ch. X) my presentation is very close to Williams' work on the Elema, although it departs from that on the Orokaiva. Similarly, I have drawn on his writings on 'sex affiliation' among the Koiari and 'dual division' in the Gulf District, on disease at Lake Kutubu and so forth, thus bringing to bear the insights of Williams' maturity on Orokaiva material.

These are the minor tasks. The major one is to continue the search for system in New Guinea societies on the basis of these insights and of the theoretical discoveries of the last thirty years. Thus this book is in a sense a dialogue with Williams to which I contribute new data that seem relevant.

IV

The ethnography is divided into three parts. In the first part, after providing a brief general sketch of Orokaiva culture, I shall examine the 'starting mechanisms' of Orokaiva exchange cycles, both in traditional institutions (Ch. III) and in institutions developed since the British-Australian conquest (Ch. IV). The second part of the study is concerned chiefly with objects of mediation: land, taro, pigs, minor foods and ornaments (Chs. V–IX). In the third part the focus shifts to the relations between exchange partners mediated by the prestations analysed in the preceding chapters.

Although my presentation of Orokaiva social structure in this part of the work is not intended to be controversial, the focus differs from that of earlier ethnographies and here and there earlier findings had to be questioned in the light of fresh evidence. Orokaiva society contains several types of groupings (clan, local clan group, lineage, plant emblem group) whose members, according to informants, are recruited exclusively on the basis of agnatic descent. Earlier investigators have emphasised these patrilineal characteristics by equating the lineage and clan emblem group, proclaiming them both to be segments of local clan groups, and by treating the local clan group as something like a segment of a clan. My own analysis, however, will be concerned more with clan fusions and fissions, with irregular recruitment within the plant emblem group, and with the lack of evidence for agnatic connection between lineages and local clan groups. My evidence shows that the non-agnates recruited into these putatively agnatic groupings are mostly uterine kin. But above all I shall try to establish that these departures from the supposed agnatic norms are not cases of irregularity or deviance, but an integral part of the Orokaiva kinship system. I shall suggest that normally clans are not intrinsically agnatic but rather that they arose out of alliances between smaller groups whose original link was affinal. The effect of this argument is to show the narrow limits of range and scope within which Orokaiva patrilineal corporations operate, and thus to emphasise the importance of the exchange system as a principle of social structure.

As soon as we extend kinship analysis beyond the conjugal family, we observe that mediation is carried on not only through non-social objects used as gifts or prestations, but also through social objects used as intermediaries. Thus, in the relation between sister's son and mother's brother there is an intermediary who is mother of one of the partners and sister of the other. Similarly, the relation between two brothers-in-law is mediated by a woman who is wife of one and sister of the other. Men also often act as mediators between exchange partners when these are not linked by kinship, or when the exchange partners are female.

The principles of exchange are the same whether the objects of mediation be social or non-social. In both cases there are two partners, *ego* and *alter*, who establish or maintain a social relationship. The object of mediation, whether social or non-social, is so chosen that both *ego* and *alter* are — or become — closely identified with it. If *ego* and *alter* are male non-agnatic kinsmen, the mediator must be a woman· if they are female non-agnatic kinsmen, the mediator must be a man. In either case, the concept of an object of mediation implies that at the beginning of the transaction *ego* had some exclusive claim upon the man or woman who is being 'transferred', but as the result of the transaction this claims passes to *alter*.

The most familiar example of such a transfer is that of a woman who is 'given' by her brother to her prospective husband. When Lévi-Strauss developed the exchange or 'alliance' theory of social structure, he mainly discussed this type of transaction, whereby a social relationship between two male partners is created by the transfer of a woman from the control of one to the other. It is clear, however, that for every man who marries, a new relationship is also created between women who become sisters-in-law. In a very significant sense, the wife has taken the man from the sister. The Orokaiva acknowledge this aspect in two ways: by the gift of a pig made by the wife to the sister, and by the term of address *bi* (= penis) used between sisters-in-law.

We may thus see social structure as the product of a web of mediation. The usefulness of such a concept depends very much on the extent to which these intermediaries are institutionally involved in dealings between partners. Among the Orokaiva, their roles as intermediaries in exchanges between men are well articulated. As wives, as sisters and as mothers they link the very small patrilineal kinship groups into social units of a viable size. The system of marriage is a rather involved one, containing elements of restricted as well as of complex generalised exchange. Once this system of marriage is fully understood (Ch. X), the basic workings of Orokaiva society stand fairly clearly revealed. The study of Orokaiva exchange would not be adequate, however, without a brief consideration of the independent friendship network and the system of ranking, especially as it has affected recent Orokaiva-Australian relations (Ch. XI).

We thus return, though with a slightly more specific methodology, to Mauss' concept of exchange as a 'total phenomenon', in the sense that we posit the interrelations of notions of exchange occurring at any level of conceptualisation, social and non-social. It is in the very pervasiveness of such notions throughout the culture that we find evidence for its dominance in Orokaiva thought and institutions and for its power to mould social life.

REFERENCES

1   I refer especially to the discussion of the 'starting mechanism' of exchange in Gouldner 1960 and to Blau's (1964) criticism of Gouldner. My own view is that the approaches of these two authors are complementary.

2   Cunnison's translation (1954) suppresses in many passages Mauss' concern with economic and psychological factors. Compare Mauss: 'Quelle est la règle de droit *et d'intéret* qui, dans les sociétés de type arriéré ou archaïque, fait que le présent reçu est obligatoirement rendu? ' (1966:148) and: 'In primitive or archaic types of society, what is the principle whereby the gift received has to be repaid? ' (Cunnison 1954:1). Compare also: 'ce type de droit et d'économie' (Mauss 153; Cunnison 5); omission by Cunnison of the last paragraph of Mauss 173; 'ces concepts de droit et d'économie (Mauss 267; Cunnison 70); 'en règles de droit, en mythes, en valeurs et en prix' (Mauss 275, Cunnison 77), etc. Recent criticism of Mauss by economic anthropologists sometimes reads as though it is based on translation rather than original.

3   For Lévi-Strauss' discussion of the notion of mediation see *La Pensée Sauvage*, Ch. VIII and *passim*.

4   For Williams' work on the Orokaiva see Williams 1925, 1928, 1930. There have been numerous recent studies of special aspects, e.g. Baxter 1969 on Isivita settlement patterns, Belshaw 1951 and Keesing 1952 on the eruption of Mount Lamington, Crocombe on cash cropping (1964), modern feasts (1966) and enterpreneurs (1967); Crocombe and Hogbin (1963), Morawetz (1967), Rimoldi (1966) and Waddell and Krinks (1968) on land utilisation and productivity; Hogbin (1966) on a modern wedding, Dakeyne (1966) on co-operatives and Reay (1953) on social control. See also Schwimmer 1967, 1969, 1970.

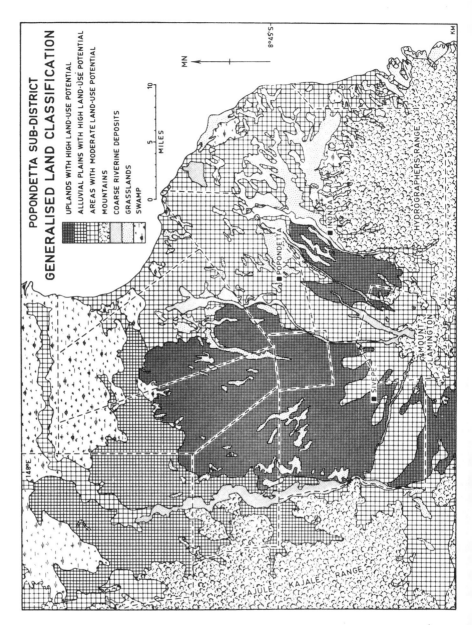

Fig. 1.   Popondetta Sub-
District: generalised land
classification

12

CHAPTER II

THE SETTING

1. *Geography*

Although several good descriptions of the physical environment and general
culture of the Orokaiva are available (e.g. Williams 1930, Waddell and Krinks
1968), a brief sketch of the setting of this study may be convenient. The
Orokaiva live in the Northern District of Papua, a district bounded on the
south-west by the Owen Stanley range, on the west by the Mandated Territory
of New Guinea. Although the administrative centre of the district, Popondetta,
lies only about 150 miles from Port Moresby, there is no road connection, so
that the only communications with the outside world are by air and sea.

The Orokaiva live on the footslopes of Mount Lamington and on the plains to
the north and east of these footslopes. This region is, by New Guinean standards,
highly favoured by nature, as Brookfield recently emphasised (1966). In a
classification of the natural resources of New Guinea according to the degree of
limitations to land use[1], Brookfield describes a large territory surrounding
Mount Lamington as 'suitable for cultivation with a mild degree of limitation'.
This comprises 'some of the largest tracts of such good land in the whole
country' (*ibid*. 47–8).

One distinguishing feature of the region is its lithological composition: there
is an abundance of Pleistocene and recent volcanic deposits. The total area of
such recent ash and lava deposits found in New Guinea is small, but notably
fertile. Brookfield maps the annual rainfall of the region as between 100 and 150
inches. This is not so high that the land becomes permanently or semi-perma-
nently waterlogged. On the other hand, the region mostly lacks well-marked dry
seasons during which the soil would rapidly dry out. With regard to terrain, the
region has extensive areas of low and moderate relief and good drainage. As for
density of population, Brookfield paints a somewhat idyllic picture that needs
correction: 'the greatest concentration of population, rising locally to 60 per sq.
mile, lies on the best land in the area – the little-dissected footslopes of Mount
Lamington, where smooth topography is combined with fertile soils and good
drainage' (*ibid*. 64).

We find, in fact, that local densities of 200 and more per sq. mile are not at
all rare (Rimoldi 1966: 4). In two villages I surveyed, I found population
densities to be 180 (Sivepe) and 135 (Hohorita) per sq. mile. Rimoldi's analysis
shows that the Sivepe population density is close to the upper limit the land can
sustain with present technology and social organisation. The sample he chose (50
persons of the Jegase and Timumu clans) happened to have under-average land
holdings, of 138 acres. Rimoldi shows that 110 of these acres are needed for

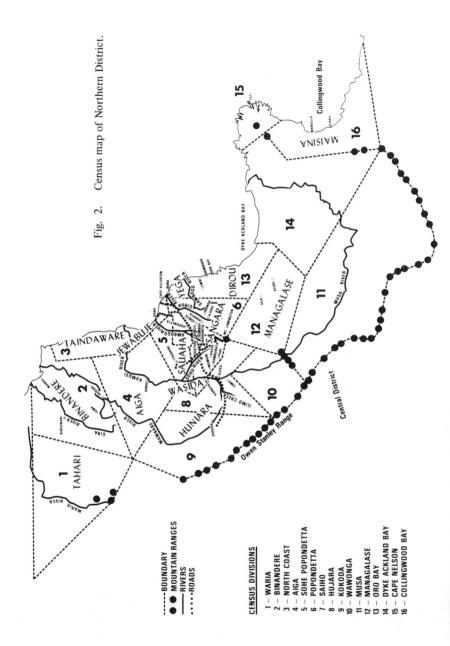

Fig. 2. Census map of Northern District.

CENSUS DIVISIONS

1 – WARIA
2 – BINANDERE
3 – NORTH COAST
4 – AIGA
5 – SOHE POPONDETTA
6 – POPONDETTA
7 – SAIHO
8 – HUJARA
9 – KOKODA
10 – WAWONGA
11 – MUSA
12 – MANAGALASE
13 – ORO BAY
14 – DYKE ACKLAND BAY
15 – CAPE NELSON
16 – COLLINGWOOD BAY

---- BOUNDARY
● MOUNTAIN RANGES
● RIVERS
···· ROADS

subsistence shifting agriculture alone. This leaves hardly any margin for land unsuitable for cultivation, for bush land needed as a source of building materials etc., or for unequal distribution of land as between families.

We may divide the land occupied by Orokaiva into two broad sub-regions. The first is made up of the foothills themselves which have an 8 to 12 inch very dark brown top soil, rich in nitrogen and phosphorus. The fine-textured subsoils range from 10 to 22 inches in depth. This sub-region coincides approximately with the Saiho census division which had a population of 8,211 in 1966 giving a density of about 55 per sq. mile. The second sub-region, situated to the north and east of the first, consists of poorly drained but readily improvable plains. Here the population is very much sparser. Most village domains contain only a fraction of immediately utilisable good cultivation land and even this does not have the special fertility of the volcanic loam on the mountain slopes. The soils of Inoda, a village situated in this sub-region, have been discussed in much detail by Crocombe and Hogbin 1963, quoting the Commonwealth Scientific and Industrial Research Organisation (C.S.I.R.O. [1954]). This sub-region forms part of the Sohe-Popondetta census division which, as a whole, has a population density of about 20 per sq. mile. Villages are smaller and more dispersed.

The boundaries of what we may call the Orokaiva tribal area are probably best determined by the criteria used by the Papuans themselves, namely linguistic criteria. Orokaiva is part of the Binandere group of eight languages (see Wurm 1960) spoken in most of the more densely populated parts of the Northern District; of these languages, Orokaiva is spoken by the greatest number, but only about half the population in the Ovokaiva-Binandere area. The only language of this group for which a reasonably full description (grammar and dictionary) has been published is Binandere (Copland King 1927), a language spoken around the lower part of the Mambare and Gira rivers. Other languages of this group are: Orokaiva, Notu, Aiga, Huniara, Yema, Taindaware. While there are considerable vocabulary differences between these languages, there is a close resemblance in grammar and enough resemblance in vocabulary to make a very limited degree of intercommunication possible. (Chinnery and Beaver 1916 and an unpublished manuscript by Capell [n.d.]). We do not know much more about the Binandere group of languages except that it is a Papuan grouping (Grace 1968).

It seems to me that dialect divisions within the Orokaiva language area which have been noted at various times (Beaver 1916, Williams 1930) are rather minor. A fairly accurate idea of the boundaries of the Orokaiva language area may be obtained by identifying this area with the district administered by the Higaturu Local Government Council which covers the Saiho and most of the Sohe-Popondetta census divisions.

Williams (1930: 157–9) attempts to distinguish the Orokaiva language speakers from other tribal groupings by listing cultural differences (notably in dress and ornaments) but these are not pronounced and, under modern conditions, may be observed only on ceremonial occasions when headgear and bark-cloth are worn.

Prior to European contact, the normal mode of settlement was in hamlets containing 6 to 12 houses and surrounded by land used for shifting agriculture.

TABLE II/1

NORTHERN DISTRICT: POPULATION 1966
(*Source*: Department of District Administration,
Popondetta)

Popondetta Sub-District

Afore
Musa	2509	
Managalase	5550	8059

Ioma
Aiga	2384	
Binandere	3693	
Waria	1717	7794

Popondetta
North Coast	4660	
Sohe — Popondetta	3588	
Popondetta	3533	
Oro Bay	5181	
Saiho	8211	25173

Town
Locals	900 (approx.)	
Europeans	300	

Rural
Locals	800 (approx.)	
Europeans	260	2260

Total		43,286

Tufi Sub-District
Cape Nelson	3642	
Collingwood Bay	2936	
Dyke Ackland Bay	1724	
Europeans	20	8322

Kokoda Sub-District
Kokoda	2018	
Hujara	3195	
Wawonga	1227	
Europeans	30	6470

Total		58,078

TABLE II/2

POPULATION BY AGE, SEX, MARITAL STATUS AND CLAN

(a) Comparison Between Inonda and Sivepe, 1951 and 1966

	Inonda		Sivepe				
			1966				
	1966	1951	Sorovi	Seho	Jegase	Total	1951
Male Adults (Total)	10	5	6	8	14	28	15
Widowers	2		1	–	2	3	
Married, residing with wife	7		5	7	8	20	
Single	1		–	1	4	5	
Female Adults	10	8	5	11	18	34	25
Widows	2		–	1	3	4	
Married, residing with husband	7		5	7	8	20	
Single or living without husband	1		–	3	7	10	
Children	22	35	15	27	33	75	59
Total	42	48	26	46	65	137	99

(b) Sivepe male adults, by clans and age groups

Age Groups	Sorovi	Seho	Jegase	Total
16–25	–	1	3	4
26–35	2	–	2	4
36–45	2	2	4	8
46–55	1	5	1	7
Over 55	1	–	4	5
Total	6	8	14	28

Note: For the purpose of this table, I have included entire households with the clan of the household heads. The breakdown of female population into clans must be understood as meaning: 'Attached to a household of Sorovi, Seho or Jegase clan'.

17

Though Monckton reports (1921) a few large villages in the early post-contact period, it is only recently, in response to Australian pressure, that multi-clan villages, with populations ranging from 100 to 500, have become common. Most of the plantations found in the Northern district have been established by Australian ex-servicemen supported by government loans. A number of Orokaiva have been drawn to work on these plantations, others to jobs in Popondetta, others again to service with the police, the armed forces or employers outside the district. Such migration has substantially reduced the proportion of the male village population group.[2]

2.   *Technology and Aesthetics*

We possess only the briefest description of Orokaiva industry (in Williams 1930). Although I did collect additional data, the traditional technology has been transformed to such an extent that my data must needs be fragmentary. The only axes and adzes now in use are made of steel; most of the various stone-made cutting tools described by Williams are no longer in use, being replaced by the ubiquitous bush knife wielded by young and old, male and female. One exception is worth noting, if only to emphasise an element of continuity: cockle shells are still used for the scraping of coconuts and for the shaping and decorating of pots. Most of the needles used by women are still made of flying fox bones (*poma*), even though a few needles have at times been obtained from the Mission. While files for sharpening tools are necessarily made of steel, rough leaves still serve as tools for scraping pots, smoothing down wood, etc. The same mixture in the use of basic tools is found in agriculture, hunting, and fishing: we still find the digging stick but also the axe; traditional hand nets and fishing spears (with steel tips), but also snorkels. For hunting, traditional devices have been almost entirely replaced by the shot gun. The old technology is still basically intact in those few industries which are directly related to ceremonial life: the making and decorating of loin cloths, feather headdresses, ceremonial weaponry, musical instruments such as drums. Certain other specifically feminine artifacts (mats, baskets, string bags) are still produced and in use, while much of the contemporary Orokaiva house-building technology is traditional, Fine wickerwork for ceremonial objects (armlets, spear decorations, etc.) is still made by some of the older men. Orokaiva women have almost stopped making pots, though this was an important industry in pre-contact times. While trade goods are used for everyday purposes, such pots as are still made serve as gifts to women at the time of marriage. They are kept for sentimental reasons, but we were able to see only very few.

An everyday Orokaiva meal consists of taro, often with a few vegetable condiments: coconut milk, cordyline tips, or edible pitpit,[3] or one of a number of herbs, sometimes of supposed medicinal value. Much care is devoted to the cooking of the taro and variety is provided partly by a choice from many varieties of taro growing in most gardens. In the dry season, any of a number of subsidiary foods (sweet potato, German taro, yam, banana, breadfruit and several others) may be added to make the taro stretch further. Meat or fish is eaten only rarely, usually on festive occasions. Foods like tea, sugar, bread and salt are also reserved for such occasions. Although several traditional methods of making salt were described to me, the housewife depends mainly on trade salt. Meals never consist of more than one course. Plates, forks and spoons are owned by all households but people do not always use them. While boiling is the most common way of preparing food, bananas, yams and breadfruit are usually roasted. Meat is often preserved by daily smoking, sometimes for long periods. There is a rule against eating meat 'in lent' and this is kept very strictly, but probably for traditional religious reasons to be discussed later. The main drink with meals is a soup consisting of the water in which the vegetables and herbs were cooked.

Foraging.   A good deal of plant and animal food is obtained from foraging, especially in the tropical rain forest which covers most of the Northern District. Among foraged animal foods I would mention especially grubs, frogs, snails, rats, bush eggs and lice. Foraged plant foods are especially valued during the dry season when roots, leaves and fern fronds may make up part of a meal. Savoury herbs and leaves, however, are collected at all times of the year. Some food plants, though growing in the forest, are owned by individuals so that the gathering of these plants may be better described as harvesting than collecting. The most important are the *tauga* and *puga* nut, sago, breadfruit, wild fig, and fruiting pandanus.[4]

Hunting.   According to Waddell and Krinks, about two man-hours weekly are spent on hunting (3.7 hours by men and 0.3 hours by women). Hunting patterns on the Mount Lamington foothills differ widely from those on the alluvial plains where kunai grass is widespread. On the foothills, there is hunting in reverted gardens and in very limited areas of virgin bush. The usual quarry consists of small marsupials and birds. If a pig is encountered, it is invariably a village pig whose owner has a claim to the carcase. The game population was virtually exterminated after the introduction of guns in the 1950s. In the kunai country, on the other hand, hunting land is abundant. The technique is by firing the kunai so that the animals can be shot when they escape. Such a hunt requires a large number of men who ring the burnt-over area. Not only marsupials but also pigs are killed, either by gunfire or by being roasted alive in the kunai grass. By no means all animals killed in the fire are retrieved. Fires tend to get out of hand and to spread over surrounding bush land which then is often covered with kunai grass and so is useless for purposes of cultivation.

Fishing.   The supply of fish has suffered greatly with the introduction of snorkels after the Second World War, as this equipment enabled the Orokaiva to fish out their rivers almost completely in a very short time. Fish is still an important resource, however, in the lower reaches of the huge rivers which run through the Northern District: Kumusi, Ambogo, Girua, Sambogo, etc. In Inonda, the village studied by Crocombe and Hogbin (1963) and Waddell and Krinks (1968), 3.8 man hours per week are spent on fishing, mostly with spears, and the product is used not only for consumption but also for trade. (Inonda people also trade meat and bush eggs.) Many of the villages near the mountain, such as Sivepe, have very little fish. Apart from a few eels and crabs, the rivers contained a small supply of two-inch-long fishes caught in April with a small hand-net used as a scoop. (See Williams 1930:53 for description.)

Animal Husbandry.   There are three kinds of domestic livestock: pigs, dogs and fowls. Every man still has one or more small dog which he uses for hunting but which, as Williams says in his discussion on Orokaiva domestic animals (1930: 60–3), are all ultimately destined for the pot. The fowl population has likewise remained more or less constant for some time (e.g. about 30 in Inonda, 40 in Sivepe). The birds are useful not only as a source of meat and eggs, but also of cockerel feathers which are plucked and used for decoration on headdresses, spears, etc. Unlike the dogs, the fowls are no longer a purely indigenous variety: they have been crossed with Rhode Island Reds introduced in the 1950s.

A few years before I did my fieldwork, the government began a vigorous campaign to eliminate pig husbandry from Orokaiva villages, in an attempt to improve village hygiene. Though this campaign generally was not very successful, domestic pigs had all but disappeared from the villages where I stayed. Like the other domestic animals they were left to forage for food most of the time but were also fed with pieces of taro and other left-over food, as well as pawpaw, coconut, etc. They mostly slept under the houses, but were free to roam. Males were castrated and females were fertilised by boars roaming in the bush. A close *quasi*-kinship link was assumed to exist between the pig and its keepers, and this was emphasised by taboos on eating a pig reared by a close relative. Techniques of domestication will be discussed below.

Horticulture.   The Orokaiva word *pure* has at least two important meanings: 'work' and 'garden'. As elsewhere in Papua—New Guinea, the garden is a centre of sexual, social, religious as well as industrial activity.

The main product is taro which occupies perhaps nine tenths of the area. But a great variety of other plants are also found: banana, sugar-cane, edible pitpit, German taro (*xantosoma*), a few introduced vegetables such as pineapples, tomatoes, beans, and some sweet potato. Some trees may also be planted though these will not bear until long after the garden has been abandoned: breadfruit, *tauga*, coconut, areca. In addition there are always some herbs and medicines, and if the gardener is a professional medicine man there will be a great many of these. Yams are grown in separate gardens.

Very full data on the size of these gardens have been provided by Crocombe and Hogbin (1963) and Rimoldi (1966). A household tends to establish something like one and a half to two acres of garden per year. A garden is never used for more than one taro season, but as planting and consumption of the taro each tend to be stretched over most of a year, almost two years elapse between the clearing and final abandonment. This gives time for the bananas and sugar-cane to reach maturity too. Once a garden is abandoned, it is not used again for at least eight years or so. The usual swidden agriculture techniques are used, burning, clearing, careful removal of 'rubbish' remaining after the burning process, planting with a digging stick, periodic attention to weeding and heaping up of earth around growing taro, removal of corm-bearing bases of petioles of mature taro for removal and planting in a new garden. The Orokaiva practise no irrigation, no form of terracing or drainage, no manuring, no measures against parasites. Sometimes a fence is made out of tree trunks to keep pigs from breaking in. This is usually done only after a pig has made its first expedition, and only on the side where the pig entered.

While planting and harvesting proceeds almost throughout the year there are important seasonal variations that should not be ignored. There is a dry and a

TABLE II/3

FOOD PLANTS PER HOUSEHOLD: INONDA AND SIVEPE COMPARED

(*Sources*: Crocombe and Hogbin, 1963: 8; Rimoldi, 1966: 17)

Crop	Inonda		Sivepe	
	Average	Range	Average	Range
Taro (*colocasia* sp.)	1.3 acs.	2.6–0.4 acs.	0.97 acs.	0.39–2.30 acs.
Sweet Potato	0.2 acs.	0.4–0 acs.	0.07 acs.	0–0.20 acs.
Corn	72 plants	140–0 plants	223 plants	0–442 plants
Bananas	81 trees	145–12 trees	71 trees	35–126 trees
Pitpit (*ina*)	56 clumps	181–4 clumps	88 clumps	0–400 clumps
Sugar	71 clumps	167–34 clumps	34 stools	11–54 stools
Yams	24 vines	61–0 vines	65 vines	0–136 vines
Manioc	10 plants	27–4 plants	a few	
Taro (*xantosoma* sp.)	5 plants	25–0 plants	28 plants	0–91 plants
Native Cabbage	—	—	22 plants	0–100 plants
Pawpaw	—	—	17 trees	5–32 trees
Beans	a few		17 plants	0–110 plants
Cucurbits	2 vines	10–0 vines	13 vines	9–28 vines
Shallots	a few		a few	
Ginger	—	—	a few	
Tobacco	—	—	18 plants	0–59 plants
Pineapples	1 plant	7–0 plants	no data	
Tomatoes	a few	—	no data	

wet season throughout the Northern Territory. On the Mount Lamington foothills, the dry season is comparatively short and somewhat undependable, but it is usually over by the beginning of September. Here cultivators must be sure to have enough dry weather for a successful burn prior to planting. 'A significant proportion of the mineral energy upon which swidden cultivates draw for their growth comes from the ash remains of the fired forest, so that the completeness with which a plot is burnt is a crucial factor in determining its yield, a fact of which probably all swidden cultivators are aware.' (Geertz 1966: 22–3) Furthermore, it is unwise to leave the burn until too late in the dry season, for if the soil has dried out (which it does quickly in the tropics), taro plants develop few shoots, so that the gardener may be short of shoots for planting out. Hence, I was told, a very substantial amount of clearing and planting needs to be done between June and August. There is thus a flush of produce nine or ten months later, i.e. from April to June. The same rhythm also applies in drier areas, nearer the coast, such as Inonda, because there the danger of the soil drying out is even greater and the dry season much longer. When we find that the principal Orokaiva feasting season is from April to June, we can see that this is ecologically determined, as it is then that taro is most plentiful.[5]

While most subsidiary crops are grown in the taro garden, it is a fixed rule that taro and yam should never be grown together. While taro is usually grown by individual households, yams are planted and harvested by co-operative groups, around the same time as the main taro planting and harvest, but yams are usually stored for several months until the next dry season. Yam houses are built in yam gardens and used for the storage of no other crop.

Arboriculture.   Although the Orokaiva traditionally planted coconut, betel-nut and a few other trees in gardens, villages and in the bush, their arboriculture used to be rudimentary in comparison to their precise and detailed attention to tubers, especially taro. The Australian authorities had hardly established themselves in Papua before they began to press the population into extensive arboriculture that would yield a cash income. One of the early 'native regulations' (No. 121, passed in 1903), compelled all Papuan villages to grow a stipulated number of rubber trees. Three such rubber stands were established at Sivepe, ranging from one half to three acres in area, all village men supposedly sharing in the work. Rimoldi (1966: 86–93), who describes in detail the vicissitudes of exploitation of these trees, shows how ill-adapted communal rubber stands are to a society lacking institutions for the distribution of corporate assets to its members. Nonetheless, a further stand was established, this time quite voluntarily, in 1964. They are known as the 'company trees', have not yielded any cash, and will be discussed in detail below as the land transactions involved cast light on the ideology of contemporary Orokaiva co-operative movements.

'Communal' village plantations for coffee were established in the Northern District under the same regulations as applied to rubber, but all producing trees in the villages I visited had been grown on quasi-individual holdings. First plantings were around 1955. On a rough estimate I would say that the number of trees in Sivepe and Hohorita, two villages on the foothills, were 3,500 and 15,000, while Inonda, on alluvial plains, had 800. Coffee is one crop that actually has provided the Orokaiva with a reliable and substantial cash income for some years. This is true to a very minor extent for the third cash crop promoted on a major scale, copra, which was grown especially near the coast. The coffee is processed and sent to a co-operative factory as parchment, for which purpose many villages own one or more hullers. Copra is supposed to be dried in driers built in the villages, but the one I saw in Inonda had broken down and seems unlikely to be repaired.

Clothing. The traditional Orokaiva costume was a skirt for women and a perineal band for men (Williams 1930: 32—4). Boys went naked until some time before puberty, girls until after puberty seclusion. These garments were made of barkcloth obtained from trees which were mostly grown in gardens for this purpose. Larger garments were used for wrapping round the shoulders in cold weather, and also for shrouds. This mode of dress was abandoned in the 1950s, so that today the Orokaiva buy their clothes almost entirely from trade stores and at mission bazaars. Traditional dress is used for dances, initiation ceremonies and other special occasions. For this reason bark-cloth trees (such as the *ajimo*) are found rather infrequently in gardens today. Bark-cloth is still being painted with decorations in traditional style and with a mixture of traditional and trade dyes.

Housing. Villages are in flat clearings where the grass is kept scrupulously cut and from which the women regularly sweep away rubbish. Houses (*bande*) are built in two facing rows, each house normally being occupied by one nuclear family. The roof of sago thatch slopes down from a central ridgepole. Wall construction has been in various styles since Australian contact, but today vertically set sago-branch midribs are becoming old fashioned in some areas and vertically laid shingles, about 6 ft. by 5$\frac{3}{8}$ ins., are being adopted in villages desiring to show they are tuned in to modern life. A great number of tree species must be used for the various parts of the house. Materials are taken as much as possible from reverted gardens which contain small trees. For a number of purposes large trees with trunks of high-quality slow-growing wood are considered essential. These trees have to be obtained from areas of bush much older than the usual reverted gardens. On the Mount Lamington foothills, such areas are very scarce. Trees of this quality tend to be the subject of gift exchange as between families, a subject to be discussed below.

Though it is each man's responsibility to build his own house, it is usual to call on helpers, especially sons, brothers and brothers-in-law, to help with construction. Recent changes in house construction include the increasing use of nails, though not for flooring; a remarkable increase in house sizes; the change in wall construction already mentioned, and a number of measures to 'improve' hygiene: lavatories, rubbish holes, pens for chickens, windows. The windows, an innovation promoted by the government to combat tuberculosis, are considered too uncomfortable in cold, wind or rain. Accordingly, they are always covered over with pieces of timber which can be removed if the patrol officer insists.[6]

Bachelors' houses (*oro*) are of precisely the same size and construction as the ordinary *bande*. The more prominent men of the village build themselves small meeting platforms, covered with a roof but lacking walls, for the entertainment of visitors (*arara*). In the gardens, we find small houses with an earth floor, no walls, but a platform just below roof level. People sit in these garden houses

TABLE II/4

CHANGES IN HOUSE DESIGN, HOUSE CONSTRUCTION AND DOMESTIC AMENITIES IN SIVEPE, 1936–1966
(Comparison between standards reportedly applied on four successive village sites)

Elements	1. Pusahambo (pre-war)	2. Pamba (between war and eruption)	3. Old Sivepe (after eruption, until 1965)	4. New Sivepe (1966)
Floor level	Raised on posts	Raised on posts	Raised on posts	Raised on posts
Flooring material	Betelnut, wide gaps	Betelnuts, no gaps	Some betelnut, some blackpalm	Some betelnut, some blackpalm
Windows	No windows	No windows	Small windows	Large windows
No. of rooms	Three	Three	Three	Three
Walling material	Split sago	Split sago	Split sago	'Timber'
Nails: Framing	Nil	Younger people	General	General
Nails: walls	Nil	Nil	Nil	General
Shrubs	Beside houses	Beside houses	Beside houses	To mark paths
Betelnut	Planted	Planted	Planted	Planted
Coconut	Few	More	More	More
Waste disposal	In gully	In gully	In gully	Rubbish holes
Pigs	Present	Present	Present	Absent
Hen houses	Absent	Absent	Absent	Pens built
Lavatories	Absent	Absent	A few	General
Floor area	'Very Small'	'Bigger'	'Much bigger again' (200 sq. ft.)	'Big' (375 sq. ft.)

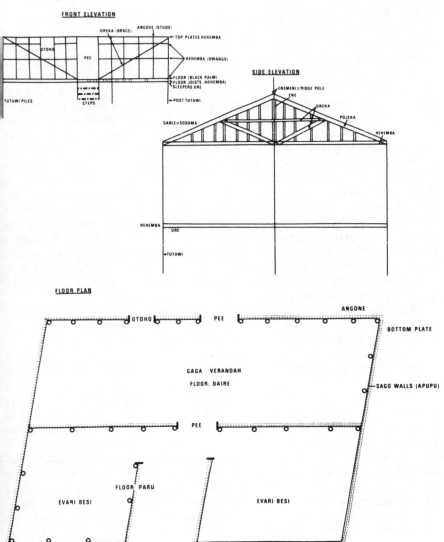

Fig. 3. Construction of a modern Orokaiva house.

(*harau*) in the heat of the day, and sometimes sleep there at night. Yams are stored under the roof.

Plastic Arts. As Mauss (1967: 96) has suggested, the best starting point in the description of plastic arts is the decoration of the body. Even though the elaborate hair dressings described by Williams are no longer seen for everyday wear, every opportunity is taken to decorate the hair in some way, especially with a few feathers. It is at the ceremonial dances that the full range of body decoration is seen: face painting, feather head-dresses, ornaments. The latter are worn on the forehead, held in the teeth, suspended from ears and nose, as necklets and as armlets.

73015

The head-dresses (*di*) and ornaments (*hambo*) are themselves artistic creations. A full feather head-dress is composed of some two dozen strands of feathers, each strand consisting of a dozen or more feathers. The strands are carefully made, sometimes from artistically shaped and trimmed feathers, while short down of striking colours may be tied to the tips of feathers. The order and arrangement of the strands making up the headdress is to some extent determined by custom but mainly by the artistic sense of the decorator, who may spend days working out the precise effect he wants. Similarly the *hambo* are often composed of a variety of objects — dog's teeth, shells, pieces of crocodile skin, a special kind of banana seed, for instance. The decorator aims at a pleasing design but is always aware of the effect of the total object as body decoration in relation to the skin, face and body of the wearer. While the objects themselves undoubtedly have magical significance, and much might be discovered about the symbolism of *di* and *hambo,* my informants were far more interested in talking to me about the aesthetics rather than the occult significance of these decorations. I surmise that the magical efficacy is actually thought to inhere in the beauty of these objects rather than in the specific qualities of component parts. Women are as lavishly decorated as men. Though some *hambo* are reserved for males only and others are characteristically female, decorations are usually interchangeable between the sexes.

Music, Dance and Song.   Today the great occasions when body decoration is performed mainly coincide with Christian festivals — Christmas, Easter, and name days of saints. But these dates tend to be close to the festive periods in the traditional Orokaiva calendar. For instance, Easter occurs around the beginning of the traditional feasting season, while Christmas is close to the rituals performed to stimulate the filling out of the taro tubers planted in the period before the rains. It is on these great occasions that the major dance cycles are performed, accompanied by entirely traditional songs and drum music. But 'practising' for these performances proceeds for months before and after Christmas, and again between Easter and the end of June. In Lent, all this is strictly prohibited, for reasons that again go back to taro magic. At any time of the year but this, one hears almost every able-bodied male in the village, from the age of two upwards, practising the dance, with or without the accompaniment of songs, while every village has its original poets who compose new songs every year. Dance 'practices' occur rather frequently, about four times a week in the two months or so before a performance. They tend to start in the early evening and continue until after midnight. Some of the dancers wear a few decorations when practising. But these 'practices' occur only if a large group can be mustered.

The Orokaiva mostly dance in pairs one behind the other, forming double file. The pairs always consist of persons of the same sex, men or women, who form more or less permanent partnerships. The dances themselves are described in some detail by Williams (1930: Ch. XIV), whose useful account would be even more valuable if he had not attempted to make up some kind of synthesis of the dance and drama of three somewhat different tribes (Orokaiva, Aiga, Binandere).

In Sivepe there were two dance leaders, one from each of the major clans, who danced as partners. They had the final say about the programme; their body movements were more extravagant and exciting than those of the others; they were allowed, and did, break out of line for extra flourishes that took their fancy while still remaining true to the spirit of each type of dance. A notable feature of the dances is the identification with spirits and animals on the part of the dancers. Mistakes in drumming and dancing are thought very inauspicious for the well-being of the community. Although men and women do not dance as partners, the dances give men a chance to show off their attractions, while the women give signs to men who impress them.

3.   *Economics*

Production.   The Orokaiva work force involves, in some ways, everybody from the age he can walk almost until the day of death. The very young and the very old are expected to make whatever contribution they are capable of. The division of labour between the sexes has been the subject of enquiry by Williams, Waddell and Krinks. A sex basis in the division of labour is obvious in a great many activities, as the charts clearly show.[7] But even where activities are 'shared' between men and women, it is most common to see each sex group work at a different aspect of the task; they rarely do exactly the same job. Calculations by Waddell and Krinks show that the Orokaiva are fairly fully occupied in terms of the number of weekly working hours. Their calculations suggest that, given the present technology and social organisation, there is comparatively little slack in the working week that could be taken up by cash cropping activities on a major scale.

The working group is most frequently the household, occupied in the *pure*. Sometimes close relatives work together on larger tasks, helping each other in turn. Although old men do maintain their own gardens, they tend to receive frequent help from sons, sons-in-law and sometimes sisters' sons. Co-operation between men is also common during hunting and housebuilding. Co-operative groups of five or more men or women are also seen occasionally, e.g. for making roofing for a house, planting and harvesting yams. Co-operation of a total village is rare, but there are co-operative fishing and hunting expeditions. Activities related to feasting tend to be communal also.

Distribution.   The Orokaiva have a subsistence economy where the bulk of goods produced are consumed by the household of the producer. Though patterns of exchange will take up a good part of the present work, it is necessary to state at the outset that only a small percentage of everyday produce enters the exchange system in any way. Waddell estimates that only 4.1 per cent of taro produced in Sivepe is disposed of by sale, gift exchange or barter. While the proportion is twice as high in Inonda, this is due to quite recent changes in the economic network in that area. One is bound to agree with Waddell that food exchanges, whatever their economic utility, are no great drain on Orokaiva resources. Of the produce entering the exchange network only a minute proportion leaves the village where it is grown. At a comparatively large feast I saw in Inonda in 1967, I estimated that Inonda was giving away, at the very utmost, 5 per cent of its annual production. As plantings are always made on a scale sufficient for survival *even if the harvest is poor*, there will be a surplus of at least 5 per cent after a good growing season. Unless the growing season is good,

TABLE II/5

SIVEPE: THE DIVISION OF LABOUR BY SEX
(*Source*: Waddell and Krinks 1968: 100)

	Men	Women
Total hours active	13,934	15,041
Total weeks present	349.7	363.1
Mean activity week	39.8	41.4

Activity	Total hours	Percentage contrib.*
Men		*Men*
Rubber – harvest	157.4	100
Recreation	194.7	97
Hunting	1,289.3	93
Preparation of tools & equip.	198.1	91
Church work	182.0	88
Construction	1,160.5	87
Coffee – market	77.9	85
Other crops – plant	41.8	84
Sago-making	319.7	81
Yams – plant	225.4	81
– maintain	45.3	79
Purchasing	273.6	77
Taro – plant	1,714.9	75
Social obligations – other	732.7	73
Women		*Women*
Sweet potato/yam – market	51.2	100
Cooking	3,442.0	97
Sweet potato – harvest	900.2	92
Care of the sick	172.5	90
Taro – market	54.3	90
– harvest	2,133.4	87
Washing	117.5	75
Both		*Men*
Rubber – market	36.1	66
Fencing	45.7	64
Coffee – harvest	353.1	62
Miscellaneous	260.6	62
Clearing	2,614.7	61
Coffee – maintain	74.5	60
Social obligations – marriage	32.7	60
– visiting	873.9	56

TABLE II/5 (*continued*)

Activity	Total hours	Percentage contrib. *
Both		*Men*
Paid work	1,128.8	56
Other crops — harvest	1,109.0	54
Sick — personal	442.6	53
Yam — harvest	412.6	53
Coffee — process	398.4	53
Collecting firewood	234.1	52
Social obligations — mourning	783.9	51
Other crops — market	66.9	51
Church services	1,946.2	46
Meetings	898.7	44
Fishing	165.0	44
Council work	824.2	42
Taro — maintain	2,551.6	37

* Where one sex carries out more than two-thirds of the work and where the total amount exceeds .01 per cent (29.0 hours) of the total hours active for the whole sample.

there is a ritual prohibition, for which I shall later quote the mythological charter, to hold a feast at all.

In any case, there seem to be two basic limitations to the size of a feast. First, the custom of restricting the number of guests to the inhabitants of *one* village, usually of about the same size as the inviting village. There are of course many variations to this custom but the principle of limitation is usually present. Secondly, the generosity shown to the guests, though outwardly most impressive, is restricted by the amount the guests can physically carry away. Though the food lying on the feasting platform looks inexhaustible to the observer, and the guests are capable of carrying away a heroic amount of food after a feast, the overall economic impact is minor.

Waddell remarks most interestingly that, in comparison with the main crops (taro, bananas and sugar-cane), a far higher proportion of dry season crops enter the exchange network. This applies especially to sago, breadfruit, sweet potatoes and yams. Waddell does not discuss nuts, but these are often given to friends and function as the small change of sociability. Both *tauga* and *puga* are stored for the season of shortage; betelnut is a traditional trade item. All vegetable produce is nowadays considered suitable for marketing. Villages near Popondetta have far more opportunity to sell or barter produce than the villages on the Mount Lamington foothills.

It is customary for animal food to enter the exchange network, either as a gift or as part of a festive meal to which guests are invited. Meat is ceremonial food, eaten for instance to mark the settlement of a quarrel. It is considered somewhat

0748338

TABLE II/6

DIVISION OF LABOUR BETWEEN THE SEXES AMONG THE OROKAIVA
IN 1923
(*Source*: F. E. Williams Papers W.5, dated Wasida 5.10.23)

Women
Planting and small cleaning in garden
Fishing for small fish
Cooking
Cleaning house and surroundings
Pottery
Bark cloth and painting of same
Look after pigs and dogs
String bags
Mourning vests of Job's tears
Mourning neck ornaments, of Job's tears
Armlets of Job's tears
Make shell and string belts

Men
Clearing of gardens
Hunting
Large fishing
Building
Make spears
Make clubs
Make cane belts
Make woven armlets and leglets
Make shell and string belts
Make wooden belts

Day's work of woman
(Ejiro of Borugata)
Sometimes in garden . . . sometimes in village . . . but more often than not
   goes to the garden
Going in the morning she will clean . . . plant . . . dig up taro . . .
In afternoon she collects firewood . . . water (in a gourd, scooping it in with a
   folded leaf), . . . taro, etc. in her string bag (*eti*) and return 'at four
   o'clock'.
Then she cooks for husband and children . . . after that *kaikais* betel and stops
   nothing

improper to eat meat without introducing some element of gift exchange, very much like 'party food' in our own society.

In general, people take any wood they need from their own land. The only record I have of transactions involving wood concerns the obtaining of less common building materials for houses. My informants made a clear distinction between gifts of bush trees and gifts of sago. The former kind create no specific debt but whenever sago is taken a return gift is expected, because, I was told, sago is a cultivated plant.

With regard to feathers and *hambo,* attitudes differ as between areas where raw materials are plentiful and areas where they are rare. On the Mount Lamington foothills they seldom enter the exchange network — perhaps once a generarion, during a ceremony of uncommon importance. On the alluvial plains, they are a frequent trade item.[8] Of other items of traditional trade, betelnuts and lime are the most important. Betelnut grows only on the foothills; lime is made of shells collected on the seashore. It was, and is, therefore common to exchange one for the other, as betelnut can be chewed only together with lime and betelnut chewing is as popular a social activity among the Orokaiva as it is throughout New Guinea and Indonesia. A peppery plant called *hingi* (piper betel) is always chewed with the other two ingredients. This again grows best on the hills, so that it is often exchanged with the betelnuts. The alluvial plains are in a poor bargaining position with regard to the betelnut complex as they produce none of the ingredients from their own land. It may be partly for this reason that they are accustomed to accumulating animal products and to using these as objects of trade.

By far the largest number of exchanges take place within a village, only a minority of transactions occurring between members of different village

TABLE II/7

ACQUISITION OF 'HAMBO' AND 'DI'
(*Source:* Crocombe and Hogbin 1963: 51; Rimoldi 1966: 80)

	Sivepe		Inonda	
	Hambo	Di	Hambo	Di
Inheritance, cash value ($)	48.40	17.60	18.60	5.70
Percentage	53%	40%	17%	12%
Cash Purchase, value ($)	9.30	4.50	36.10	2.00
Percentage	10%	10%	33%	4%
Bride price or other exchanges, value ($)	17.70	6.50	48.30	17.90
Percentage	19%	14%	44%	38%
Made or caught, value ($)	16.60	15.40	5.90	21.10
Percentage	18%	35%	5%	45%
Total, value: ($)	92.00	44.00	108.90	46.70

communities. When these do occur they are usually between neighbouring communities, as Waddell and Krinks have clearly demonstrated.⁹ Intertribal trade, though small in volume, was politically important in that it provided a motive for terminating, or at least interrupting, warlike disputes. Intertribal trade was mainly in animal products, betelnut ingredients, feathers, *hambo,* and certain artifacts which were known to be of high quality in particular districts, e.g. Binandere pots were exchanged for Yega loincloths; only mountain people could supply cassowary feathers, and so on. Such exchanges may, under modern conditions, take the form of gift exchange, barter or sale but it may be doubted whether barter was ever as clearly institutionalised and differentiated from gift exchange among the Orokaiva as is the case in many other parts of Melanesia.

Money. With a few reservations, one could describe the role of money in the modern Orokaiva economy in much the same terms as Salisbury used for the Siane (1962). Salisbury distinguishes between three nexuses of activity. One is concerned with the production, distribution and consumption of subsistence goods, another with luxury goods and a third with ceremonial goods. The three nexuses involve not only categories of goods but also different types of social groups. Among the Orokaiva as among the Siane, money mainly enters the luxury and ceremonial nexuses. As with the Siane, the Orokaiva tend to store pound notes in treasure boxes, with *di* and *hambo,* and to keep them for special purposes which are often ceremonial (payment of brideprice, giving of feasts and church donations), but sometimes utilitarian (payment of taxes). Purchases in trade stores are mostly for luxury items, i.e. objects which the Orokaiva use only when there are guests to be entertained (tinned meat and fish, sugar, tea, batteries, cartridges, kerosene and tobacco, for example). Foods like rice, bread and flour are classifiable as luxuries among the hill people, as here they are used exclusively as guest foods. It is clear, however, from Waddell and Krinks' statistics that on the alluvial plains near Popondetta, rice and flour is bought in far greater quantity in months when taro is in short supply. These products are thus taking the place of subsidiary crops. People in this area prefer to make money from cash crops and services and to spend some of their cash on supplementary staples. The Siane, at the time of Salisbury's research, did not depend on cash as a source of staple food.

The use of money for capital goods merits some attention. Salisbury defines capital as a stock of goods, present before a productive act is performed, used in production and 'immobilised' from direct consumption while the act is in progress. Tools and implements are classed as 'durable instruments of production.' Houses and clothing, etc., are called consumer's capital because they 'produce' services for their owners while they exist. It is interesting to compare, in respect of monetary input, everyday consumer goods and the types of capital just mentioned. While the former have generally remained outside the cash economy, it is precisely in the sphere of capital goods that the traditional industries have been largely or wholly replaced by cash-purchased innovations such as trade, store clothing, agricultural, hunting and cooking implements. Totally new items — radios, flashlights, wrist watches, pressure lamps, sewing machines and guitars have been added. Locked suitcases, for the storage of valuables, are very popular, indicating that safe storage used to be a vexing problem.

Most of these capital goods enter the village by gift or gift exchange. Some types (e.g. kitchenware and clothes) may pass from one village to another by way of brideprice, but other types of gifts (e.g. radios) are hardly ever made in a ceremonial context, but only to close kinsmen. I am not at all sure whether, in Salisbury's terminology, the latter type should be classified as a luxury or a ceremonial item.

One conclusion emerging from the various studies made in the 1960s is that total village income has risen rapidly among the Orokaiva. The sources vary. it may be due to outside employment of persons still ordinarily resident in the village, to increased cash cropping, to sale of food surpluses or to increased remittances from local men employed away from the village.

4. History

The main object of this section is to provide some background for the study of Orokaiva exchange, especially between tribes and between Orokaiva and Europeans.

In physical constitution, Williams considered the Orokaiva to be 'midway between the typical Papuan and the typical Melanesian'. Dupeyrat, who has recently (1965) surveyed the evidence, considers the Orokaiva 'basically of the Papuan Mountain type', but mixed with Polyno-melanesian elements, late-comers in Papua, who spread to the Northern District via Maisina and Manigela. It is certainly true that one notices more Polyno-melanesian features along the coast (e.g. among the Yega) than inland.

In the period just prior to European occupation, the most notable aspect of Orokaiva history that can be reconstructed is pressure from the dense population on the Mount Lamington foothills upon the sparser populations surrounding the mountain on all sides, but especially to the north and east. These sparser populations (to whom Williams gives the common name Sauaha) pressed upon the still sparser populations dwelling in the still less fertile country on their own northern and eastern borders (see Chinnery and Beaver 1916; Williams 1930: 152–4; Monckton 1921: Ch. XXIV; Crocombe and Hogbin 1963: 14–16).

In 1888, in response to Australian pressure, the British government annexed Papua. The first administrator, Sir William McGregor, made many arduous exploratory expeditions while establishing his rule in this vast unknown territory. On one of these expeditions he ascended the Mambare river to its highest navigable point, a few miles above Tamata creek, where he discovered the existence of gold in the sand and shores of the river (Monckton 1921: 78; Murray 1912: 326–8). This was the first discovery of gold in Papua with important commercial prospects, and led to a major movement of prospectors and miners to the Northern District. Relationships with the Papuans were bad from the beginning, and there were numerous killings by both sides. In 1900 150 miners were working on the Yodda river; the Yodda and Gira goldfields together produced 15,000 oz. of gold (Murray 1912: 333). In order to stop the bloodshed, resident magistrates were stationed at Ioma, along the Mambare and at two places on the Kumusi river, which was for some years the access route to the Yodda field.

The early relationships between Orokaiva and Australians may be gleaned from the three books of memoirs written by Monckton, who was resident magistrate in the district until his immoderate punitive expeditions led to his being eased out of the service in 1907. His most memorable achievement was the building of a road from Buna through Orokaiva country to Kokoda, near the goldfields. This road, slightly modernised, is still the main line of communication in the Northern District today. By the time it was built (1904), the sanguinary battles between Monckton and the Dobodura and others had taken place, so government patrols were treated with much circumspection. Nonetheless the tribes around Mount Lamington were still 'fighting like Kilkenny cats' (Monckton 1922: 142). Monckton's comments on the road are interesting.

> Yodda Road is tabu to the tribes and is traversed in perfect safety by single white men and their unarmed carriers. Never since I broke the Dobudura and Sangara has there ever been a theft upon it. It is a sanctuary for any and everyone; the wildest tribes only visit it in peace to trade food and goods to passing travellers. They rather like it, as small parties of hostile tribes can move freely about on it in safety with their women and children. (1934:41)

While the road was being built 'no hostilities took place between my working parties and the local inhabitants' (*ibid.* 63). It was thus described not only by Monckton, but also by Lieutenant-Governor Murray who wrote:

> The Wasida and Sangara have been particularly active in forming markets along the road which leads from Buna Bay to the Yodda Goldfield, and in supplying carriers with taro and other food in exchange for articles of trade, such as tobacco and glass bottles, which are much prized for the manufacture of razors. (1912:105)

The Protectorate of British New Guinea became Australian territory by the passing of the Papua Act 1905 by the Commonwealth Government of Australia. The new administration adopted a policy of peaceful penetration and the Monckton type of massacres were not repeated. Nonetheless, these early excesses are now forever part of Orokavia history. In the period that followed Papua presented 'in many ways an example of enlightened rule' (Mair 1948: Ch. III). Many measures of social and economic native development were introduced, though these invariably took the form of 'native regulations', for the breach of which a penalty was attached. The principle of coercion was applied over a remarkably wide and ever widening field.

From the days of McGregor, local control was in the hands of 'village constables, paid servants of the Crown. They were intermediaries between government and people, chosen by European officers.' From 1925 onwards, one or more 'village councillors' were appointed alongside the village constable. These were not paid servants of the Crown but were intended 'to be the representatives of native opinion'. In the Northern District I found they had generally been regarded as constables' assistants or subordinates. No indigenous officials had any judicial powers, as Murray felt such powers would lead to corruption.

In the period of Murray's rule (1907–40), the government's basic objective was to turn the Papuan into a keen and efficient indentured plantation worker. In that role, he was assiduously protected by measures which effectively minimised alienation of Papuan land and controlled recruitment, payment of wages and the employer's treatment of labour.

No money was devoted to public education under Murray's rule. Social improvement programmes were largely confined to village inspections, at which law and order, hygiene and road maintenance were imposed by patrol officers under penalty of prison sentences. Hamlets were consolidated into larger villages, as these were easier to patrol. Villages were ordered, for their own good, to plant commercial tree crops.[10] Education was entrusted to the missions; health services were left either to missions or to employers. In 1919, a head tax was imposed upon the Papuans.

By a gentlemen's agreement between the Protestant denominations, a specified portion of the Territory of Papua was given to the exclusive pastoral care of each of them. North-East Papua, from Cape Dulcie to the German border, became Anglican territory. The centre of the mission was at Dogura, Milne Bay District, where the first Bishop of New Guinea, Montagu Stone-Wigg, established his court in 1898. That year, missionaries were sent to set up stations all along the coast of the diocese, at Cape Vogel, Manigela, Gona and as far north as the Mambare River.

The New Guinea Mission soon set about adding to its staff by building one more advanced school at Dogura, to which it sent the most promising students from the village schools, in the hope that these could be trained as priests and deacons. The Mission thus offered responsibility to Papuans very much earlier than any other White institution in the Territory. In 1967, the bishop of the Northern District diocese, as well as a number of priests and virtually all mission teachers were Papuans, often drawn from the Northern District tribes.

Experience with miners, government and mission in the Northern District led rather quickly to the emergence of adjustment cults, notably the Baigona and Taro Cults[11] arising respectively in 1912 and 1914. Though Worsley (1957: Ch. III) classifies them as non-millenarian, he recognises them as having been a political threat to the Australian authorities. Doctrines of unity, co-operation and comradeship between formerly hostile tribes were central to the Taro Cult. Cult leaders dissociated themselves from the Christian missions and claimed a special bond with Jesus Christ. Although the Northern District never developed cargo cults of the classical type, even in later years, there is a constant undercurrent of what one may call millennial thinking, which is of great concern to the government even today.

The Second World War. A new era in Papuan history began when the Japanese invaded New Guinea in January 1942 and, in June 1942, landed at Buna, in the Northern District, with the intention of crossing the Owen Stanley Range and taking Port Moresby. They were checked at the Kokoda Trail by Australian and American forces who by January 1943 drove them from the Paupan mainland. According to Lucy Mair the Japanese were not unpopular until they began to plunder gardens and round up pigs, a course to which they resorted when the Allied navy blocked their supply lines (Mair 1948: 199). The Orokaiva mostly took to the bush where they lived in temporary shelters and grew German taro.

Army administration introduced a new tone in human relations. Australian troops, in their dealings with Papuans, applied egalitarian attitudes prevalent in their home country. American troops, by their equal treatment of Negro soldiers, created the impression that racial barriers had no place in their society! The troops' friendliness to the Papuans was tangibly expressed by gifts, not only of tobacco and other small luxuries, but also of discarded tools and equipment still used in villages today. It is in these events that the Orokaiva saw the portent of the coming of a new era.

The Eruption of Mount Lamington.   In 1951, a Peléan eruption occurred on Mount Lamington. The *nuée ardente* produced by this eruption completely devastated a surrounding area of 68 sq. miles (Taylor 1958). Almost 4,000 people were killed and there were hardly any survivors of the numerous Sangara tribe. Those who did survive were provided with food, medicines and other comforts by the government and were for some time maintained in evacuation camps. The evacuees were not at once allowed to return to their villages as the authorities feared further explosions in the mountain. Some officials saw in this sequence of events a chance to create Papuan model communities with up-to-date socio-economic institutions. These plans for village reform, whatever their merits, were not realised at that time, partly because the danger of further explosions was soon greatly reduced, in the view of vulcanologists, so that the people were allowed to go back to their old village sites; partly also, because the reforms were not favoured by the Australian administration which assumed power after the defeat of the Labour Government in 1951.

Intensification of Development Policy.   Large scale, expertly planned social, economic and political development did not start in Papua until around 1960 (Parker 1966:189). In the economic sphere the first major development success was the building up of a coffee industry based on the production of indigenous growers using their own village land. While by far the largest quantity of this coffee is grown in the Highlands, the yield in the Northern District was enough to assure to any Orokaiva who entered the scheme an income of something like $60–100, in the year 1966–67. During that year all the villages I visited, both on the foothills and in the plains, were producing coffee. It was an activity in which any able-bodied man resident in a village would normally engage to a greater or lesser extent. Several factors aided the development of this industry.

Agricultural extension work to train the population of the Northern District in coffee growing began immediately after the eruption. A training school was set up in Popondetta. Papuan agricultural assistants were trained to give basic instruction and to distribute seed. These assistants spread knowledge not only while they were employed by the government, but even more when they went back to their villages and grew their own coffee.

Title improvement work is also beginning to contribute to agricultural development. Until 1956, the government kept entirely aloof from indigenous tenure problems and passed no ordinances enabling it to adjudicate in land disputes. By that time, however, it had become obvious that commercial arboriculture could be developed only to a limited extent unless a land registry was introduced and the traditional Orokaiva principle of maintaining residual rights in land was adandoned. Though the first attempts to change the land tenure system were unsuccessful, in 1967 it looked as though a very satisfactory procedure had been worked out. (See Ch. V.)

Road improvement was another necessary preliminary to significant village

TABLE II/8

ENROLMENT IN PRIMARY SCHOOLS OF THE
ANGLICAN MISSION IN THE NORTHERN
DISTRICT

(*Source*: Department of Education, Popondetta)

	1966	1967 (Est.)
Preparatory Classes	1,775	1,845
Standard 1	1,290	1,307
Standard 2	1,563	1,581
Standard 3	1,278	1,298
Standard 4	1,275	1,310
Standard 5	693	708
Standard 6	488	498
Total	8,362	8,547

Note: Some schools offered classes up to Standard 2, some up to Standard 3, some up to Standard 4, while only a few schools offered classes beyond that level. Children unable to obtain transfers to schools offering classes at a higher level might stay at school for a year or more after finishing the highest available grade. This explains the unusual statistical pattern.

development. By 1967 two important moves had been made: the arterial road between Buna and Kokoda was being rebuilt and linked to the main coffee-producing villages by a system of access roads, built with the assistance of taxes raised in villages.

The educational services have not, so far, been very closely integrated with economic development goals. Many of the schools in the Northern District are conducted by the Mission. While the objectives of many of the Mission schools are still primarily religious, and the teaching staff has only rudimentary training, some of them do prepare students for further education at the secondary level, and provide recruits for skilled occupations. The Sasembata school attended by Sivepe children falls within that category. Chances of passing a qualifying examination for secondary schooling are good and from that point adequate financial assistance is usually available to students. Villages such as Hohorita and Inonda, lacking such opportunities, and having access to only two or three years of elementary schooling, cannot hope to have any but the brightest students advance to secondary education. As the language of instruction is English in all schools, those who do not advance beyond elementary grades do not become acquainted with concepts relevant to development objectives.[12]

Local Government Council. The Higaturu Local Government Council, formed in 1956, serves about 15,000 Orokaiva, comprising the Popondetta, Sohe-Popondetta and Saiho census divisions. In 1966 the main activities of the

TABLE II/9

REVISED ESTIMATES OF HIGATURU LOCAL GOVERNMENT COUNCIL
FOR JULY 1966–JUNE 1967 (*abridged*)

Revenues		Expenditures	
Tax: 2000 males	$16,000	*A. Personal Emolument*	
1000 females	1,000	Council President	$ 156
Truck Hire	13,000	Council Vice-President	108
Aid Post Orderlies		Councillors	1,560
		Exec., Fin. Ctee	108
Subsidy	1,250	Council Clerk	1,170
Water Supply Subsidy	3,320	Messenger	390
Aid Post Subsidy	240	Landrover Driver	500
Adult Education		Truck Drivers	1,450
Subsidy	780	Agric. Fieldworker	234
		Market Manager	260
Miscellaneous	2,900	Aid Post Orderlies	2,500
Total	$38,490	*Total*	$ 8,692
		B. Revenue Expenditure	
		Council Administration	$ 1,000
		Transport	5,000
		Drugs	720
		Adult Education	780
		Other Items	1,686
		Total	$ 9,186
		C. Capital Expenditure	
		Drivers' houses (2)	$ 2,200
		Council Staff House	800
		Council House Furniture	500
		Market Building	1,500
		Staff, House, Health, Personnel	800
		Water Supplies (16 villages)	6,565
		Clinics (3 villages)	900
		Roading (3 projects)	6,070
		Other Items	2,099
		Total	$21,434
		Grand Total	$39,212

Council were road building, improvement of water supplies, building medical aid posts, maintaining produce markets at Popondetta and Saiho and the operation of trucks to provide extra revenue. Most revenue was derived from a head tax of $8 per annum for every adult male and $2 per annum for every adult female. The central government paid a 50 per cent subsidy on certain Council projects. Between 1959 and 1962, the Council also ran the coffee processing factory operated for Orokaiva producers, but this was transferred to the control of an

Orokaiva Coffee-Grower Society, a producers' co-operative formed for the purpose.

The Council is made up of twenty-six Orokaiva members who are paid a monthly stipend. However, in practice a government adviser attached to the Council appears to determine policy. Indigenous attitudes to the Council are analysed in detail in Schwimmer 1967. Together with the Coffee Society, it has offered the Orokaiva some political participation and the importance of this new departure is vividly recognised by the people.

The New Age. Since the Second World War, a great many ideas from the outside world have been communicated to the Orokaiva. I have already mentioned economic, and some political ideas; in addition, the Anglican mission began to attract many converts, especially after the Mount Lamington disaster. By 1964, the great majority of Orokaiva were baptised.

The establishment of the House of Assembly in Port Moresby, giving limited powers of political decision to Papuan representatives elected by universal suffrage, has introduced new patterns in village life: meetings with the local member, with other candidates, and with organisers acting for these candidates and presenting political argument. The personnel of the local government council tends to be deeply committed in national politics and to talk about political affairs when visiting villages.

During such discussions, the Orokaiva are beginning to learn that an end to Australian rule is conceivable and that they will have some voice in decisions relating to the independence of their own country. They fully recognise that this makes an immediate difference to the balance of power between themselves and

TABLE II/10

EDUCATION AND OCCUPATIONAL EXPERIENCE OF THE
JEGASE AND SEHO CLANS OF SIVEPE COMPARED –
ADULT MALES ONLY

Approximate Period	*Education*		*Occupational Experience*	
	Seho	*Jegase*	*Seho*	*Jegase*
Nil	6	6	4	5
1 year	–	1	1	2
2 years	–	2	1	–
3 years	–	1	–	–
4 years	–	2	–	2
5 years	–	–	–	1
6 years	–	1	–	–
7 years			–	–
8 years			–	–
Over 8 years			–	4
Data vague	2	1	2	–
Total	8	14	8	14

TABLE II/11

HOHORITA MALE ADULTS IN SKILLED
OCCUPATIONS

Occupation	Resident	Non-Resident	Total
Teacher	9	1	10
'Medical'	3	–	3
Driver	2	2	4
Shopkeeper	4	–	4
Other	2	2	4
Total	20	5	25

the Australian rulers, although they also know that so far the difference is not great.

Finally, broadcasting services and the messages transmitted by councillors have greatly increased their knowledge of the outside world. Through their transistor radios, they become aware of, and discuss, the affairs of the independent nations of Asia and Africa. They are thus beginning to feel part of the modern world.

5. Field Locations

I spent one year in the Northern District, travelling through it a good deal. My detailed data come mainly from three villages which I shall now describe briefly.[13]

Inonda.   This was the first village I visited; I stayed there for eighteen days, returning later for a few brief periods. The village was previously reported on by Crocombe and Hogbin, Krinks and Waddell. It lies eleven miles from Popondetta, on the road to Oro Bay, has seven dwelling houses and a population of forty-two. At the time of my visit, there was only one politically significant clan represented in the village, namely Andiriha, who had been driven from the foothills of Mount Lamington by the Sangara tribe some fifty years earlier. Inonda, like other Orokaiva villages, was laid out in an elongated rectangle, with the dwellings spaced at equal distances. Neat rows of palms, shrubs and floral borders interspersed with trees subdivided the central area between the houses so as to give each family a semi-private space. The village had an Anglican chapel, made out of a corrugated-iron storage shed, where a lay preacher gave services. There was also a corrugated-iron copra-drying plant, no longer in use. Just behind the village was a slab of concrete laid down by the army during the war, and now being utilised as the floor of a women's club house that was being built at the time.

Unlike the other villages I visited, Inonda is only partly Christianised, four of the households being pagan. Coffee gardens have been established only by the Christian families and the women's club, which is one of a number organised by the government for social development purposes, and is supported exclusively by the same families. Inonda was also unusual, at least in my experience, in having one leading family in control of virtually all forms of community organisation.

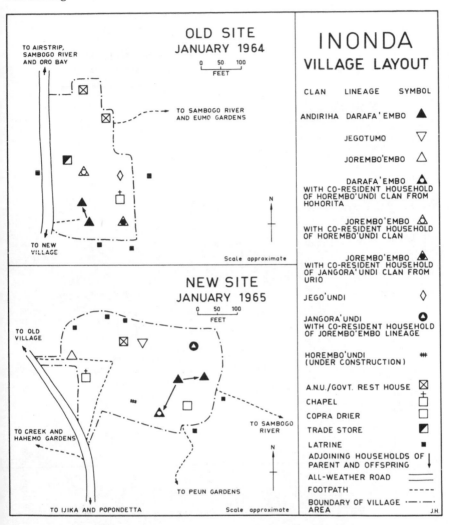

Fig. 4.   Inonda village layout.

The leader, a government driver, earned about 65 per cent of the total cash income of the whole village, not only in wages but also through various enterprises on the side. He was the lay preacher as well. The only limit to his influence was the unwillingness of the pagan faction to become involved in 'modern' activities of which he was the champion.

Ecologically, Inonda is characteristic of the alluvial plains region to the east of the mountain. It lies between 200 and 300 feet above sea level, and has a comparatively low rain-fall and long dry periods. Its population density is low: 42 people on a village domain of 2850 acres (less than 10 per square mile). The best Inonda land is 580 acres of coarse-textured recent riverine deposits, covered with forest or regrowth and lying beside the Sambogo and Girua rivers.

42

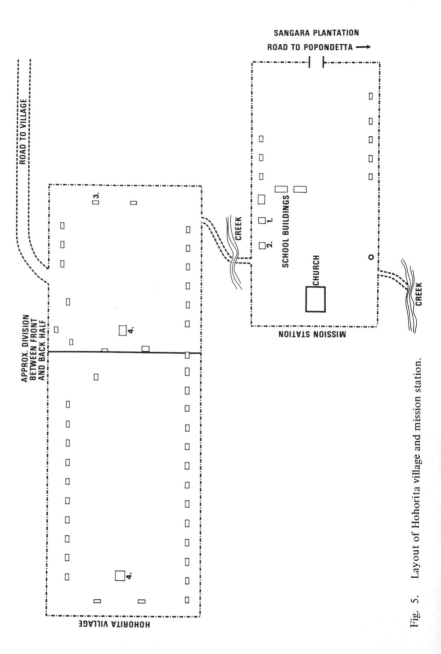

Fig. 5. Layout of Hohorita village and mission station.

Hohorita. My stay in Hohorita lasted for a month, and I made several return visits. This village lies thirteen miles from Popondetta on the road to Saiho, has forty-one dwelling houses and a population of 358. Hohorita and three contiguous hamlets are the home of the Sangara who survived the Mount Lamington disaster. The Sangara population was reduced by the eruption from some 3,000 to 195 people, who stayed together in the evacuation camp and later founded Hohorita, where the remnants of about a dozen clans may be found. By far the strongest clans in this village are those whose homes, at the time of the eruption, were at the outer edge of the devastation area and who were able to run away from the *nuée ardente* before the searing blast could reach them.

Hohorita, though built much earlier than Inonda (1957), was not beautified with the same care. The area between the two rows of houses was bare, except for some coconut and betelnut palms. The village was divided into two rectangles by a short row of houses. The front and back part were settled at different times and different clans were dominant. When I was working in the front half I would meet hardly anyone from the back half and vice versa. A feast house had been built in both the front and the back sections of the village. The feasts had been held just a few weeks before my arrival, to entertain neighbouring villages. Originally a combined feast had been planned, but disagreement had prevented it. There was no chapel in the village, but a mission station just next to it, with a white mission teacher, a mission school and several Papuan teachers who were in charge of church services. This was a contrast with Inonda, which was several miles removed from a school and even further from a mission. There was a woman's club with a small club house, but again this was supported by only a small minority.

Hohorita was entirely Christianised, in the sense that everyone had been baptised. A number of the older men had been educated in a mission station prior to the eruption and had become mission teachers while evacuated. When coffee became a lucrative cash crop — more lucrative than teaching — many of them had retired to the village. As a result the leadership pattern differed sharply from Inonda. About twenty men in Hohorita had held down occupations requiring some European skills, and these men tended to work out together the everyday and long-range decisions required in the village. The leading personality was, at that time, a well-educated man, who for years had been the chairman of the Higaturu Local Government Council. In Hohorita virtually everyone was growing coffee. Some men worked in the plantations nearby.

Ecologically, Inonda is characteristic of the alluvial plains region to the east Lamington foothills. Before the eruption, the concentration of population was entirely on the higher reaches of the tribal domain as rainfall and fertility are higher there. The lower portion of the territory, away from the mountain, was used for hunting. But the government discouraged reoccupation of the higher land, for fear of further eruptions. Hohorita is lower down than the old villages. The more elevated land is used a little less than before, and often for coffee rather than subsistence crops. The topsoil is volcanic loam; the rainfall is probably between 120 and 150 inches per annum. Population density is 135 per sq. mile. This is a little less than is usual on the Mount Lamington foothills, but prior to the eruption the population must have been very dense indeed.

Sivepe. I stayed in Sivepe for about nine months, from September 1966 until June 1967. Previous intensive studies had been made there by Rimoldi and Waddell. Sivepe is twenty-four miles from Popondetta, but this distance represents a drive of two to four hours in a Landrover, according to the time of year. The village lies on a side road, serving a population of some 2,000 living in the valley of the Sasembata (or Hembe) and Sohu rivers, two tributaries of the Kumusi. This side road runs from the main road in a south-easterly direction as far as Kendata. The Sasembata-Sohu valley combines all the most favourable ecological conditions: heavy rainfall, deep volcanic loam, excellent drainage, easy contours. The first time I drove to Sivepe was during the dry season. Turning from the main road, I found myself on a slightly improved grass track, with villages built right across it, the sweet aroma of coffee trees (which, incidentally is strongly disliked by the Orokaiva) pervading the atmosphere, lush vegetation, and a life-style on which the Europeans had apparently made much less impact.

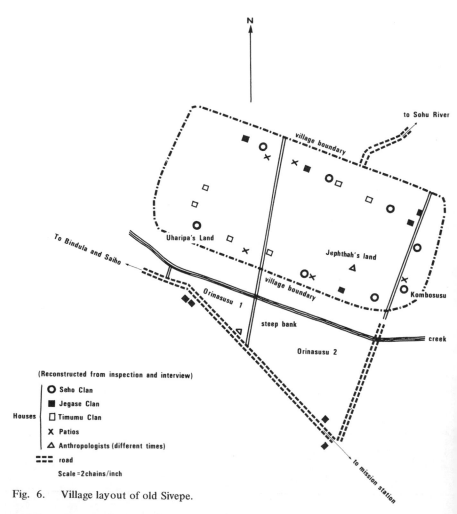

Fig. 6.   Village layout of old Sivepe.

Sivepe has twenty-four dwelling houses and a population of 137. The two politically dominant clans are Jegase and Seho, but some families from the Sorovi clan had not long ago migrated to Sivepe from a neighbouring village (Garombi). Sivepe had been shifted recently to the present site so that decorative borders were not yet established, though such improvements were started during my stay. It was planned that the village would be rectangular in shape, with two long facing rows, as in Hohorita and Inonda, but a third row, supposedly temporary, had been established on the hill behind the planned site. In other respects, however, the same standard of village layout had been followed. The houses were roomier than in the other villages and had walls of horizontally laid shingles, an innovation of which the villagers were rather proud.

Sivepe has no chapel, but the Anglican mission station is less than a quarter of a mile away from the village. The school conducted on the station is one of the best in the Northern District; it teaches up to grade six and many of its students qualify for admission to secondary schools. The station also maintains a small field hospital, with a Papuan assistant medical officer in charge. For more serious cases the large government hospital at Saiho was used, a facility serving the whole of the Northern District, but in practice out of reach of distant villages like Inonda. Hohorita people, however, use it frequently.

Sivepe has been Christianised only very recently. There were no baptisms until after the eruption and the Seho clan did not join the Church until about 1963. Today very few pagans are left and they do not form a political or other faction. Leadership is shared between several strong personalities. Sivepe lacks residents who stand out by superior wealth or European education, but is rather more homogeneous in that respect than either of the two other villages. Money comes mainly from coffee and from remittances sent by relatives working outside the village.

Sivepe, like most of the Sasembata-Sohu valley, has an extremely dense population — about 180 per sq. mile.

REFERENCES

1   Brookfield uses the Klingebiel and Montgomery (1961) classification of land which distinguishes land areas by the degree of limitation to land use imposed by geographical conditions. Limitations may be due to terrain, lithology, soil, or climate. A large territory surrounding Mount Lamington falls in classes I to III (which means it is suitable for cultivation with a mild degree of limitation), as contrasted with most of the rest of New Guinea, where the limitations are much greater.

2   Figs. 1 and 2 give a general impression of the geography of the district: land systems, natural features, settlements roads, tribal areas, etc. Table II/1 shows the distribution of population in the Northern District of Papua. Table II/2 shows the age breakdown of the population in Sivepe and Inonda. Table II/10 shows rather strikingly how suddenly labour migration began: the men of the Seho clan of Sivepe were just a little too old to have been involved, but the Jegase clan, whose members were slightly younger, mostly spent some time on jobs outside the village before or shortly after marriage.

3   Orokaiva: *ina*; botanical: *sacharum edule*.

4   Orokaiva: *tauga*; botanical: *cycas media*; Orokaiva: *puga*; botanical: *terminalia okaria*. There are two varieties of breadfruit, called *oga* and *eumba*. They are both somewhat unusual but I failed, in spite of sending samples, to obtain indentifications.

5   Details of garden production are given in Table II/3. Rainfall at Sivepe and Inonda is shown in Rimoldi 1966:109; Crocombe and Hogbin 1963:100.

6   A plan of a contemporary Orokaiva house is shown in Fig. 3. Recent changes in house design, house construction and domestic amenities are summarised in Table II/4.

7   See Tables II/5 and II/6. Williams' data are taken from an unpublished manuscript and appeared first in Schwimmer 1969:226. I have discussed the Orokaiva division of labour in more detail in Schwimmer 1969: 145–50 and explained the apparent discrepancies between Williams' table and Waddell's and Krinks' statistics.

8   Crocombe and Hogbin (1963) provide a list of prices prevailing in this trade. They report that there is still some trade in shell ornaments from the coast and in feathers for head dresses from the mountains. Informants at Eroro, on the coast near Buna, gave me details of their traditional trade with Managalasi of the nearby mountains. A Sivepe man who has hunting rights to land near Ajoro goes there to hunt birds and sell the feathers. His chances of finding any of the more valuable birds near Sivepe are remote. The difference in Sivepe and Inonda patterns (i.e. the foothills and the alluvial plains) appears from the data in Table II/7. It will be seen that Sivepe stock is to a far greater extent inherited, whereas Inonda stock is to a far greater extent acquired through brideprice (value $13), barter (value $21.60) and other exchanges (value $13.70).

9   Dr. Waddell has provided a detailed statistical table of the geographical distribution of subsistence produce (Waddell and Krinks 1968:218). This table provides clear and detailed information on the geographical range of the Sivepe exchange network. A full descriptive account may be found in Schwimmer 1969: 41–69.

10   An interesting picture of this period of Orokaiva history is drawn in Beaver, 1916.

11   Full information on these cults will be found in Chinnery and Haddon (1917) and Williams (1928). If has escaped previous commentators that Bia, who started the taro cult, was employed for some years by Monckton, and participated in various punitive enterprises with an alacrity most pleasing to his master. He was described in Monckton's books in rather revealing detail (e.g. 1921: 185, 268, 269, 295, 308; 1922: 10, 13, 65, 136, 172, 214, 216). For the present relationship between the Orokaiva and the missions, see Schwimmer 1969; 123–33.

12   The general subject of Orokaiva economic development since 1951 is very fully covered in numerous bulletins published by the New Guinea Research Unit from 1963 to the present, and also in Schwimmer 1969. A general indication of the investments in socio-economic development is given by a table of public expenditure in the territory of Papua for the years ended 30 June 1961 to 1965 (Commonwealth of Australia: *Annual Report of the Territory of Papua for the period 1 July 1964 to 30 June 1965*, 179). The growing emphasis on educational services is perhaps the most notable aspect. Table II/8 indicates the pattern of school attendance. Table II/9 summarises the activities of the Higaturu Local Government Council; roads, water supplies and clinics are perhaps the projects most relevant to development.

13   The three villages have been sketched in figures 4, 5 and 6. Education and occupational experience at Sivepe and Hohorita are analysed in Tables II/10 and II/11.

CHAPTER III

THE IDEOLOGY OF INTERTRIBAL EXCHANGE

1. *Experiences with the Exchange System*

Many authors have been fascinated by Melanesian ideas of reciprocity and exchange. Malinowski was the first to show in detail that these ideas are a central theme in Melanesian cultures; his lead was followed by Bateson, Belshaw, Burridge, van der Leeden, Pouwer, Reay, Sahlins, Salisbury, Strathern, Wagner, Young and many others. The literature on Orokaiva exchange, however, is less comprehensive than for some other parts of Melanesia. Williams, the principal ethnographer, has written a great deal on reciprocity and marriage exchange among Papuan groups, but this was mostly in his later works (1934, 1936, etc.), which do not deal with the Orokaiva. Some phenomena, as he records in his later ethnographies, might in some instances just as well have been found among the Orokaiva, and here it will be my role to fill in the record. Very recently, Waddell and Krinks (1968) have collected detailed statistical data on Orokaiva exchange. Valuable as this material is, it is concerned with economic geography rather than social organisation and ideology.

All ethnographers who have worked among the Orokaiva seem to be well aware of the importance of the exchange system. Whenever I met one he soon came up with the key question: 'How did you get on with *hoija*?', *hoija* being an Orokaiva word meaning 'exchange between non-kin'. Fieldwork in any area probably has its tensions; among the Orokaiva the initial distrust of, perhaps the hostility towards, the fieldworker finds its expression in the rather aggressive offering of (sometimes unwanted) gifts and services, followed immediately by peremptory demands or ceaseless wheedling for return prestations. Every fieldworker thinks of some 'solution' to this problem: accepting everything (because according to Mauss the acceptance of gifts is obligatory), accepting just a little from everyone, accepting prestations from only a carefully defined and limited group, or maybe accepting nothing, though I cannot imagine this. What all these anthropologists are talking about, though from a purely practical rather than a theoretical viewpoint, is how they should behave as exchange partners, given their own peculiar status. It should be a comfort to them that Firth has recently (1967) challenged Mauss' proposition that the acceptance of gifts among primitives is obligatory. They will now probably have fewer uneaten potatoes and German taro lying on their verandahs!

In all the villages I visited events followed the same kind of sequence. I always received an effusive welcome and many gifts for which no return was asked. This phase would last about two days. Villages where I made very brief visits never passed beyond that stage, thus remaining in my memory as exceptionally endearing in their generosity. Before I understood the system, I harboured romantic notions of going to live in these villages. In the second phase there would be frantic *hoija*. Everyone brought gifts, asked for tobacco, salt, kerosene and rides in the car. People appeared to be most hurt when I would not drive into Popondetta every day, and take the whole village with me. Whenever I was offered any gifts or service during this period there would be an immediate demand for some desired benefit.

After some weeks, this rather aggressive barrage diminished. I found myself with a number of regular exchange partners who brought me what it was presumed I needed and who asked me for more or less standard return benefits. Two sorts of partnership developed: one type of partner expected a return gift immediately upon bringing me his own; the second type made gifts for which he asked nothing — they were represented as gestures of pure affection. Yet in the future an occasion would arise when I would be asked for, or would spontaneously offer, something in return. But this second type of partnership was far more similar to the kind of gift exchange the village people had among their fellow villagers or close associates. As more and more people shifted from the first to the second type of partnership, I could see something like a genuine exchange network building up. People trusted me enough to allow me to be in their debt for a while. I was thus approaching the stage when I would be regarded as a desirable exhange partner, or, to put it in Orokaiva terms, as a man of some moral virtue. It seemed to me that it was on my behaviour as an exchange partner that my status would ultimately depend.

Most of the significant events in which the village was involved were also concerned with exchange. While marriages, deaths, feasts and initiations were all occasions for ritual and magic, the gifts always loomed largest in everyone's interests. It would usually take at least a year, but often far longer, to accumulate the gifts needed for such occasions. During this period members of the family, local clan branch or village (whichever was the donating group) would be constantly on the lookout for money or gift objects that could be stored up. People would go looking for jobs. They would keep unused some clothing they had been given by a relative. Whenever a visit outside the village was contemplated, an essential part of the preparations was the getting together of the gifts that would have to be taken. Or when a visitor arrived, there was stealthy activity in the background to prepare the gifts without which he would not be allowed to leave. The size of the gifts would always be carefully planned, in accordance with the importance of the visit, the extent to which it was thought politic to do homage, and the availability of supplies. But the making of the gift would always be done in so casual a manner that one might easily believe it was totally spontaneous.

This manner must be affectionate and humble. But the wise man, in making a gift, puts his partner in his debt as much as possible without suffering undue expense, while at the same time enhancing his own status. At a later time, he will use his status as creditor to the best advantage. His concern is to foster a social relationship while at the same time seeking the acquisition of some scarce resource. Social and economic ends are pursued simultaneously. Thus Melanesian gift exchange differs to some extent from the Western exchange of Christmas presents with which it is sometimes compared. In the former, as opposed to the latter system, the acquisition of desired scarce resources is a most important consideration; the fostering of social relationships is equally important in both systems.

Westerners often criticise Melanesians for being too grasping and mean in gift exchange. Absurd though this criticism may seem, it arises from a real cultural difference: Westerners depend on institutions other than gift exchange for the acquisition of desired scarce resources. Hence the institution of exchanging Christmas presents need serve no other end but the fostering of social relations. For the Melanesians, with a rudimentary market system, gift exchange must serve economic as well as social ends. This lack of differentiation leads to the necessary consequence that social exchange is rarely effective unless prestations of economic value are exchanged between the partners and both sides are satisfied with what they receive.

Orokaiva regard exchange relations as the *causa efficiens* of social relations; they cannot envisage any significant social relations in the absence of exchange relations and they ascribe all breakdowns in social relations to an antecedent breakdown in exchange relations. They support this view with cogent and sophisticated arguments, which will be presented throughout this work. Here, I shall quote only a few examples of their reasoning so as to give it some *a priori* plausibility.

One evening a women's dance practice was interrupted by an angry man calling his wife to come home. It turned out that his son's wife, who lived with the couple, had run off and returned to her village. The immediate cause of this escape was clear: he had tried to seduce her. He considered himself entirely justified in doing so as the young woman belonged to his son. To which his wife retorted that the son was hers also. The loss of the young woman, for whom bride price had been paid and whom the son would certainly expect to be reserved for him, was very serious and led to a meeting involving his clan, his wife's clan and the son's wife's clan. This meant that all of Sivepe was there, as well as a number of people from neighbouring Sasembata, the son's wife's village. A councillor was invited to adjudicate. The Sasembata people's arguments were interesting but not relevant here. The meeting was mainly concerned with what was regarded as the key problem: the conflict between the older couple. Their marriage had been unhappy for some years. The wife had been away to Port Moresby for a long time; when she returned the husband had gone away, also to Port Moresby. When he came back he found his wife was having an affair with another man. He himself was constantly chasing his three daughters-in-law.

The meeting addressed itself to the question of what had caused this marriage breakdown. The husband had been wrong to pursue his daughters-in-law; the wife had been wrong in committing adultery, and so on. But how did it begin? Why had the wife gone to Port Moresby in the first place? So she told the tale. She had had diarrhoea; her husband had become angry. But she kept on going out of the house. She then took some of his betelnuts to chew, and he told her in a fury that he did not want her to go to his garden any longer. She did not get food for a day and a half and then left for Port Moresby.

No further questions were asked. Once the husband had confirmed this account, the meeting ruled that the cause of the marriage breakdown was the husband's refusal to allow her to enter his garden. The attempted seduction, the adultery, the escapades to Port Moresby, the violent words and acts that had characterised the marriage over the years were all declared to be blameworthy, but the most serious of the offences was the husband's act in denying his wife entry to the taro garden. This signified the breaking off of the basic exchange relation in a marriage whereby the man clears the garden, the wife harvests the taro, and cooks it, and the husband and wife both eat it. I was told that when this exchange relation is broken, the marriage itself breaks down.

Why it is the taro garden where exchange between husband and wife is so important will be discussed in Chapter VI. I am concerned here to show that in tracing the cause of a marriage breakdown, what the Orokaiva seem to be looking for is evidence of a breakdown in the area of gift exchange. As long as the husband still gives his wife taro, there may be considerable difficulties between them, but these are not *defined* as a breakdown in Orokaiva culture unless there is a breakdown in Obligatory exchange.

Another such case was that of a man who took sides in a quarrel between his brother and another man who had been trying to rape, i.e. seduce by force, that brother's wife. I thought that the village generally would be on the brother's side, as rape is disapproved of, but almost everyone took the side of the rapist and the man who took the side of his brother had to leave the village. The man who was expelled had a long history of trouble making. During my stay he had been involved in every fight except those between husbands and wives. He had also committed rape, his victim being a prohibited partner under the incest rules. His trouble was, so I was told, that no woman wanted him. I asked my informants why this was. The reason was that he had been married previously, he had maltreated his wife and she had run away. Now nobody would help him. And why would nobody help him? Well, brideprice had been paid for his first wife; it had been lost through his fault, and that was the 'real' reason why nobody supported him in the quarrel. Here again we notice that the cause of the trouble was the breakdown of an exchange cycle. When a man has been helped in paying brideprice he has an obligation towards his clansmen to hold his wife, raise a family and be a support for the others. He must manage the relationship with his own affines properly and make them into valuable exchange partners.

In both instances a basic exchange cycle had been broken and that was thought to constitute the essence of the relationship. In the first case this was the exchange between man and woman in making their own contributions and deriving their own benefits in the taro garden — a cycle of exchange which parallels the cultivation cycle of the taro itself. In the second case it was the exchange between clansmen which is complete only when the man who received the brideprice provides recruits for the clan, as well as a steady new affinal alliance. It does not concern me here whether psychologists would, in such cases, accept the exchange breakdown as the real cause of the social breakdown; I have illustrated that the Orokaiva view social breakdowns in this manner.

2. Folk Explanations of Exchange

Having noted how the Orokaiva diagnose cases of social conflict, let us now explore the social philosophy underlying these diagnoses. My argument will be in three steps. First, I shall restate in a more generalised form the Orokaiva ideas hinted at in the previous section; secondly, I shall express these ideas in the form of a more abstract model; thirdly, I shall show how the Orokaiva justify their ideas in terms of their own religio-philosophic system.

Orokaiva social philosophy differs from our own, in the first place by its refusal to recognise the authority of anyone outside the individual's extended family, a characteristic to which I shall give more attention later. If the Orokaiva, by and large, order their lives by the same moral principles, they would explain this by their common belief in certain demigods whom they all regard as their ancestors and as sources of authority, and who created certain institutions embodying moral norms to which they all subscribe. Not only do they obey the precepts of these demi-gods, they also re-enact their feats in ritual and identify with them during ceremonies, and in many of their regular expressive activities.

I shall therefore attempt to reconstruct what these demi-gods are said to have taught the Orokaiva about social relations. This reconstruction requires a brief analysis of some myths in which these teachings are contained. The myths all refer to events in original time. I was told that men, in their primordial or pre-cultural state, were living by the top of Mount Lamington (*Sumbiripa Kanekari*), which is traditionally regarded by the Orokaiva as the centre of the universe (Schwimmer 1969). I collected a number of myths explaining the origin of death, strife, fire, houses, marriage, clothing and several other elements of culture. The demigods who transformed human life by introducing these gifts came 'from the mountain'; Sumbiripa himself was the first man to die. He retired inside the mountain and all those who died later are said to stay with him inside the mountain. Hence the rumblings and tremors emitted by the volcano. Two published sources (Tomlin 1951, Benson 1955) show that these beliefs antedate the eruption of 1951.

While men lived by the top of the volcano, there was, according to the myths, no disunity, no quarrelling and no warfare, and men all ate with one another. As they multiplied greatly, so one of the tales records, some of them settled in an unoccupied place at the foot of a *barivo* tree. There they collected saplings, thatch and lashings to build themselves a village. One man stole lashings prepared by another and used them to build his own house. When the owner of the lashings found the thief, the two started to fight. The men present, one and all, became separated into two contending sides which never stopped fighting. *Emboavo aramiko tiketo ijunu avunu ena*: 'Therefore, from that time onwards, they dwelt separately down-valley and up-mountain.' Having started thus, they continued to be alone (*oenga oenga*) and to fight (*isoro ue mitiatera*). Separately cornered they captured, killed and ate each other and thus they then remained. In a final sentence, the narrator of the myth adds that permanent peace has now come and fighting (*isoro*) is finished.

I could not obtain data that would confirm that this stolen cord represents an umbilical cord and that this myth is about the birth trauma. However, the myth says that at the end of original time, warfare became an intrinsic part of social life. Two more specific messages emerge:

1. The institution created by the thief was *isoro* (intertribal warfare) which was cogently distinguished by Williams (1930: 160—6) from *embogi* (inter-clan fighting). *Isoro,* as opposed to *embogi,* takes place between groups who are geographically fairly distant, are often the speakers of different languages or dialects, and who do not usually maintain close social relations. In *isoro,* but not *embogi,* men fight to kill and eat each other. The myth therefore provides a charter for an institution by which social groups are in permanent strife with one another and permanently seek to kill and eat each other.

2. The myth states that this trife, in particular, divides the people from up-hill and down-valley. I have already pointed out that the main immediate cause of warfare around Mount Lamington was pressure of population generated on the fertile foothills, which led to groups being driven downwards, while these groups in turn drove the valley people further and further from the mountain to less desirable territory.

The social philosophy expressed in this myth is therefore based partly on the observation of ecological realities. Given a fertile centre and an increasingly infertile, but practically boundless periphery, strife is indeed endemic between social groups because the centre will continue to develop a denser population than it can support, and will always be able to muster much bigger raiding parties than the sparsely populated hinterland. It may lose battles now and then but in the long run it must be able to drive its excess population downwards. Thus the opposing forces will tend to be placed, as the myth says, up-hill and down-valley. The historical facts, as reported by Chinnery and Beaver (1916), Monckton (1921, Ch. XXIV) Williams (1930: 152—4), and Crocombe and Hogbin (1963: 14—16), all suggest that valley populations such as Aiga, Sauaha and Dobudura originally lived near the mountain and were driven off.

So far, Orokaiva social philosophy looks notably like Hobbes' view of social life as it would be in a state of nature. Between the warring groups, certainly, there appears to be no justice or injustice, but only war, and 'force and fraud are, in war, the two cardinal virtues'. How can fiduciary social relations be established at all in a world of this kind? As we know, Hobbes argued that it could be done only by the establishment of central authority, a step the Orokaiva did not take.

In order to present, as fully as possible, how the Orokaiva answered this question, I shall begin by quoting a myth told to me by Gideon of Hamburata, a village in the Sasembata district.[1] I had asked Gideon to tell me the origin of feasts, then taped the reply and translated it from Orokaiva:

> I shall tell you how feasting began.
>   Three men, after marrying wives, set out and settled by the root of a *barivo* tree. They had twelve children. When they had enough children, they built a house and founded a village. Then, deciding to leave, they made a feast by the root of that tree.
>   They all collected taro, made a platform, prepared all the food and got ready. Gasi, the last-born son, tied together his taro for the feast, intending

that it be there for his mother and father to eat. As he slept that night before the feast, Ombota stole the food. That man's garden was empty. He had no food, so he had nothing for the feast. Therefore, looking for food, he had stolen that taro for his mother.

The day broke, the feast was in progress and Gasi's mother and father were very hungry. Then Gasi looked about for them. Straight away his parents asked: 'Where did you prepare food for us? We are now very hungry.'

That boy asked in reply: 'Where is the taro I fetched for you?' – 'We have no taro and we are very hungry.' Upon returning inside the house to look, Gasi then saw that the taro had gone. So he went round the houses to look for that taro and saw it lying in Ombota's house.

As Ivi and Gasi quarrelled with Ombota, the mother and father went down to Erehata creek, taking with them their entire small house, as it stood on its posts. They floated down that stream until it met the river Embara. The woman's name was Jomiko and her husband was Sirere.

They stopped when they had reached a place called Sorovi-Ereremba. Meanwhile their sons, about to give the feast, inquired where their parents were but could not find them. When the battle (*isoro*) was over, Gasi and the oldest son, Havurure, went away to find their mother and father. Upon arriving at the place called Sorovi-Ereremba, they saw them where they had come to a stop. Their parents told them: 'We are staying here but you must go back and feast.' The sons then went back, but their mother and father stayed behind.

At that time, their parents' words were as follows: 'We are staying here. In bad times you will hear no speech from us but if times are good, and you intend to hold a feast, then listen to our speech.' Thus they spoke.

Sirere turned into a stone which is still there today. In time of hunger we do not hear his speech. In good times, when a feast is about to be held, we hear his speech.

My small tale about feasts is finished.

Before discussing the meaning of this tale, I should explain briefly some ethnographic details. It is customary to hold a feast on the occasion of a departure, so the brothers' decision to hold one agrees with modern custom. On the other hand, it is irregular indeed to hold a feast unless it is known in advance that there is enough food for all the guests. A feast is always preceded by elaborate and highly ritualised checks to make sure that the supply of taro is abundant. We may regard the tale quoted here as a mythological charter for these ritualised checks which are discussed in detail in Chapter VII. It is still usual, however, for guests at a feast to be fed in the individual households where they are staying. Thus the taro used for cooking would be kept, as in this tale, in individual homes. The gift taro, laid out on platforms, falls in a different category.

The house in which the parents floated away must be understood as the prototype of the feast house. This is a small structure placed at one end of the central plaza (*araha*) of a village. It is built a few weeks before the feast and it is in front of and in the feast house that rituals are performed during the whole of the period that ceremonies last. We may take it that Jomiko and Sirere are demigods who are believed to have stablished the institution of building a feast house. As this couple were in the feast house during the fight, it may be assumed that they were, in a ritual sense, the feast-givers. A modern feast also always has a person occupying the office of feast leader who is charged with the ritual as well as the organisational tasks of the feast. This leader (*pondo kiari embo*) is a man acting alone, and there is no mention that his wife has any function. This is a curious discrepancy between myth and custom, especially as elsewhere in New Guinea the feast-givers are often an elderly couple (e.g. Landtman 1927).

I was told that the people of Hamburata, before holding a feast, always consult the stone mentioned in this tale. When the wind blows through it, it makes a whistling sound, and is the sign that a feast may be held. This may be regarded as part of the ritual precautions necessary to ensure that a feast will be successful, but it is a purely local custom. The rule that a feast may not be held in hungry times is quoted and observed by all Orokaiva informants, of whatever locality. For the purpose of my analysis it is more important than the rule concerning the stone.

This tale resembles the one previously quoted in that both are concerned with a quarrel (*isoro*). The affair at the feast was not just an ebullient sham fight (*embogo*), but a serious battle, as the term *isoro* implies. But the messages of the two myths differ, in fact they seem to contradict each other. The message of the feasting myth may be summed up as follows:

1. In original time, men might hold some kind of feast at any time, but since the days of Jomiko and Sirere such permanent amity was no longer permitted. The *isoro* ended it.

2. Feasting was henceforth permitted only after special precautions had been taken and special permission obtained from the demigod. It had become an exceptional event, for which a special feast house had to be built.

3. The main criterion for the appropriateness of a feast was abundance of food.

4. A feast could be permitted only if perfect peace reigned among the guests. If the guests quarrelled the demigod's spirit would at once depart and the feast would be ritually void or even calamitous.

While the *isoro* was mentioned in the myth of the stolen lashing leads to a permanent state of war, the *isoro* in the feasting myth leads only to a restriction on the occasions when feasts may properly be held, and a rule to keep the peace for the feast's duration. How can these two apparently discrepant ideas about the nature of *isoro* be reconciled? My Orokaiva informants considered the two myths as stating different aspects of the same principle. Certainly *isoro* is (or used to be, before the Australians came) an expression of mutual anger that will never end. But it may be briefly interrupted, and it is good that from time to time the anger should cease and that men should then come together for a common feast.

Williams describes these interruptions exremely well:

The lively monotony of warfare was broken by intervals of peace. A truce-making was called *peka,* and the first emissaries were women who, born members of one tribe, had married into or been captured by the other. . . Two or three from either side would spend a few days and nights with the opposite party, and after this the two tribes would meet in armed force on some common ground between their territories to exchange gifts of pigs and ornaments. . . . (1930: 166)

Williams emphasises that such *peka* were precarious and often mere stratagems for killing more enemies. Nonetheless, feasts were held at intervals, former enemies were invited to them, and when they did happen the slate of old hostilities was wiped clean. No doubt, hostilities of the same kind would often occur again once the feast was over. Nonetheless, if there was no treachery, the feast was an occasion when the estrangement existing between social groups could be overcome in a communion ritual in which primeval amity was restored.

The notion of the feast as communion ritual is most clearly stated in a series of myths, of which the most widely known is that of Totoima. Some of the most celebrated stories about Totoima — his practice of killing men and eating them while wearing pig's tusks, and of killing and eating his children as soon as they were born — are reserved for other chapters of this work. All the stories about Totoima, however, have a similar ending: by some trick (his son stealing his teeth, his son feigning death and concealing a spear, his wife or sister raising many children out of blood from a cut finger so they could murder him) Totoima was killed in revenge for his iniquities. In many of the versions, which we shall discuss in Chapter VII, Totoima is neither fully a human being nor fully a wild pig but rather an undifferentiated pig-man partaking of the nature of both.

Totoima's body was cut into the joints into which pigs (and presumably slain humans) were traditionally subdivided prior to being shared out between guests at a feast. Those who ate the joints multiplied miraculously so that their descendants peopled practically the whole of the Northern District. Usually, at a feast, the joints would be given to the heads of different nuclear or extended families. In this case, the family head who received the right fore-leg became the ancestor of all the Mambare people; the recipient of the left fore-leg became the ancestor of the Opi people; the right hind-leg became Sangara, the left hind-leg Isivita, the head became the coastal people, the back Kokoda, the belly Togahou and the 'liver' Angerita. One might say therefore that Totoima was the primal ancestor of all these warring tribes, and as Williams shows (mostly in his unpublished manuscripts) all the tribes listed here have retained some similar story.

But Totoima was a primal ancestor in a special sense. Strictly, in most of the versions, he was not the sire of the people who ate his meat. He is not, therefore, an ancestor in a genealogical sense. But it was his meat that miraculously caused these small families to multiply into tribes. Thus it was his strength, his *ivo,* entering the bodies of those who ate him, which really caused the tribes to multiply. The tribesmen became the inheritors of his *ivo* and it was from this that their power arose. Totoima was their ancestor in the sense that they had his *ivo.* We are thus led closer to the underlying pattern of Orokaiva political philosophy. As a result of the primal quarrel, the affair of the stolen lashing, social groups were separated by a permanent *isoro.* At the same time they are bound together by a primeval communion, the common eating of

Totoima's body, from which all derive their *ivo*. The feast seems to be the occasion *par excellence,* at which the primeval communion is re-enacted. This is, of course, a point that needs careful empirical demonstration, which will be given in Chapter VII. All I wish to suggest at this stage is the existence of at least one ritual device whereby the state of permanent *isoro* between social groups can be overcome, the re-enactment of a communion for which the Totoima myth provides the mythological charter. Such a communion may be brought about only by a long series of economic and ritual preparations, such as a feast requires; there must be an abundance of taro and of pig, there must be feathers and ornaments, new loincloths, musical instruments and guests willing to share in the communion. Above all, there must be skilful magic. Even then, the success of a feast is never predictable, and always hangs in the balance. Thus the communion between social groups, in this philosophy always remains prob- lematic but, for various practical reasons (the need for alliances in a world at war) it is frequently attempted. The social philosophy of the Orokaiva, then, starts from the assumption of the gulf that yawns between man and man, and proceeds to delineate various techniques (of which the feast is one) to bridge it.

We are now able to see more clearly why among the Orokaiva social exchange is rarely effective unless prestations of economic value are exchanged between partners to mutual satisfaction. Relations between social groups are generally unsatisfactory and hostile, but they can be made harmonious if one side gives the other a feast, which the other side must reciprocate. The harmony thus established is an extraordinary state which is sure to be interrupted by subsequent conflicts, so that feasts must be held periodically to keep group relationships within the bounds of amity.

Relationships between individuals follow the same pattern, though gift exchange here takes the place of the larger and more formal feasts. If no presents pass between two individuals for some time, this is thought to signify a breakdown of amity and the gradual re-establishment of the *natural* hostility between man and man. Only gift exchange prevents Orokaiva society from presenting the perfect living model of Hobbes' war between all and all. It is largely for this reason that I have chosen gift exchange as the basic principle in my analysis of Orokaiva society.[2]

3. Towards a Model of Exchange

The feasting myth quoted in the previous section seems to me to embody the essence of Orokaiva social philosophy, in as far as it explains the basic nature of gift exchange relations. My next task will be to translate this myth into the more abstract language of social science, as must be done if its ideas are to be made part of anthropological discourse.

A feast tends to be held by two social groups between whom relations have turned somewhat sour. There may have been a war, or a murder, or some other grievous act of violence or there may have been no more than minor friction between them. One side may suspect that the other performed black magic against them. Generally speaking, however, by the premises of Orokaiva social philosophy, both sides will have been storing up some grievances against the other. Often neither side will be willing to admit to the major responsibility for the ill feeling that has built up; usually any attempt to assign guilt would lead only to further conflict, as the record is too tangled to be satisfactorily sorted out. The party which decides to hold the feast and to invite the other side may or may not admit that it regards itself as guilty, and that it owes the other side a debt. The past is simply set aside and the host acts as though the feast is a free gift, an expression of disinterested love and generosity. The guest at the feast accepts the same fiction.

Accordingly, if we regard a feast as an occasion for social exchange, as the Orokaiva undoubtedly do, the basic objects of exchange are repentance and forgiveness. Sometimes a few words are exchanged between host and guest to express this notion of forgiving and forgetting, though I do not suppose this is invariably the case. On one occasion I invited a man to have a feast with me, after some months during which he had been acting unpleasantly towards me for reasons I did not quite understand. I must have unwittingly offended him. After the meal he said: 'I did not really know you before now.' This implied that he was willing to forgive and forget whatever had previously annoyed him. At the same time, the fact of my inviting him indicated that I was sorry for whatever I had done wrong. What we were really exchanging was a willingness to change our attitudes to each other, which involved some effort for both of us. Whether this is, in practice, done genuinely or only ritually does not concern me here as I am discussing feasts from the viewpoint of Orokaiva collective representations. When two groups feast together, each has the obligation to feel sorry for any offence he has caused and to forgive any offence caused by the other side. It is only thus that the feast can interrupt the inherent enmity between man and man. Through the sharing of meat the two sides re-enact the communion existing in primordial times when men, as brothers, shared the body of Totoima.

An essential part of any feast is that the host should offer meat to his guest. But it is a total misapprehension of Orokaiva social philosophy to believe that it is the meat that is being exchanged for forgiveness. If that were so, it would not be essential for the two parties to consume it together. Certainly, if I have offended another person, I may make him a gift of meat in reparation. This is often done. But the reconciliation between the parties is not effected by such a gift alone. There must in addition be commensality (the common eating of taro) and communion (the common eating of meat). The meat used in such a communion is not an object of exchange. It is better described as a mediating element which makes possible the actual transaction (i.e. the exchange of repentance and forgiveness). Orokaiva are quite definite that there can be no true repentance and forgiveness between men unless meat is consumed between them. One may therefore regard meat as a *necessary* mediating element in this transaction.

Perhaps the most useful insight to be derived from Orokaiva social philosophy is that the natural form of a social relationship is cyclical and moves regularly from hostility to reconciliation and back to hostility. In other words, the Orokaiva do not see the model of a friendship, as do Westerners, in the form of a perpetual harmony, so that every conflict that arises is regarded as a deviation from the model. On the contrary, Orokaiva consider conflict as intrinsic to the model. This is true also in the discussion of quite intimate relationships: father and son, husband and wife, and so on. The perfect relationship is not one where no quarrels occur (Orokaiva do not seriously envisage such a relationship), but one where quarrels are resolved before they have gone too far. The Orokaiva would feel more affinity with the sociology of Simmell and Blau than with that of Weber and Parsons. A bad relationship is one where the cycle *reconciliation – quarrel – reconciliation* is interrupted, and the relationship is broken off, or the quarrel intensified until one of the parties resorts to sorcery.

We may express this view of social relations diagrammatically in the following simple model, where (*a*) stands for exchange partners, (*b*) for objects of exchange, and (*c*) for mediating elements.

MODEL 1

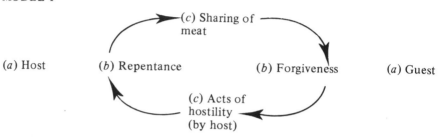

This model, first of all, contains three binary oppositions. The exchange partners are represented as opposed to one another. This corresponds to empirical reality because at any feast the persons present always belong in one of these two categories. Secondly, there are two objects of exchange between which a conversion takes place. One partner gives repentance and receives in return forgiveness. I have already pointed out that in practice both parties may feel guilty so that both may be offering repentance and forgiveness at the same time, but this is not essential and not included in the model. Furthermore, I have assumed that the host is the repentant party. This assumption is made because the person who gives the feast demonstrates thereby that he is more anxious than the other to restore the relationship. It is he, therefore, who is playing the humbler role and this is expressed in the model by making him the 'repentant' party.

It will be clear that an expression of repentance does not necessarily imply that the other party will offer forgiveness. A man may invite another to a feast and the other may refuse to come. In that case there has been repentance but no forgiveness and no feast. The exchange cycle has been interrupted by the other's refusal. But if the guest comes, he indicates that he is at least willing to forgive. Even then, the transaction may break down. There may be angry words between host and guest; the guest may expect some additional reparation and not be satisfied with what he gets. The ideal model of Orokaiva social relationships, however, assumes that the conversion will be successful.

The third binary opposition is between the mediating elements. I have already said that Orokaiva social relations move from a state of permanent strife marked by acts of hostility to temporary reconciliations mediated by the common eating of meat. There is justification for treating these concepts as binary oppositions. I have demonstrated that the common eating of meat is a mediating element because without it no exchange of repentance and forgiveness takes place. It goes without saying that acts of hostility are also mediating elements as, in their absence, there would be nothing to repent or to forgive.

In addition to three binary oppositions, the model contains a cyclical movement. One may start reading the diagram at any point on the cycle. For instance, one may start with acts of hostility, *isoro*. (According to Orokaiva philosophy, such acts require no special explanation.) These are followed by repentance, shown by the host in inviting the victim of these presumed acts of hostility to a feast. The sharing of meat follows, after which the guest, either in words or gesture (and probably by subsequent actions), indicates that he has forgiven whatever he had been angry about. Then, sooner or later, social relations lead to new acts of hostility and the cycle starts again.

While this model expresses adequately the Orokaiva view of social relations, we must admit at once that the feasting myth from which it was derived communicates a more complex message than this. It deals, in fact, with two exchange cycles at once, but overtly the myth does not mention the sharing of meat at all. On the contrary, it is concerned only with the sharing out of taro. The exchange partners are again host and guest; the exchange, as told in the myth, is between a shortage of taro provided by the hosts and a fight provided by the guests. The mediating elements are: the removal of the taro by a thief (arising out of the shortage; bringing about the fight) and the removal of the demigods responsible for the feast. The exchange cycle created by these elements reproduces the sequence of the myth:

MODEL 2

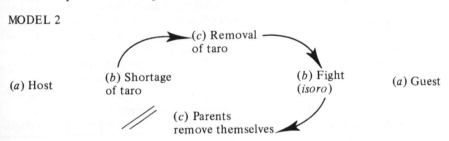

(*a*) Host   (*b*) Shortage of taro   (*c*) Removal of taro   (*c*) Parents remove themselves   (*b*) Fight (*isoro*)   (*a*) Guest

It will be noticed that the exchange cycle is incomplete. In the next section of this chapter, I shall show that exchange cycles in myths are always incomplete, and I shall explain why this is a special characteristic of myths. Indeed, the chief message of the feasting myth is that the incomplete cycle shown above should *not* be repeated; instead it is the following cycle that has become institutionalised:

MODEL 3

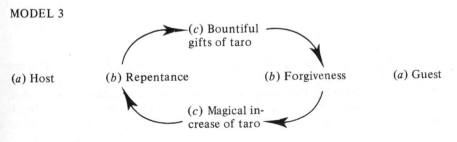

(*a*) Host   (*b*) Repentance   (*c*) Bountiful gifts of taro   (*c*) Magical increase of taro   (*b*) Forgiveness   (*a*) Guest

This model is very similar to the exchange cycle in which meat is served as the mediating element. I have already pointed out that taro, displayed on a huge and impressive platform, is an essential part of the gifts offered at a feast. I did not then quote the folk explanation of this. I was told that harvest feasts are beneficial to the donors because feasts make the taro grow well. On further enquiry I found that the Orokaiva believe that taro *always* grows well except if sorcerers from other villages put a spell on it. One of the rituals at a feast is a kind of rain-making ritual performed by medicine men from among the *guests*. When I asked: 'Why the guests?', I was told that they would be expert at removing the bad magic from the gardens because, in all probability, it was they who put it there! We can now see why it is that the guests' forgiveness, in the model, leads directly to a magical increase of taro. I was also told that the increase in the taro harvest would enable the hosts to give another feast soon afterwards. As this second feast would normally not be given to the same group as the first, the idea suggested by the model is that successful feasts enable a village to give an infinite series of feasts, thus attracting an infinite number of allies, one after the other, and becoming infinitely powerful.

In reality, however, this infinite series is interrupted by disappointing harvests and other misfortunes. Such misfortunes are ascribed to the sorcery of enemies, and in order to remove this sorcery, a *peka* is made with the enemies. A feast is held; and it is thought that matters will again improve. There is a periodicity of shortage and abundance, coinciding with the quality of external relations. Prior to the *pax Australiana*, bad external relations caused frequent warfare, the marauding of gardens or the lack of attention to gardens. Feasts had to be held occasionally so that the intensity of warfare would not lead to a serious depletion of food stocks. Feasts thus produced an abundance of food, because they provided peace, or at least a respite from war. The institution of feasting kept the scale of warfare down to a level which the people could economically afford. This ecological basis of the cyclical movement between war and peace is well documented in Rappaport's book about the Tsembaga (1968).

In terms of the model developed in this chapter we may express this cyclical process as follows:

MODEL 4

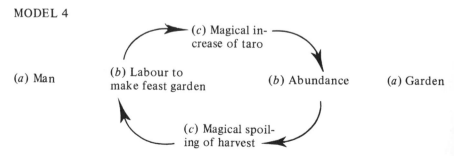

This exchange cycle belongs to the level of ecology rather than of social relations. The exchange partners in the model are man and his garden. The objects of exchange are the man's extra labour, needed to make a feast garden, and the abundance of taro that his garden can provide in good seasons. But it will not do so merely in response to man's labour. Labour alone cannot guarantee success. The transaction between man and his garden must be mediated by the holding of a feast that will dispel noxious influences by which sorcerers have, in the past, spoilt a man's garden. After the feast, the garden will produce abundantly, but this abundance will not last. In fact, the resumption of social relations will lead naturally to hostility; again sorcery will spoil the harvest. Sorcery mediates between man and his garden to impel the gardener to make a new feast garden; thus the cycle is repeated.

This model (No. 4) expresses a point to which my Orokaiva informants returned time and again. The most important benefit an Orokaiva expects to get out of a feast is not improved social relations but a better taro harvest. The rituals of repentance and forgiveness which entered into models 1 and 3 are magical performances with improvement of the harvest as their ultimate purpose. Thus it is wise not to restrict our study of exchange to the social and economic levels only, because the basic transaction may occur on a quite different level, in this case between man and his garden. The method of analysis I am proposing here has the advantage that it moves with equal ease on all levels at which collective representations exist.

4. The Starting Mechanism

In this chapter I first sketched Orokaiva social philosophy; I then abstracted some simple diagrams to represent this philosophy. Some elements of the exchange cycles represented by these diagrams are found in all or most cultures. All cultures have transactions between hosts and guests; all agricultural societies have transactions between man and his garden. Exchanges of social objects such as repentance/forgiveness, labour/abundance arise out of universal tendencies of man or nature. There is, however, nothing universal or logically necessary in the particular mediating elements appearing in these diagrams. Meat and taro, good and bad magic, *peka* and *isoro* – these are all peculiarly Orokaiva means for the mediation of social exchange. When Homans and Blau developed their (sociological) theory of social exchange, they gave no systematic attention to mediating elements, and rightly so, because their interest was universal laws, and mediating elements are never universal. However, for the anthropologist, who usually treats cultures as a significant variable, the mediating elements are of special importance.

Nonetheless, even if particular mediating elements are not universal, the use of mediating elements is a universal characteristic of social exchange. Sociologists, by ignoring this fact, have occasionally found themselves in difficulties, as for instance in their discussions about the 'starting mechanism' of social exchange. Gouldner posed the problem clearly in his essay on 'The Norm of Reciprocity' (1960: 177):

> Let us suppose two people or groups, Ego and Alter, each possesses valuables sought by the other. Suppose further that each feels that the only motive the other has to conduct an exchange is the anticipated gratification it will bring. . . . At least since Hobbes, it has been recognised that under such circumstances each is likely to regard the impending exchange as dangerous and to view the other with some suspicion. . . . Thus the exchange may be

delayed or altogether flounder and the relationship may be prevented from developing.

Gouldner's answer to this dilemma was that there must be a 'norm of reciprocity', internalised in both parties, which *obliges* the one who has first received a benefit to repay it at some time. Other sociologists, such as Blau (1964: 92–3), do not accept this particular explanation, because they do not believe that all social constraints are normative 'and those imposed by the nature of social exchange are not, at least, not originally'. Blau argues, in short, that the advantages to be gained from entering into exchange relations are psychologically so compelling that dangers and suspicions are insufficient obstacles. Even those who fully agree that not all social constraints are normative may feel dissatisfied with this psychological non-explanation.

Let us now consider how the dilemma can be solved in terms of Orokaiva social philosophy as presented in previous sections of this chapter. Orokaiva recognise that social exchange is precarious but claim to have various (magical) devices which are successful if properly used. These devices appear in my model as mediating elements. Why do Orokaiva believe in their effectiveness? They do so because the mediating devices have been instituted by demigods whose heroic feats they re-enact in their rituals. There is a strict code saying what should be done and how it should be done. The exchange fails if the code is not followed. What we have is not, as Gouldner suggests, one norm of reciprocity, but a wide range of codes deriving their authority from mythical demigods. The 'starting mechanism' is, in effect, the whole of Orokaiva mythology. I have been unable to find a charter in this mythology for any rule that a person who has received a benefit should repay it; in other words, I do not know of an Orokaiva mythical charter for a norm of reciprocity. All I have encountered are rules stating what acts are necessary if certain types of exchange are to be effected successfully.

I shall clarify these generalisations by giving a brief account of the nature of these demigods and of the rules they instituted, so as to be able to set out more clearly their role in the Orokaiva exchange system. The demigods of the Orokaiva resemble those found throughout Melanesia. Not all the cultures who believe in such demigods have a generic term for them. The Marind-anim of Western New Guinea, however, use the term *dema* to refer to all beings who lived in original time, to whom the creation of a feature of the cultural order is ascribed, and who are celebrated in myth and ritual. I shall follow Jensen (1960) and borrow the Marind-anim term, though other terms used in anthropological literature (culture hero, transformer, etc.) have a somewhat similar meaning.

Jensen presents a useful generalised portrait of these *dema*, as they are found in cultures of tropical tuber cultivators. In general, they are not creators of the natural order but rather of the salient features of material, social and religious culture. Very often it is not through his deeds that a person becomes a *dema* but through the circumstances of his death or departure, which make his *dema*-like nature apparent and give rise to an institution. Thus, Totoima became a *dema* as the result of his body being shared among his people; Jomiko and Sirere became *dema* after departing, in their peculiar way, from the world of man. Similarly the coconut *dema* is a girl who was killed and from whose body a coconut grew. Thus she gave the coconut to mankind and, by this gift, acquired the status of *dema*. Jensen quotes numerous examples of this kind from all parts of New Guinea; one may find further examples in recent literature (e.g. Newman 1965: 81; Serpenti 1965: 217f.; Held 1857: 287, 316f.; Oosterwal 1961; Williams 1940: 118—20).

Not only are *dema* commemorated in myth, but collective ceremonies are held in their honour. Man celebrates them by identifying, during these ceremonies, with the *dema* of original time. Newman, in describing a Gururumba ritual, shows how far this identification can go:

> The rite begins with men going into the forest for several days to hunt for various small animals and birds. While the men are gone from the villages, taboos are placed on those remaining behind against 'doing things the ancestors did not do'. It is believed that in the time of the ancestors man lived in a technological and social state much simpler than today, so that there are taboos against making new fire or working in the gardens because the ancestors did not know how to do these things. When the men return from the forest, the animals they have collected are allowed to decompose partially and then are eaten in a village feast where the unsavoury food is gobbled up in what the Gururumba consider a crude and disgusting fashion. (Newman 1965: 70)

Although I did not see anything so extreme among the Orokaiva, in various parts of traditional feasting ritual (the men's crude way of harvesting the feast taro, the eating of raw meat by the first-born, the throwing of raw and bleeding joints at the guests) the celebrants identify with and imitate what they believe to have been the ways of their primal ancestors. A person who dances in full costume, with head-dress, paints and ornaments, is regarded as a spirit and identified with man of primordial times. The sound of drums, flutes, bull-roarers and the reed-like tone of traditional songs all evoke the world of spirits and involve identification with primordial beings. The same significance is given to the narcotic effect of *areca*.

In all such rites, it is understood that the *dema* is dead and that it is only his spirit, preserved in taro, pig, coconut, the technique of cooking pork, the rules of marriage, the rituals of feasting, etc., that is still alive. Thus one cannot serve the *dema*, nor sacrifice to him; one can only identify with him. As Jensen puts it (*op. cit.*: 103—11), the *dema* is immortal but his active efficacy is limited to original time. Upon his death, he tends to be metamorphosed into useful plants, animals, or implements. Often these metamorphoses are simple, as when a coconut palm grows out of the grave of the coconut *dema*, but sometimes they can be complex and instructive, as in the case of the death of Totoima, to whom I have already referred briefly. Totoima, in all the myths, is represented as a man, but when he went on his murderous expeditions he wore pig's tusks which he took off when he went to sleep. When he killed men, it was with his pig's tusks. His son stole the tusks; then killed his father with a club. The meat from his father's body was shared among the people. Like some other myths, to be discussed in Chapter VII, this one has to do with the differentiation of species. Totoima was neither pig nor man, but pig-man. Pig-man killed human beings. After he was killed, pig-man ceased to exist, and instead there were two entirely separate species: man and pig. Whereas pig-man killed his enemies with tusks, the son (a man) killed his father with a club, a human weapon. Furthermore, the order of superiority was reversed: it was now no longer man who was killed by a tusked being; man became the killer, pig became the quarry.

From this analysis it would appear superficially that it is not Totoima but his son who ought to have been revered as the *dema*. It is he, after all, who has effected the differentiation between man and pig, who has provided man with pig as his quarry. But this is not how the Orokaiva reason. It is the same with the *dema* Pekuma to whom the technique of meat-roasting is ascribed. Pekuma is not the man who invented, by his own ingenuity, the technique of meat-roasting. He was the victim of another man who played a trick on him, dropped him in a hole, and roasted him. He tasted delicious. The Orokaiva remember Pekuma because he *was* the first roast meat and Totoima because he *was* the first quarry. The gift for which they are celebrated is not their inventive ingenuity but their body, in the form of food. Like the victims of cannibal raids, to whom Jensen devotes a lengthy discussion, the *dema* release their spirit power by the deed of being sacrificed, and this spirit power then becomes available to the killers and to all men.

We have seen, however, that the killing of Totoima was not an isolated event; it was done in response to Totoima's own murderous activities. As Jensen points out, in the life history of the *dema* some fault usually occurs, either committed by the *dema* or someone else, which is represented as the cause of death. We may thus, to some extent, view *dema* myths as a special kind of truncated exchange cycle. Totoima's story, for instance, might be represented in the following diagram in which Man and Totoima are the exchange partners, both of whom offer their body as an object of exchange (or sacrifice):

MODEL 5

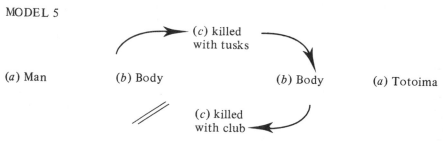

In this as in all myths, the exchange cycle is incomplete, as the completing of the cycle in the model would imply that the cycle is intended to repeat itself *ad infinitum*. But the whole point of the myth is that after Totoima it is no longer normal for man to be killed by a pig's tusks, but that pig becomes the normal quarry of man. The world, indeed, has been completely transformed as a result of pig having become man's quarry. Man is now able to multiply rapidly, deriving a great new strength from the pig-meat he is able to acquire. The exchange cycle shown in model 5 has therefore, since that time, been replaced by institutionalised feasting where pig sacrifice appears as an essential mediating element (model 1).

We may therefore regard truncated exchange cycles such as are shown in models 2 and 5 as the starting mechanism of Orokaiva exchange. To put this more concretely, let us consider the large platform heaped with taro that is exhibited at every feast for guests to take home. This is an essential mediating element in the social exchange between hosts and guests, and appears as such in model 3. But why does this taro have to be there? What does it do? Why can it function effectively as a mediating element between guests and hosts? The answer to these questions lies in the myth about the origin of feasting (model 2). This myth tells the Orokaiva that if they have a big heap of taro at a feast, they *can* have effective social exchange between hosts and guest. The myth also tells them that this heap of taro is essential. The starting mechanism thus provided by the myth for the social relationship is essentially a magical one. It is a magical code rather than a moral norm, even though it has become institutionalised almost like a norm. Of course, the starting mechanism, like all magic, can fail on occasion. But unless the magic is used, there can never be social relations.

REFERENCES

1   For location of Hamburata, see Fig. 10.
2   After writing this chapter, I found that Sahlins has also been interested in Hobbes' social philosophy as in some way anticipating contemporary ideas about primitive exchange ('Philosophie politique de l' "Essai sur le don" ', 1968). Especially close to Mauss' thought is Hobbes 'Fourth Law of Nature – Gratitude' (*Leviathan*, Part I, Ch. XIV).

CHAPTER IV

THE EXCHANGE SYSTEM AND THE NEW AGE

1. Cultural Changes

Many significant changes have occurred in Orokaiva society since European contact. The introduction of cash cropping has made the Orokaiva, to some extent, into a peasantry, depending to a limited degree on monetised marketing. Furthermore, there has been a large amount of labour migration, mostly by male workers whose families stay behind in villages. Even in the villages, technological innovations have been influential in raising productivity and improving standards of living, while sharply reducing the game population. People have become accustomed to the existence of a specialised political authority, wielded by Australians but supported and assisted by Papuan functionaries. Inter-village and inter-tribal warfare has been effectively suppressed. The Orokaiva give at least nominal allegiance to Christianity, and thus to the principle of obedience to an omnipotent god.

These changes have profound implications for Orokaiva political philosophy. As we have seen, the Orokaiva recognised the importance of Hobbes' question: how can a man avoid a perpetual war between all and all? The answer, briefly, was that social order can be created by a system of exchange partnerships. But this was not Hobbes' own answer nor that of the Australians who now rule New Guinea. If the changes pursued by the colonial government are wholly successful, it is clear that exchange partnerships, as the basic source of social order, must become subordinate to legitimate central political authority and the modern market economy. In other words, there is what Gluckman calls a 'contradiction' (1965: 109) between Australian policy and the exchange-oriented Orokaiva social philosophy. It is possible, but cannot be predicted, that this 'contradiction' will eventually lead the Orokaiva to abandon their traditional exchange ideology. In the meantime, however, it is already clear to the Orokaiva that their world view is being seriously challenged by white wealth and power.

The effect of pressure on the exchange system is evident in many spheres. In the economic sphere, the Orokaiva still carry on most of their non-monetary transactions by the traditional system, using gift exchange between consanguines, affines and bond friends. Furthermore, gifts of money are being made along traditional lines, money being used either as a substitute for *hambo* and other valuables, or as gifts from urban migrants to country kin. On the other hand, store-bought goods are, by a general convention, excluded from the full operation of the exchange system, only a minority being distributed as gifts. The tendency is to use money income to purchase goods needed for daily life but obtainable in the subsistence sector of the economy (Waddell and Krinks 1968: 192). Only a small minority of the goods used by Orokaiva fall into this category, but if the tendency to exclude most store-bought goods from the gift exchange system continues, we may expect that system gradually to decline in importance as the monetary sector of the economy increases.

In the political sphere, the traditional system of control is still generally in operation at the village level. Under this system some men may exert great influence over a community, but they cannot enforce compliance by physical sanctions. While the Orokaiva generally maintain this system, an exception is made for councillors and committee men acting under delegated power from the government. These men may lay complaints with Australian authority and in practice do not always disdain to do so. Among the New Zealand Maori, any leader who so much as threatens to invoke European authority risks being nicknamed 'Mr. Government' and losing all influence. Not so among the Orokaiva; the argument is that it is better for such powers to be used by an Orokaiva official than by the government itself. Nonetheless, use of authority outside the extended family goes against the Orokaiva ethos and undermines the exchange system in a minor way, because an official, by invoking his *authority*, can obtain something from Alter without becoming indebted to Alter. A traditional leader, under the same circumstances, might have incurred a debt or drawn on a kind of credit balance. Here again, the departure from the traditional exchange system does not greatly intrude in everyday affairs, but is symptomatic of the type of changes social development would bring. There has thus been a growing inconsistency between the norms of the traditional exchange system and the facts of labour migration, cash cropping, adherence to the Christian Church, attendance at meetings called by councillors, school education, use of medical services, changes in house architecture, participation in women's clubs, savings and loan societies, rubber co-operatives and the like. How, if at all, did Orokaiva thought cope with these basic inconsistencies?

I have explained how traditional institutions are accounted for. When I inquired why it is that mankind wears clothing, makes fires, contracts marriages, I would be told myths about the *dema* responsible for these institutions. I would also be told that after the *dema* had shown men how to act in these matters there had never been any change. There was primordial time during which men lived, one might say, in the state of nature. In spite of the absence of strife and death that era was not invariably represented as a happy one. Women were desolate because they had no men to marry, no fire to cook with, no houses to live in. In spite of most obstinate and desperate efforts, graphically described in the myths, mankind failed to get the things it needed. The *dema* thus brought release from suffering when they introduced cultural goods, techniques and rules of behaviour. But after the *dema* died, nothing ever changed again.

While such beliefs belie any suggestions that the Orokaiva are without history,[1] it remains true that the Orokaiva repertoire of historical explanations is very small. The actions of the *dema*, the scission of lineages comparable to the branches of a tree, the settlement of villages by men sleeping under a *barevo* tree — this completes the set of traditional historical explanations of which I have knowledge. How could the Orokaiva, confined to this set of concepts, find a rationale, satisfying to themselves, for the behaviour patterns they are now adopting in response to the impact of the white man's power? This is the question to be explored in the next section of this chapter. I shall put foward the suggestion that the Orokaiva actually developed an interesting and satisfactory explanation of recent cultural changes, using the concept of a new *dema* who set new exchange cycles into motion. In demonstrating this point, I shall quote at length from informants' statements so as to indicate clearly the nature of the primary evidence on which I have drawn.

2. *A New Starting Mechanism*

I shall begin by quoting a tape-recorded speech made by a member of the Higaturu local government council at a meeting held at Torogota village, Sasembata valley.[2] The reader may well doubt the sincerity of this speech, as I did myself when I first heard it. I discovered, however, that councillors frequently address meetings in similar terms. Trusted Sivepe informants told me that the recorded speech is typical of what that councillor usually said. It was elicited when I asked the men of Torogota for tales about olden times (*iji matu*).

The councillor started with a sketch of the wars of his forebears. His 'grandfather' Bohuka, with a group of migrants from Waseta, and other villages, drove off the inhabitants of a village called Hingo Kakasita and settled on the land of that village:

> Today his grandchildren call this our land, but they are weak grandchildren of strong ancestors. . . . All this is communal land (*company enda*) conquered by our forebears. As a new day has now arrived, I tell you to be united. Therefore you must follow my instructions. The councillor for Sasembata is speaking. Everybody who speaks north, east, south or west should now stop.
>
> Now I am speaking about this old village here. I am Councillor Ase. I am saying: follow this word and hear it. I shall therefore tell you how they (i.e. the Europeans, the *taupa*) talk: 'Those men were all felling the tree. The man whose name I mentioned was a fighting man. His enemies killed the wayfarer like a dog. The Waseta people beat and chased them, came here and stayed.'
>
> I am councillor Ase. Here we live, people, in this very old village. We are the descendants of fighting ancestors, therefore we live here. We say that we live in the land where the *seha* grows (a useless bush tree) or where the *inota* grows (a useless cane looking like a sugar cane) or on *gindiri* (i.e. sandy, infertile) soil. We stay in an old village, but people are saying we are living on communal land; we are staying on a place we took during a raid. They are saying: 'The Waseta men had weak descendants. They stayed here because they were defeated.'

A little later during the same recording session, Councillor Ase spoke again. This time he started with a description of various magical powers traditionally possessed by the Orokaiva. He continued:

> In those days people did these things. They did not take jobs for only Jesus Christ gave jobs that people could take. The village constable bound people (with handcuffs) and took them if he believed they were telling lies. He took them to Kokoda and Court was held; then they would start work . . .

When a summons was issued by the village constable, then those magic things were put to work (to save the accused from conviction) . . .

In those days men worked for a while but then stopped shifting the earth. The village constable bound them and they went to court in Kokoda. If the court thought they were lying or if they said 'I don't know,' they were taken away and the governor stopped their work. This is the tale of those men of olden days.

Although the passages quoted here are full of obscurities, the situation in which these speeches were delivered makes them worthy of careful analysis. The councillor, who was born in Torogota, had recently moved to Kongohambo, a neighbouring village built in modern style. Some families had accompanied him, but he wanted Torogota village to be abandoned altogether and the whole population transferred to Kongohambo. In his first speech, he gave reasons with which he hoped to persuade his people. We are thus given a glimpse of the social philosophy of his listeners. Although the latter had no intention of leaving Torogota, they did share the basic sentiments to which the councillor appealed. They agreed communal ownership of land was no longer quite fashionable, the village was getting too old, too much land was lying idle, it was bad for labourers to be unreliable, it was bad to kill wayfarers like dogs. They desired to emulate the feats of their ancestors and they knew this could no longer be done by raiding neighbouring villages. This traditional road to renown is no longer open; obviously, new roads have to be found.

The main burden of the councillor's speech was that his people had not found these new roads to power: *ivo ambupu-ta ahihijera*. (Strong ancestors have reared feeble descendants.) *Ivo* (strength, power) is a basic concept in Orokaiva thought, and is somewhat similar to the Polynesian concept *mana*. It is the quality that enables man to be successful in 'ways with which ordinary technique cannot cope' (Firth 1967: 191). It is transmitted to a man by his father at the time of conception, and is augmented by the fact of success, and particularly by the killing of an animal or an enemy, the eating of meat, or the making of gifts. Bohuka, the ancestor of the councillor's lineage, and his companions, undoubtedly had *ivo* which was augmented by their conquests, but his descendants who inherited this *ivo* stood to lose it unless they themselves achieved something of commensurate importance. The Orokaiva, unlike the Tikopia, do not think of this magical efficacy as being essentially an attribute of chiefs or leaders, though men of influence do have *ivo* to an exceptional degree. In the terms of the theory developed in the present work, *ivo* is always an object of exchange, received from an exchange partner, often in the form of meat, as will be shown in Chapter VII. The ultimate source of *ivo*, however, are *dema* figures such as Totoima and Pekuma who first gave *ivo* to man.

The councillor's second speech is one of several pieces of evidence that lead me to suggest that the Orokaiva regard Jesus Christ as a *dema* figure and a powerful source of *ivo*. A Papuan pastor was the first to put this idea to me when we discussed an Orokaiva dance performed at his Church during the Christmas service. The dancers, dressed in traditional garb and beating drums, filing in a wide circle past the cross erected on the mission station, sang a traditional chant originally performed after a victim had been killed in a cannibal raid. The pastor drew my attention to the similarity between the killing of such a victim and Christ's Passion. He also pointed out that by performing this chant, the dancers were sacrificing their bodies to Christ. There was no harm in this performance, he said, because the sentiments in both forms of religion were the same.

Councillor Ase added a more earthy dimension to the pastor's words when he declared that it was Jesus Christ who had given the Papuans the benefit of wage labour. This sentiment might have appealed to Governor Murray. It completes the image of Jesus as *dema*. First, Jesus was killed and gave His body to mankind, or to His followers, by being crucified. His body is still being consumed at Communion services, the deep sacredness of which the Papuans recognise. He also left behind him immense *gifts*: the technology (cargo) of the white man, and money with which men may acquire this cargo. Wage labour is one of the means now open to the Papuans for acquiring at least a little of this money and cargo. Thirdly, like all *dema*, he left behind a set of rules which men have to follow if they are to obtain full access to the particular kind of *ivo* he bequeathed upon mankind.

It now becomes a little clearer how the Orokaiva have found a rationale, satisfying to themselves, for the behaviour patterns they are adopting in response to the impact of white power. The coming of the white man is viewed as an event of the same magnitude as the addition of a new *dema* to the pantheon. The most crucial fact about this new *dema* is that it was through his help that the white man obtained extraordinary wealth and power. It was hinted to me from time to time that the white man should have been far more generous in sharing this wealth and power with the Papuans. At the same time, however, it was emphasised that the Orokaiva had already received some substantial benefits, for example the introduction of money, wage labour and cash cropping. My informant the councillor, whose contact with white authority had been somewhat closer than was usual in the district, claimed special knowledge about how European-type power might be obtained. It was on the basis of this knowledge that he felt entitled to advise his people to shift to another village. But his audience did not really believe he knew anything.

While the councillor's competence was doubted, his basic ideas were generally accepted: Orokaiva progress was thought to depend on the following of prescriptions originating from the *dema* Jesus Christ. The white man had revealed only part of these prescriptions. (In this respect Orokaiva beliefs resembled those reported by Burridge 1960, 1969.) It was thought, moreover, that these rules prescribed ritual acts performed for the first time by Jesus Christ and now imitated by those who are fully initiated in His mysteries. While these Orokaiva beliefs may impede their understanding of the workings of white society, they do provide a rationale for those white behaviour patterns which Orokaiva are able to observe. They also provide a charter for the changes Orokaiva are actually adopting in their exchange system and elsewhere.

One experience at Hohorita made me aware how closely the introduction of Western culture is identified with the action of traditional *dema*. Due to the death of most of the older men of the Sangara tribe at the time of the eruption, their descendants grew up at Hohorita without much knowledge of myths and traditions. Nonetheless, when I visited the village, a number of men spent several nights with me telling me what they knew. Their information would mostly be dismissed by a seeker of ancient lore, but contained some myths of obviously recent vintage which helped me to understand contemporary Orokaiva thought. I was told that before the Europeans came, the Orokaiva used to make only very small gardens. They were in constant danger of starvation and depended greatly on wild fruit. I copied the names of these, but was told that many of them were never eaten nowadays. (Many are inedible.) In those days, people did not make feasts as they did not grow enough food. The large gardens people have at the present time were introduced only when the Europeans brought steel axes and knives.

In other villages I was told similar stories about a primordial state of wretchedness when people cultivated no taro but ate wild fruit now considered inedible. But this period ended when the *dema* introduced the elements of traditional Orokaiva culture. In Hohorita, culture history had become fore-shortened. Other Orokaiva distinguished the traditional *dema* stories which occurred in the dim past from the stories concerning the arrival of the Europeans; they recognised in fact *two* periods of fundamental change: one ancient and complete, the other recent and incomplete. In Hohorita tradition, these two periods have to some extent become fused. The premature death of men born between, say, 1890 and 1910 deprived the men of today of any factual knowledge of the coming of the European: it has already been turned into myth and placed, so to speak, *in illo tempore*. But this unusual development only emphasises how closely the gifts of European culture are identified with those of traditional *dema*.

The chairman of the Higaturu Local Government Council, who also happened to live at Hohorita, had long conversations with me about the constitution and activities of the council. On one occasion I wished to discover to what extent the council had been set up in response to popular aspirations and to what extent the councillors (as opposed to the Australian adviser) made decisions on basic policy. Answer: because the government had a council at Rabaul, it decided to have one in the Northern District as well. Did the people want the council? They had been given schools; they had been given coffee to market. They therefore thought the council would also be good. Would it not be better for the people to decide for themselves how their problems should be solved instead of leaving all decision-making to the government? The council did not come from ourselves but from the administration. We do not know about the council. It belongs to the administration and it was given to the village people.

The Department of District Administration had recommended this informant to me as being the most knowledgeable in the district on the subject of the council. I found his knowledge of the facts to be most accurate, and at council meetings he was the only man who dared to argue with the advisory officer. But when I questioned him on the level of social philosophy, he fell back on the standard Orokaiva explanation: power and strength come to us not from things we have invented or made ourselves, but from things that have been given to us by our exchange partners. This is precisely what Councillor Ase said: if the Orokaiva of today desires to have an *ivo* equal to that of his ancestors, he has to follow the instructions of the council, i.e. to build a new village, grow coffee, individualise land titles. This, at the present time, is his best available source of power and strength. In other words, it is not a matter of villagers independently working out a development policy, but rather of obeying a sacred formula that came to the Australian authorities from a *dema*-like source and was then passed on as a gift to the Orokaiva.

Are all these gifts derived ultimately, in Orokaiva estimation, from Jesus Christ, or are there other *dema* figures as well to whom these gifts are ascribed? Who would they be? This is a hard subject for a white anthropologist to inquire into. Informants answer: 'We do not know. Nobody has told us.' The anthropologist feels uneasily that if anyone knows the source of Western wealth and power, it ought to be himself rather than his informants.

3. New Exchange Cycles

The image of post-contact history reconstructed here from statements by Orokaiva informants seems unduly dreamlike and idealised. This is because they are statements about the metaphysical starting mechanisms making social relations possible. Turning to the relationships themselves, I find that they are often marred by a severe conflict of interests and values. For the purpose of a brief overview, we shall consider relationships with representatives of three types of European-introduced institutions: church, commerce, and government. Following our theoretical scheme, we shall be especially interested in the objects that are exchanged in these relationships and in the mediating elements that make possible social exchange.

An employer of Papuan labour is interested chiefly in obtaining the compliance of his workers by the payment of money. Usually he is not at all interested in social exchange, but in a contract whereby he acquires the total work output of the worker for the period he is on the job. The Orokaiva, however, regards all the work he does as part of a social relationship with the person for whom he works. First of all, he expects that person to feed him while he is working. This is because he has been prevented by the person he is helping from going to his own garden. The employer in New Guinea usually does feed his workers, subtracting the cost of the food from the wages he pays. But secondly, the Orokaiva, lacking a long tradition of wage labour, regards his work as a long series of gifts to his employer enabling him to claim return gifts. He does not think of his wages as being a total discharge of his employer's obligations. They were promised at the beginning, but since then many unpredictable things have happened: he has loyally looked after his employer's interests in a series of small crises; he finds he has additional urgent needs he did not envisage when he agreed to come to the job; he believes his labour has yielded his employer vast profits. As the Orokaiva understand a social partnership, events of this kind all create a claim upon the person who has received help. Thus, the worker keeps on pressing his employer most persuasively for extra gifts of various sorts, in addition to his wages. This pattern is found throughout New Guinea and is known as the *baksheesh* system. Employers often give in to the demands, hand out various extras, and allow for these costs in plantation budgets.[3]

The basic significance of the *baksheesh* has already been pointed out by Mauss (1966: 250–5, 229–32); '*La chose ainsi transmise est, en effet, chargée de l'individualité du donateur.*' It rests on a notion that both worker and employer give something in excess of their contractual obligation. These services and gifts over and above the formal contract are a form of social exchange. Both parties seem to be expressing affection and solicitude for the other. The worker does this by special care for his employer's interests; the employer does it by 'baksheesh'. The latter are never just extra handouts or cast-offs, though these may also be given. They are usually responses to appeals by the worker who describes an emergency that has arisen for which he requires some object of usually quite limited value: old batteries, a little kerosene, etc. It is the employer's solicitude in response to a claim which gives these objects their special value (though, of course, they have some monetary value as well). This social exchange can be expressed in the following diagram:

MODEL 6

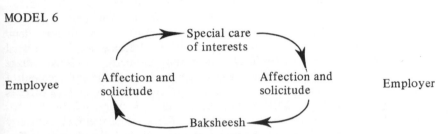

This model represents the ideal norm of the relationship, as seen by the Orokaiva. He is well aware that the reality often falls far short of the ideal norm: not all employers show affection and solicitude. It is, however, a more serious flaw of the model that the white employer would totally reject it; his ideal norm of the employer-employee relationship is a very different one that does not involve social exchange (or baksheesh) at all. There is, in fact, a conflict of ideal norms between employer and employee. The actual arrangements on the plantations, which I have briefly sketched, are a sort of compromise or accommodation between the two conflicting concepts of employment: the employee accepts the fact that baksheesh is usually rather unwillingly and rudely handed over, as being a regrettable white man's custom; and the employer somehow makes room for a minimum of baksheesh on his balance sheet.

The fact that the conflict of values remains unresolved in this relationship does not vitally threaten plantation development, but similar conflicts are not so easily sidestepped in the Orokaiva's relationship with government and the mission. Neither community development nor religious conversion will be successful without some ideological commitment on the part of the receivers of the message. Obvious though this statement is, it is worth while to spell out its implications here, as it applies to the implementation of government policy.

Policy is formulated in Port Moresby and promulgated by the Administrator in the form of ordinances and regulations. Instructions on the enforcement of these are prepared by the Department of District Administration in Port Moresby and interpreted, in the light of local conditions, by the Department's officers in Popondetta, the administrative centre of the Northern District. But how can these ordinances and regulations be enforced in the jungle by a very limited number of patrol officers? Until 1956, a rather simple procedure was used. The patrol officers appointed a large number of suitable Orokaiva as village constables, instructed them to report any trouble, visited the villages, looked for evidence of non-compliance with instructions, punished delinquents, left further instructions with the village constable and threatened further punishment. The trouble with this procedure was that the changes it could produce were of rather limited scope. All the Orokaiva needed to do to keep the patrol officer satisfied was to attend to things that could be seen on a visit (the state of the roads, houses, latrines, the grass in the villages, the quota of obligatory rubber trees, etc.) and to avoid the kind of trouble the village constable could not help reporting (murders, serious dissensions).

Social and economic development, however, depends on the communication of ideas, on encouraging regular schooling, use of medical facilities, cash-cropping, the development of markets, participation in local government, preparing the young for careers outside the district, encouraging capital formation and entrepreneurship, improvement of agricultural techniques, land titles, and so on. In the 1950s, when the government became deeply interested in these objectives, it created local government councils, abolished village constables, and rather forcefully changed its emphasis from the enforcement of compliance to the inducement of collaboration. Some of the Australian officers told me they found this shift rather frightening: if there was no jail for non-compliance, how could one be sure that the Orokaiva would take any notice? On the other hand, Orokaiva conservatives found the shift in policy frightening for the opposite reason: as they told me, the village constables left Orokaiva social life virtually intact, except that occasionally someone would be sent to jail for a while — a mere ripple on the surface of community affairs. But since the government councils were established, and the councillors came round regularly making long speeches, and since the new institutions listed above had actually been demonstrated to be useful, the foundations of the old way of life were beginning to be undermined.

With the help of the councillors, the government's ideas were certainly being communicated, but hardly ever by the government's own officers.[4] The only white officers who regularly visit villagers are young, inexperienced patrol officers, dependent on interpreters. Speech-making is only a minor part of their role and not the most successful. All the councillors I have heard, however, are master propagandists. As the government's aim is clearly the communication of ideas, it would be hard to find a more efficient method than the present one, where the government communicates to the councillors and leaves the latter to do the rest.

An interesting and somewhat unusual exchange cycle results from these transactions. The exchange partners are the government and groups of Orokaiva villagers. The objects of exchange are information (emanating from the government) and respectful attention (on the part of the villagers). I use this term 'respectful attention' as the nearest translation of Orokaiva *ingari* which means 'to hear', 'to understand', 'to follow advice' — and comes closer than any other word in the Orokaiva vocabulary to the notion of obedience and compliance. The exchange cycle may be expressed in the following diagram:

MODEL 7

The elements of mediation are entirely indispensable in this relationship. Unless there is development activity, the government will feel that the relationship has broken down. Unless the councillors intervene, the government's information cannot be communicated.

Both the villagers and the government find this exchange cycle highly precarious. It is precarious for the villagers because social exchange, for the Orokaiva, implies a state of competition between the partners. It is unprofitable to engage in social exchange with a partner unless one can hope to equal him (and even better him) in wealth and power. This desire to equal (and defeat) the Europeans competitively is an ambition of which informants spoke to me occasionally when I came to know them well. It was quite clear to the Orokaiva that they could never achieve this objective by growing coffee on small village plots. Hence, they could not regard the activity advocated by the government as being worth engaging in for its own sake. The question facing them was: will this activity serve our ultimate end of achieving equivalence or victory? The term 'development activity', as used in model 7 implies that it is thought to serve this ultimate end.

I demonstrated in the previous chapter that all elements of mediation are essentially magical. The Orokaiva similarly regard development activity as magical. In response to this notion, government officers sometimes evolve rules of behaviour that look remarkably like magical formulae. One officer in the Northern District invented a regular weekly calendar which he thought the Orokaiva should follow. Certain days of the week should be set aside for coffee growing, others for growing and marketing extra garden crops, others for cleaning and improving the village, and so on. I heard the officer proclaim this calendar; later, I heard a councillor proclaim it in Sivepe village. It was listened to with respectful attention, but afterwards ridiculed by the village men. The formula was rejected because it was thought to be useless. There was, of course, a plethora of such formulae circulating as many officers thought up their own, and most officers were rapidly transferred from one job to another. It was natural, therefore, for the Orokaiva to become selective in the formulae they adopted. Also, experience showed them that the formulae did not always work.

The difference between this modern magic and the traditional varieties lies in the greater uncertainty of the prescription. The Orokaiva habitually use an experimental approach to magic: if one medicine does not work, then try another. But all traditional medicine has at least an impeccable source: it was given by the ancestors. The magic of 'development' (money, Western technology, Western power) was, in Orokaiva belief, ultimately derived from Jesus

Christ and perhaps other supreme sources of which they have no knowledge, but these ultimate sources mostly seem inaccessible to the Orokaiva; the people know their information to be poor and unreliable. Nonetheless, as the councillor from Hohorita remarked, it has been found by experience that the gifts deriving from the government have often been good ones. The relationship is therefore worth maintaining as it may produce further valuable gifts in the future. (This widely held opinion, incidently, is the bane of Papuan progressives, who are pressing for immediate independence of the Territory from Australian rule).

Although, in an attempt to make my meaning clear, I have spoken of the magic of 'development', it is important to point out that the term 'development' has not been borrowed, to my knowledge, in Orokaiva speech. The Orokaiva term is *iji eha* (the new day), a phrase occurring, for instance, in the passage quoted from Councillor Ase's address. The *iji eha* has come about, as we have seen, as the result of the gifts of a new *dema*, Jesus Christ. One of these gifts was a permanent peace, to replace the permanent state of *isoro* of earlier days. But this gift was accompanied by new commandments. Councillor Ase emphasised the casual connection between the gift and the commandments: 'As a new day has now arrived (*oroho evi iji eha avo eto,*), I tell you to be united.' Like *isoro*, so the *iji eha* requires unity, but for the sake of struggles of a different kind: the building of a new village, the growing of coffee and rubber, the support of school education. The commandments of the *iji eha* are in effect community development.

It may thus be said without hyperbole that community development among the Orokaiva has a mythological charter – namely, the Christian religion as the Orokaiva understand it. It acts as a mediating element between the Orokaiva and the European power-bearers: it is the magic whereby a relation of social exchange may be established between the former and the latter and whereby the Orokaiva may eventually become the equals of the white man in wealth and power.

But the second mediating element in this relationship is the councillors, through whom the government's information must pass to reach the people. They do not play the role of leaders but of mediators in a rather limited sense. In their contact with the government (mainly confined to contact with the advisory officer to the council), they receive information and hear council decisions in the formulation of which they generally have no part. The flow of information tends to be from the government to the councillors rather than in the reverse direction. This one-sidedness suits both parties, but especially the councillors, who gain little but may lose much by adding to the government's knowledge. At the village level, the councillor tends to become the chief mouthpiece of the *iji eha*. He is expected to report faithfully, and in detail, what he has heard from the government. His advice will be asked on matters related to council activities, but most of the time it is the councillor himself who takes the initiative and harangues the villagers. He does not expect all his advice to be accepted; he may even have private doubts about some of what he is transmitting. A Sivepe ex-councillor even had the habit of reporting on all council matters in Motu, a *lingua franca* used at council meetings because the advisory officer does not know Orokaiva. Most Sivepe people understand some Motu. By speaking in Motu to his fellow-villagers, the councillor built up his own status while at the same time establishing some distance between his official performance and his private self. Even when a councillor does not resort to so extreme a device, his role is a highly formalised one, as the values underlying his message are very strange to him. The *iji eha*, as communicated at the council meeting, is almost outside his mental grasp. He has heard the details but cannot see the pattern. (The council meetings are not suited to the communication of the complex patterns of Western civilisation.) Fortunately his audience is usually warm and sympathetic to his message and shares with him the mood, the 'feeling' of the *iji eha*, if little else.

4.   *The New Day, the Mission and Divine Retribution*

Relationships with the mission in the Northern District have usually been of two main types. When a mission station was first established, exchange relations between Orokaiva and the station began immediately. The mission offered schooling, medical services and largesse of various sorts. The Orokaiva offered land and labour. These were direct exchanges requiring no mediating elements. The mission was usually in no great hurry to begin baptising converts, preferring to let interested persons rise gradually from the status of hearer to catechist and conferring baptism some years later. Although coastal stations were established around the turn of the century, it was only after the Second World War, when a considerable number of stations and outstations were established inland, that the majority of Orokaiva came within reach of mission influence. The Sasembata station[5] serving Sivepe was not opened until 1945 and had no baptisms until 1953. The bulk of the population of that village was converted between 1953 and 1964.

It was then that the second, and more complex, phase of the relationship started. In the first phase there had been a great deal of contact between people and mission station, especially because of the educational services that were offered, but it was only in the second phase that these contacts became religiously significant. We may express the emerging relationship in the following diagram:

MODEL 8

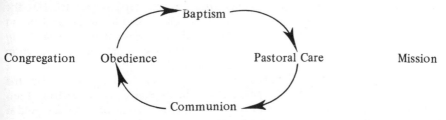

Although this exchange cycle seems, on the surface, to represent more or less the relationship between any Christian and his Church, it seems arbitrary to select from the complex set of mediating elements enriching the fullness of such a relationship as commonly understood just these two sacraments, important as they are. It is only in the light of the Orokaiva understanding of the Church that these two sacraments became pivotal, while the rest of Church life, however deeply experienced, seems to be a supplementary benefit. I am speaking, be it understood, of a group of rather recent converts.

When I asked informants why they had joined the Church I was given one invariable answer: 'to receive a new name.' The meaning of this is clear and unequivocal, and follows from information already published by Williams (1930: 97, 175–7). An Orokaiva, under the traditional system, might have three types of name: (1) a 'name proper' (*javo be*) taken from a stock of names used by his father's or mother's patrilineage and conferred at birth; (2) one or more nicknames (*javo isapa*) which may be acquired at any age; (3) assumption by the slayer of the name of the slain. Williams reported that there was also a common habit of bestowing the victim's name upon the child of the slayer. The name of the slain is adopted as a distinction, and as a means of acquiring the latter's *ivo*. Baptismal names fall within this third category, for what the Orokaiva regards as obvious reasons.

First of all, baptismal names are never Orokaiva names, but are chosen from a large stock known to servants of the Church. Some are recondite names (Cephas, Stanislaus, Gemima), other are a combination of the Christian and surnames of missionaries (Dick Stafford, Nancy White). All these names, used by the mission for baptismal purposes, are reasonably regarded as names belonging to Jesus Christ. Now, Christ was slain by His enemies. After His death, those who adopted one of His names were saved and obtained great wealth and power. White men are powerful because they obtained the *ivo* of this slain Man. The mission gave Orokaiva the opportunity to acquire one of these names too, if they obeyed its rules. Thus a baptismal name fulfils the same function as was fulfilled by the adoption of the name of the slain. *Ivo* can now be obtained without the need to kill a human victim; in fact, it has now become not only useless but evil to kill people in order to assume their names. The baptismal name has taken their place.

An important parallel between the two kinds of name is that a person cannot confer either upon himself. This can be done only after a person has gone through rituals of purification by a man of great purity and renown. The eating of the body of the slain can confer *ivo* only if this communion food is a gift from some other person; similarly, bread and wine are spiritually potent only if given by a priest in a proper ritual. I have already pointed out the similarity perceived by Orokaiva between communion and the traditional rite of eating slain victims. Communion may be called the culminating ritual of the *iji eha* when Jesus Christ fully becomes the celebrant's spiritual ancestor, much in the manner of Totoima, and with similar potent effects.

This sketch is not at all intended as a criticism of the mission. On the contrary, time probably has to pass before the Orokaiva can move from their present identification with the Church to the internalisation of its values. And it has been argued (e.g. Kelman 1962) that identification is often a necessary preliminary of change. Even the degree of change described here has been by no means easy to achieve. The ideology of the *iji eha* which underlies the present acceptance of socio-economic programmes as well as of Christianity, was long resisted by Orokaiva, even after the Second World War. A premise of this acceptance has been a growing opinion that the Western world order was indeed so formidable and irresistible as to leave open no other option. For many Orokaiva, this became a certainty only as a result of what to us would seem an entirely unconnected event, namely the Mount Lamington eruption of 1951. The effect of this eruption on Orokaiva ideology is worth a brief analysis here because it provides evidence that the 'new day' ideology is still essentially based on the traditional exchange-oriented Orokaiva philosophy. We find that the cataclysm was universally ascribed by the Orokaiva to the breakdown in an exchange relationship with some *dema,* and that many believed this *dema* to have been the Christian God. On the basis of this theory, the Orokaiva were led to search for more effective mediating links between themselves and these powers, so as to avoid similar misfortunes in the future. Development activity and baptism were the most important of the mediating elements in which they placed their faith.

As I have already published a full survey of Orokaiva explanations of the eruption (Schwimmer 1969), my summary here will be brief. In 1966, during visits to Inonda, Hohorita and Sivepe, I interviewed a number of survivors about the explanation of the disaster given by people *at the time it occurred.* All informants were agreed that at that time the increasing rumbling in the mountain, the tremors, the smoke issuing from the crater, the showers of ash, the emission of stones and fiery particles, and finally the Peléan eruption, were all ascribed to the anger[6] of Sumbiripa, the god of the mountain, though there were varying explanations of the probable cause of that anger. These statements tallied with published evidence from two clergymen, both present in the Northern District at the time of the eruption, who refer to the people's fear of the anger of Sumbiripa (Tomlin 1951, Benson 1955).

Evidence of a different kind comes from two anthropologists (Belshaw 1951, Keesing 1953) both of whom interviewed survivors a few weeks after the disaster. Belshaw summarises Orokaiva explanations as follows:

> Some people said that this was God's visitation because they had disobeyed the Bishop's instructions to build new churches. Others said that God had punished them because they had not helped the Allies sufficiently during the war and because some of them had betrayed missionaries to the Japanese. (Others again mentioned) lack of co-operation in Mission and Government plans for development. (1951: 242)

Keesing agrees with this summary, adding that the eruption resulted in 'strong feelings of insecurity and even of guilt in their retrospective look at the pre-eruption way of life'.

Many resident Europeans, including the Bishop of New Guinea, the Most Rev. David Hand, confirmed Belshaw's and Keesing's account, but the Bishop told me that the mission has since discouraged the Orokaiva from thinking that the Christian God harboured anger against them and expressed it with such indiscriminate violence.[7] Hence this explanation is no longer heard. People nowadays believe that the eruption was caused by the anger of Sumbiripa or, if they wish to display a modern scientific attitude, they will repeat what they have been told about vulcanology.

Explanations based on the anger of Sumbiripa, the government and the Christian God resemble each other in that they are all based on the concept of a social exchange relationship in which the Orokaiva thought they had defaulted. In the case of Sumbiripa, this relationship was a rather special one as Sumbiripa's gift is the safe confinement of the dead, whereas man's gift is avoidance of any disturbance of Sumbiripa's mountain. Man mediates the relationship by sending his dead to Sumbiripa, whereas Sumbiripa mediates by emitting his usually innocuous rumbling. Before 1951, Sumbiripa had never erupted in living memory. We may express this in the following diagram:

MODEL 9

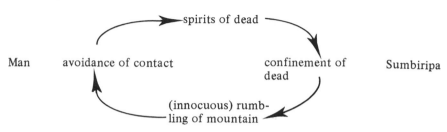

One theory of the eruption was that man had broken the exchange relationship by hunting on the mountain with guns. This disturbance angered Sumbiripa so that instead of innocuous rumbling he emitted the full blast of his immense and disastrous fury. The effect of breaking the exchange relationship with the Church was thought to be disastrous in precisely the same way. Just as the rumbling of the mountain suddenly became lethal instead of benevolent, so the 'communion' offered by the Church suddenly turned negative, dispensing retributive justice instead of mercy. Similarly, default in a social exchange relationship between human beings may lead the wronged person to give Alter misfortunes and diseases through sorcery, instead of the benefits he would otherwise bestow. If a relationship is broken, the wronged partner may respond by invoking negative mediating elements to obtain redress.

This dangerous trend may be reversed by expressing repentance, and by receiving forgiveness (see models 1 and 3). Subsequently, the offender will be more careful, if he is prudent, to stop the relationship from breaking down. Thus, after the eruption, the Orokaiva became more careful to carry out development activity (model 7) and seek baptism (model 8). The fact that the Anglican Mission denied that God had been angry would in no way diminish their solicitude, as such denials are always issued by offended exchange partners as part of the ritual of showing their forgiveness. Detailed empirical evidence given elsewhere (Schwimmer 1969) in fact shows that the eruption speeded up the development of the *iji eha* ideology among the Orokaiva. It would be wrong, however, to suppose that the supernatural fear propelling the Orokaiva towards development and baptism was due to a cruel deception by the mission or to irrational self-deception on the part of the people. It may equally well be regarded as a case of rational choice. It is not at all irrelevant to emphasise that development and baptism, in fact the whole *iji eha* ideology, was a sensible direction for the Orokaiva to take. The explanation of the disaster which they adopted was not a blind reaction to external vicissitude but rather the strategic reinforcement of a mythical charter for institutions mediating a valuable relationship. They could conceivably have chosen a different explanation which would have provided a charter for the reinforcement of quite different relationships. If the eruption had not happened at all, the Orokaiva would most probably have taken the same direction, but the charter validating development and baptism would have been weaker for some time. It may be that the exchange ideology would have weakened before development started. The eruption, however, seems to provide Church and government with a most formidable arsenal of negative sanctions in case the relationship is ever broken through the fault of the Orokaiva. We may conclude that the Orokaiva, by their belief in a new kind of divine intervention (through the *dema* figure Jesus Christ), have been encouraged to make new types of economic, social and religious exchanges, while maintaining their assumption of an exchange-oriented universe, and that their philosophy has provided them, at least for a time, with a workable rationale for the contemporary world.

REFERENCES

1.   The traditional time concepts of the Orokaiva are probably mainly restricted to what Evans-Pritchard (1939) called 'oecological' and 'structural' time. It is, however, very likely that they also had 'an historical perspective of their own, whatever its depth may be' — rather similar to the one described by M. Panoff for the Maenge (1968). Such a perspective would include not only the *dema* but also the scission of lineages and the settlement of villages. An Orokaiva described lineage fission to me by drawing a tree on the ground — using precisely the same symbolism as Panoff's Maenge informants. Orokaiva stories of the settlement of villages also abound, usually giving the name of the tree by which the settlers 'sat down' when they arrived.

Pocock (1964) has argued that as culture change becomes more rapid under the impact of European contact, traditional time concepts undergo structural transformation to make them more nearly explanatory of the actual course of events. I believe that the identification of Jesus Christ with a *dema*, as argued in this chapter, is an example of such structural transformation.

2.   For the location of Torogota, see Fig. 10.

3.   Information on this point was derived from several local planters, including Mr. C. E. Searle of Awala. See also Howlett 1965.

4.   Details on communication channels between government and people are given in Schwimmer 1967, 1969.

5.   The Sasembata mission station is not in Sasembata village but just north of Kongohambo. See Fig. 10.

6.   Reay has reported that 'the natives had no knowledge, or legend, of an earlier eruption' (*apud* Taylor, 1958: 21). My own study (Schwimmer 1969) suggests that this view, while not strictly incorrect, needs to be modified. My sources are tape-recorded myths and Miss Nancy White's manuscripts (White, n.d.).

7.   Interview with Bishop Hand, January 1967.

PART II:
OBJECTS OF MEDIATION

CHAPTER V:

LAND

1. Mediating Elements

In the preceding chapters I have set out a method for studying the working of the principle of reciprocity in Orokaiva society. I have shown in a general way how this method may be used for the analysis of traditional institutions and demonstrated that it is still applicable to contemporary institutions. In the chapters that follow I shall apply this method to elucidate a wide range of ethnographic data for some of which no satisfactory alternative explanation has yet been offered. To recapitulate, we may state the method, as set out so far, in the following provisional model:

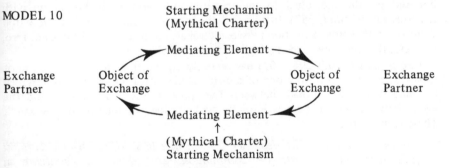

MODEL 10

Starting Mechanism
(Mythical Charter)

Mediating Element

Exchange Partner   Object of Exchange   Object of Exchange   Exchange Partner

Mediating Element

(Mythical Charter)
Starting Mechanism

There are three main constituents in this model, viz. (*a*) exchange partners; (*b*) objects of exchange; (*c*) mediating elements.

The plan of this work is to discuss mediating elements in the present and four succeeding chapters, and to deal specifically with relationships between exchange partners in chapters X and XI. The objects of exchange, some of which have been briefly mentioned in previous chapters, tend to be institutionalised social attitudes such as repentance / forgiveness; compliance / administrative or pastoral care; avoidance / preservation from harm. Objects of this kind are exchanged in virtually all cultures. In deciding whether or not they will engage in such exchanges, individuals weigh the social costs they would incur against the social benefits they might gain. Social psychologists like Homans and Blau have made valuable contributions in this field of study. In omitting consideration of it here I do not mean to imply that it is irrelevant to anthropologists, but it is difficult to develop universal propositions about human exchange and analyse universal processes governing associations, in a work whose main purpose is the eludication of a specific cultural system. The study of objects of exchange requires a book to itself.

My discussion on mediation starts from the principle that gifts are essentially similar to sacrifices. Hubert and Mauss suggested that sacrifice, beneath the diverse forms it takes, always consists in one same procedure: 'This procedure consists in establishing a means of communication between the sacred and the profane worlds through the mediation of a victim, that is, of a thing that in the course of the ceremony is destroyed' (1964: 97). In the same vein, we may say that the gift, beneath the diverse forms it takes, also always consists in the same procedure. Echoing Hubert and Mauss, we may describe this procedure as the establishment of a means of communication between Ego and Alter by the mediation of a thing from which Ego later separates himself.

One of the characteristics common to social exchange and sacrifice is identification between the donor (or sacrificer) and the mediating element (or victim). In the anthropological literature on sacrifice, one of the subtlest and most illuminating accounts of identification is given by Evans-Pritchard when he discusses the relation between men and oxen among the Nuer (1956). Here we find strong economic dependence, deep emotional attachment, the assumption of ox-names by men, religious practices (not involving sacrifice) where oxen serve as a direct means of communication with the unseen world, all of which is summed up by Evans-Pritchard as 'a moral identification, a participation imposed on the individual by his culture and inextricably bound up with religious values' (*ibid*, 257). In this and the next few chapters, I shall show that there is a rather similar relation between Orokaiva individuals and the land, taro, pigs, etc. that they use as mediating elements in social exchange.

Lévi-Strauss (1962: 294–302) has recently argued that this identification of sacrificer and victim is only one of a series of identifications by means of which a connection is established 'between two polar terms, the sacrificer and the deity, between which there is initially no homology or relation of any kind'. These identifications

> peuvent se faire dans les deux sens, selon que le sacrifice est piaculaire ou qu'il représente un rite de communion: soit donc, du sacrifiant au sacrificateur, du sacrificateur à la victime, de la victime sacralisée à la divinité: soit dans l'ordre inverse.

Here again the procedure of social exchange is essentially similar to the procedure of sacrifice. Identifications are made at every phase of an exchange cycle: the donor identifies with the mediating element, the mediating element identifies with the recipient. If the recipient is willing to return forgiveness for repentance, and to restore the exchange relationship, he follows the same procedure, in the opposite direction.

How does the mediating element 'identify with' the recipient? This process is best explained by the analogy of the 'sacralisation' of the victim in sacrifice. Hubert and Mauss distinguish two ways in which a victim may be consecrated: there may be fixed rites to confer upon it the religious condition that its destined role demands; or it may be consecrated by the mere fact that the species to which it belongs is joined to the divinity by special links (1964: 29, 122–3). Even so, one of the great anxieties in sacrifice tends to be whether the victim is really a proper one, whether it is god-like, so that the god may identify with it. The only test of propriety and perfection is the practical one of whether the sacrifice is 'accepted', whether the sacrifice actually receives the desired benefit. Success depends on the willingness of the god to identify with the proffered victim, and so can never be predicted.

It is the same with elements of mediation. Their purpose is to attract and seduce the recipient. The donor hopes that the recipient is 'captivated' by a gift, or an appealing speech, or the use of some ritual object. Thus he is induced to cede whatever the donor happens to desire. To a varying extent there are fixed rites to confer upon the mediating element the magical condition that its destined role demands. What these rites are, and whether there are any, depends on the nature of the relationship between the partners, the nature of the exchange, and the nature of the mediating elements themselves. The style of giving is arranged so as to increase the power of the mediating element to entice and seduce the recipient, to overcome him so that he in turn will wish to overwhelm the donors with his generosity.

The intent of using an object of mediation may thus be called magical in the sense of Williams' 'magic of impersonation', i.e. in a rudimentary or elaborate rite, a person identifies himself with a mythical character who has been efficacious in making the gift and obtaining the required result. Hence the mythical charter included in the model is essential to the understanding of the process, as there is no other ground for believing in the efficacy of the transaction. We may thus say objectively that within the Orokaiva cognitive system magical intent always inheres to some extent in elements of mediation.

To be sure, most transactions that actually take place are somewhat standardised and habitual. There are fixed modes of making gifts almost mechanically. Many of the transactions I shall consider are of this kind. At the same time, gift-making always remains to some extent a game of strategy, a way of manipulating an opponent, preferably at the smallest cost to oneself. But this is as true of sacrifice as it is of social exchange. Furthermore, this game of strategy always remains a very emotional one, as the breakdown of almost any social relationship is regarded as a grave threat.

An object of mediation has more than one fixed use. Just as the significance of a word in a language depends on the context in which it is used, the prefixes and suffixes attached to it and its grammatical position in the sentence, so also the significance of an object of mediation may vary according to the existing relationship of the exchange partners, the objects of exchange, the manner in which the mediating object is given and the codes and norms governing the total transaction. The description of a single object of mediation therefore involves semological operations somewhat resembling the description of words in a dictionary. I have not attempted the immense task of compiling a comprehensive catalogue of Orokaiva exchange but contented myself with a limited number of objects of mediation, sufficient to demonstrate a method and to describe some key objects of mediation in Orokaiva culture. If a complete compilation were made it would show the meaning of all gifts that are made for the purpose of mediating social exchange.

Though the concept of mediation used here is inspired by the concept of mediation as developed in the work of Lévi-Strauss and Leach, there are differences that must be clearly stated to avoid confusion. When the two earlier authors speak of mediation, they are usually dealing with real existents which appear as binary oppositions in non-empirical cognitive systems, e.g. earth /sky. The mediating element is likewise a real existent which is physically interposed between the two opposites. e.g. trees, birds. Their physically intermediate position is an empirical fact utilised in the building of cognitive systems, which treat trees or birds as mediators between earth and sky.

When Lévi-Strauss speaks of 'mediation' in the context of sacrifice, he warns that he is not speaking of the same thing: while cognitive systems are 'systems of reference' classifying real existents, sacrifice is a 'system of operations', a technique for obtaining certain results where the opposed elements are: the Self (a real existent, in this argument) and the Other — who is transcendant and may be a god postulated for the sake of obtaining the results. While trees and birds are always physically interposed between earth and sky, a pig is interposed between man and god, or between two exchange partners, purely as an operational strategem. It may be replaced by a different object of mediation (a chicken) or by anything else human ingenuity may invent. Lévi-Strauss describes the difference thus:

Les systèmes classificatoires se situent au niveau de la langue: ce sont des codes plus ou moins bien faits, mais toujours en vue d'exprimer des sens, tandis que le système du sacrifice représente un discours particulier, et dénué de bon sens quoiqu'il soit frequemment proféré. (ibid. 302)

This argument applies to social transactions as much as to sacrifice. Certainly, in social transactions *alter* is a real existent, viz. another human being or group of human beings. Yet this *alter* has one crucial transcendental[1] characteristic, namely that *ego* cannot control his will. In making a gift to *alter* we may feel that by the norm of reciprocity we ought to receive something in return, but we can never be sure that we will. Mediating elements used in social transactions therefore have an essential resemblance to sacrifices. They are real existents which are believed to have 'virtue', i.e. to elicit a desired social return, if given to certain classes of partners in certain circumstances. The purpose of the present investigation is to determine why beliefs in the 'virtue' of various objects of mediation are held among the Orokaiva.

It is readily admitted that the system I am studying here is *'un discours particulier, et dénué de bon sens'* and that it does not provide a classifactory scheme representing the universe. It merits the term 'system' only because each exchange cycle forms a system and success or failure in the use of objects of mediation is advanced by Orokaiva as an explanation of a great variety of interconnected event-structures in time. I shall return to these theoretical questions in the introduction to chapter VIII. It will be useful first to survey some of the more elementary Orokaiva magical recipes for effecting social exchange by means of gifts of land, taro and pigs.

2. Land and its Transfer: Transactions between the Sexes

The first object to be considered is land. A kind of standard profile of the general characteristics of New Guinea land tenure has already emerged from the writings of Berndt, Brookfield and Brown, Hogbin, Lawrence, Meggitt, Rappaport, Salisbury, Serpenti, Wagner and several others. The Orokaiva system falls within this general pattern, though with less emphasis on overriding rights held by clan and lineage, and more emphasis on individual rights than, for instance among the Siane and Mae Enga, less emphasis on corporate leadership than among the Garia, and more incidence of duality of rights than among the Chimbu, and so forth. Though the time has come when a comparative study of these systems could profitably be undertaken, it falls outside my present purpose which is to analyse the significance of land transactions, especially among the Orokaiva.

In order to carry out this analysis, we must first describe the basic categories of land transactions. We shall not use the term 'transactions' solely in a legal and economic sense, but more broadly in accordance with Mauss' concept of exchange as a total phenomenon. Thus, land enters crucially in 'transactions' between husbands and wives, and between men and spirits, and these 'transactions' will be considered before we turn to the more familiar topic of transactions between men. Here we have to distinguish between transactions within and outside the patrilineage. Our general argument will be that all of them occur as part of a continuing series of social exchanges, and that useholds granted on varying conditions must be regarded basically as benefits exchanged for other past or future benefits. In as much as paternal protection and filial service are very common objects of social exchange in these transactions, paternal protection being mediated by land grants, we may observe the practical operation of a system of patrifiliation.

A few words should first be said about the significance of land itself. The Orokaiva spend most of their days in their individual garden plots. They are tied to them not only by a total dependence on the produce, but also by deep bonds of affection. A man and his wife like nothing better, generally, than to spend the whole day, and virtually every day, in their garden together. These are intimate places where nobody would go without an invitation and where nobody is disturbed or called away except in a serious emergency. They are the most private places the Orokaiva has, much more private than the village houses where every sound and movement can be seen or overheard. Even so, physical privacy is secured often by no more than a narrow ring of second growth around the cultivations. Many people have a garden house, ornamental shrubs, places to rest and sit. Orokaiva gardens can be very homely and beautiful. People rest there in the heat of the day. They are favourite places for love-making.

The most ubiquitous of all social transactions mediated by the land occur between husband and wife. Perhaps the most important rights and obligations arising out of marriage have to do with garden land. Both the male and female gardening tasks are, of course, learnt before marriage. Bachelors have their own gardens in which they do all the work which is not specifically set aside for women and taboo to men. They clear the land; they help with planting (using the digging stick); they protect the land against pigs and other dangers; they weed. It is a fact, already observed by Williams, that a girl choosing a husband takes serious account of the state of the garden of her intended spouse. She does not like to marry a man whose garden is in a poor state. The bachelor is assisted by a sister, or brother's wife, or by his mother with the dropping of seed into the ground, and with harvesting, which he may not do. Upon marriage, the new wife is usually expected to garden on her husband's land. There is a fiction that, at the time of marriage, she 'does not know' the work she is expected to do on the land of her new affines. Her mother-in-law has to instruct her and it is only after such an apprenticeship that her husband's people consider her competent to tend taro on their land, harvest it and offer it to visitors in proper style. She would usually have been trained in these tasks by the women of her own clan, but the subtleties of family traditions differ.

As against these male and female obligations, we may note some clearcut rights: the man's right to his wife's labour and the wife's equally important right of unlimited access to the husband's garden land and to its produce. This right extends not only to harvesting food for the household, but also for gifts she may choose to make outside the household, providing that she manages the food supply so as to avoid shortages. A domestic dispute I observed in Sivepe (referred to in Chapter III above) illustrates the importance attached to this married woman's right. When this dispute was adjudicated, the 'explanation' of the breakdown of the marriage was found in a single incident, namely the husband's instruction to his wife not to go to his garden again. Here, in the view of everyone present, lay the 'root' of the trouble, a judgement with which the husband was willing to agree. This prohibition to go to his garden is one of the few things a husband is on no account to utter to his wife; it amounts to total repudiation of the conjugal relationship.

This brief discussion of social practices has already indicated that a garden plot is a gift made by a man to a woman, while the productiveness of the land is a gift from a woman to a man (because a man can neither plant nor harvest). Let us now consider to what extent the nature of these gifts may be clarified in the light of rituals, myths and indigenous explanations. It will be best to begin with some legal ideas about land. As has been pointed out by Salisbury (1962: 67ff.) among others, several sets of rights arise with respect to any one piece of land: rights of the village, of the clan, of the lineage, and of the 'father of the ground' or trustee. It is the last-mentioned person who assigns a piece of land (*enda*) to a cultivator for the purpose of making a garden (*pure*). The cultivator to whom land may be assigned may be either male or female. Among the Orokaiva it is common for women to have land assigned to them for cultivation in their own right, even though most land is assigned to males. They receive this land mostly from a father or brother, sometimes from their mother. When a woman wishes to have a garden established on her land, she (voluntarily) transfers the land to her husband or another male on a temporary basis so that he can carry out the crucial male tasks without which the garden cannot be made. These tasks are ritual as well as productive. It is common for the men of a clan to hold a feast together and to kill a pig from which they eat and obtain strength (*ivo*), before clearing new ground. The fertility of the soil depends greatly on getting a good burn after clearing, and a good burn depends on climatic conditions that can never be wholly predicted. I was unable to find out much about the ritual connected with clearing but gather it had to do with control over the sun and the rain. Another magical danger that arises in new gardens comes from the ghosts (*sovai*) lurking in the reverted gardens or bush that is being cleared. The garden thus established is the gift made by the man to the woman; the *pure* is felt to be a feminine thing. In the myths it is the mother who buries the taro shoots (her children) and covers them with leaves and earth which are equated with her body. I shall show this in more detail in the next chapter.

In Williams' report on the division of labour, planting is shown as a female task, whereas the time studies of Waddell and Krinks suggest that the activity is actually shared by the couple. There is no real contradiction here, nor much evidence of change, as the man's task is to pound holes into the soil with his digging stick whereas the woman does the actual planting, or burying (*kovari*) of the seed.

Unless the normal rules are suspended, as happens at feasting time, men do not harvest taro or other products of the *pure* where taro is planted. (The rules are different for the yam garden as we shall see later.) The explanation that is given of this rule is that only the women know how to harvest crops to best advantage, i.e. at the right time and in the right quantities. If men harvested, the supply would never last through the lean season. The woman is responsible for nurture, in the widest sense. It is her task every day to bring home garden food in the large string bag suspended from her head. Contrary to what white observers have sometimes believed, this is not a symbol of female slavery, but rather of female power and it is done proudly. When my wife started to bring home produce from our own garden in Sivepe (in a different kind of bag), the women crowded round excitedly and congratulated her. The food gifts that are constantly sent from one household to another may be, at least partly, regarded as a display by the women of their own success. The products of the taro garden (though not the yam garden) may ultimately be regarded as a gift from women to men. We may summarise the total transaction as follows:

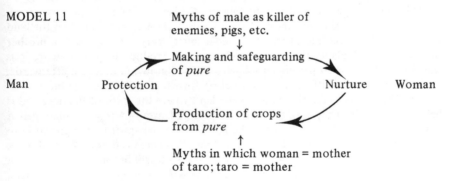

MODEL 11

Myths of male as killer of enemies, pigs, etc.

Making and safeguarding of *pure*

Man   Protection   Nurture   Woman

Production of crops from *pure*

Myths in which woman = mother of taro; taro = mother

On the basis of such a model, what precisely is the nature of 'rights' in land enjoyed by husbands and wives? A simple analogy would be a jointly owned machine of which one party controls all the bolts and the other controls all the nuts. The assets of neither party have any value independently of the other. Value can be created only by the co-operative *action* of screwing together bolts and nuts. Land transactions between Orokaiva husbands and wives are similarly a sequence of cumulative co-operative actions, such that each move by one party calls forth an appropriate response. The only 'rights' are 'rights' to responses once certain moves have been made. Legal disputes can in practice arise only if one party fails to make the required response. It creates a wrong impression to speak of land being 'vested' in a man if all he has (independently of some woman) is a cleared patch of ground on which nothing grows; nor is the woman in a better position as she cannot (independently) bring any crop to maturity as she needs the man's garden magic. As we shall see below, 'rights' in all Orokaiva land transactions are limited in some way similar to this.

3.   Land Transactions between Men and Spirits

A second basic transaction mediated by the land is that between the soul of a recently deceased person and a new-born infant. The Orokaiva believe in transmigration of souls. But this transmigration occurs through the mediation of the piece of land where the spirit of the dead person has taken up special residence. This is usually the garden he or she was cultivating at the time of death. It is a fact of Orokaiva life that old people do not stop gardening as long as they have any strength left in their bodies. Waddell's study of time allocation in Sivepe showed that after the age of fifty-five, time spent on productive subsistence activity, especially in the garden, declined only slightly, whereas non-productive activity (e.g. social obligations, dealings with external agencies) declined very sharply (1968: 104). Old people devote their reduced energies almost exclusively to their gardens, grow progressively closer to their gardens and away from the social network, until finally, after death, their spirit becomes still more closely attached to the land. Their souls re-enter association with the village through transmigration.

Crops from the garden cultivated by the deceased may not be eaten by any member of the deceased's lineage. They are harvested by the heir and given away by him to persons outside the lineage. No *bere* are taken from these crops. After a suitable period of fallow, the garden is replanted, but even then the land is not thought to be free of the deceased's spirit. Very often the son or brother of the deceased plants the garden and uses the produce to give a feast. It is thought that the spirit presents no danger to food grown in that plot afterwards.

Transmigration is affected by a ritual performed shortly after the birth of an infant. The parents take the child to the land where the spirit of the deceased is believed to reside. They seek the spirit by placing leaves of a fragrant plant called *mo* in a creek which runs through the land. When the spirit is thought to have entered the leaves, the parents address it thus: 'You are dead now. We shall look after the land and we shall look after the baby so it will become big and strong. Then this child will look after the land.' The wife, in preparation for this rite, has brought the baby to the garden in a string bag, and has also brought a stick. When she arrives in the garden, she places the stick in the ground and hangs the baby in its string bag from the stick. After the ritual by the water, she drops some of the leaves by the stick, then takes the baby, the bag and the rest of the leaves and returns home with her husband. The custom is for the husband to say at night: 'I hear the baby crying.' He is expected to go back to the garden and talk to the baby that is believed to be in the stick, telling it that the parents will now look after it and there is no need to cry. He should then take the stick, with the 'baby' inside it, to his home.

The significance of this ritual became a little clearer to me through the case of a baby, named Jarata, who became sick and died at the age of nine months (of gastro-enteritis). I was told the cause of death was the father's neglect to collect the stick. The baby Jarata who died was described as a spirit baby (*meni ahihi*); the real baby (*meni be*) had been left in the garden inside the stick and was taken away by the fairies (*sovai*). When the baby became sick, the medicine man went to collect the stick, no doubt with appropriate magic, but it was too late; the 'real baby' was no longer there.

This explanation, referring to the father's neglect, was given by members of Jarata's maternal clan. But I was given a second explanation by the child's paternal clan. According to them, the child died because the mother did not look after the land properly. The assumption here is that if the garden where the child obtains what we provisionally call his soul is well tended, then the child's body will also grow well, but if the garden is neglected (horticulturally or ritually), the child will become sick and die. This intimate connection between the garden and the well-being of the soul endures to some extent throughout life but is especially critical in infancy before a child is able to walk and grows teeth.

It is clear that the 'baby in the stick' resembles what is generally known as an 'external soul'. In its more usual form an 'external soul' resides in an object which is carefully preserved from danger, for any vicissitude that may threaten the object will also threaten the life of the person to whom the 'external soul' belongs. Normally such an object is carefully buried and kept out of harm's way. It appears that the Orokaiva do believe in external souls in this sense, and that they reside in particular specimens of a plant after which a person is named, but that is not relevant here. The concept of the baby in the stick differs in interesting ways from the usual kind of 'external soul'.

The first difference is one of terminology. When I asked whether the part of the baby that was in the stick was called its *ahihi* (spirit) this was denied explicitly. On the contrary, it was the *ahihi* of the child that the mother took with her to the village after the ritual and it was the *ahihi* that the mother was left with when the child sickened and died. The child I had been looking at for several months and that died of gastro-enteritis was nothing but an *ahihi* and it was for that reason that it wasted away and could not live. The part left in the stick and stolen by the fairies was actually the child's *hamo*, its body. Emphatically, therefore, the Orokaiva believe that *ahihi* can be corporeal and that *hamo* can be incorporeal.

Let us now consider more precisely the transaction between deceased and infant that may be called transmigration of souls, which is mediated through the land. Let us start with the death of a man of the Seho clan who was called Jarata (1). Jarata's spirit stayed on the land he had been cultivating at the time of death. Some six years later, Jarata's brother lent this land for a season to Gilford, the husband of a classificatory sister. Gilford's wife was pregnant at the time. When the infant was born, it was named by the man who had lent the land, and was given the name of the dead brother, Jarata. As far as I understand, the effect of this act of naming was to attach the *ahihi* of Jarata (1) to the infant, Jarata (2). (A male infant may obtain its name from either its mother's or its father's patrilineage.) But in addition to *ahihi*, the baby had to be given bodily strength and vigorous growth, in other words, it had to have *hamo*. This could be obtained only from the garden where Jarata (1) was still present. Jarata's *hamo* was thought to inhere in his old garden plot and in the products growing there, or more specifically perhaps in the water flowing through the garden, for it is in the water that the dead tend to live, even though in a more general sense they are everywhere in the garden, as well as in the abode of the dead under the mountain and in other places also. The transfer of the *hamo* to the child is a drawn-out process that may last a year or so. It is done through the mediation of the stick. A mother carries this stick with her every day as she goes to the gardens and she is supposed to hang the child from the stick as she does her work. I have actually seen another mother do this for months. The child draws soul substance through the stick all the time and as the taro and other crops fill out and become vigorous, the child will do the same. It is through this absorption of *hamo* that the child can later fulfil the promise made to the dead Jarata, namely to look after the garden from which he has drawn his life-force.

The ritual formulae spoken by the parents in the garden and quoted above both clearly have the form of a bargain, by which the spirit of the deceased is asked to give *hamo* (a combination of supernatural protection and nutrient strength) to the infant in exchange for proper homage. This transaction may be expressed in the following exchange cycle.

MODEL 12

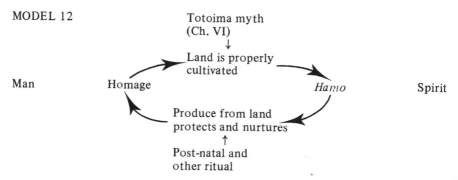

Superficially, it may appear that the exchange cycle given here offers a generalisation that goes far beyond the data I have presented. My data present a transaction between a deceased and a particular couple, with one particular child, who promise to look after the land. My model, however shows a transaction between any spirit attached to a piece of land, and any cultivator. Yet it may rightly be argued that every couple cultivates, at one time or another, a large number of plots, and that only some of these plots are linked to their cultivators through post-natal rites performed in respect of themselves or their children. This argument, however, is irrelevant. Spirits are attached to every garden plot, and there is always some person charged with the care of those spirits. The senior member of an extended family, the 'father of the ground' (*enda mama*) has the ultimate responsibility to see that the spirits are not neglected. When he gives any cultivator a usehold over a piece of land, it is understood that this cultivator takes over the care of the spirits on the land. This care includes making food offerings to the spirit on a raised platform built for that purpose. More broadly, the responsibility to the spirit also involves the proper performance of all ritual and horticultural activities prescribed as parts of the cultivation cycle.

Why does man have this duty? According to the data I have presented, the duty arises out of a promise made at the time of birth. The land is identified with the ancestor who gave the infant its body. The cultivator works not only to 'survive' but also to repay to that ancestor the debt he has incurred by being given a body.

These beliefs are relevant not only to land as a mediating element between living and dead, but also between man and man. The religious system is unconcerned with the consanguineous relationship between the living servitor and the spirit of the dead. It is the service alone that counts, while the capacity to provide the service rests on no more than the authorised occupancy of land. The implication for land transactions between men is that such transactions can never be purely economic.

In the present instance Jarata's brother, in lending his plot to a classificatory brother-in-law, simultaneously passed over the duty to care for the spirit of his dead brother, whose spirit resided on that plot. This is especially interesting as that affine (and his son Jarata (2), if he had lived) belonged to a clan different from the spirit's. Thus, on a religious level, there is no recognition of a clan's 'right' to certain land, but only of a sequence of cumulative co-operative acts between man and spirit, such that each move by one party calls forth an appropriate move in response. We shall now turn to the social aspect of these transactions, i.e. the conditions upon which authorised occupancy is granted.

4. *Transfer of Useholds between Agnates*

In suggesting that land transfers should be studied as social rather than as economic transactions, we may meet with the initial objection that land transfers occur in response to economic needs and are adequately explained without introducing social considerations. But among the Orokaiva, there are many land transfers for which an economic explanation would in practice be hard to find. Certainly there are cases where land is transferred to a household notably short of land, but I know of more cases where the purpose of transfer was to have the company of a good friend on a neighbouring plot and other cases where the only discernible purpose was to make a gift and strengthen a social bond. Crocombe and Rimoldi have recorded a large number of land transfers in Inonda and Sivepe, a large proportion of which were outside the extended family and even outside the lineage. By no means all of these were redistributions to help the deprived. Many were mainly for the sake of strengthening sociability. It is therefore reasonable to inquire into the significance of land in the mediation of social relationships.

We may, first of all, divide these transfers into two broad types: those occurring within corporate groups, and those occurring outside them. In a strict unilineal system, it would be possible to draw a land map showing areas owned by a lineage, and if the system were segmentary, one might speak of a clan domain, a tribal domain and so forth. Such boundaries would theoretically remain unchanged in perpetuity as each generation inherited holdings in the patriline or matriline. No New Guinea system of which we have a recent professional description approximates even remotely to such a model, at least in practice, as we find that many land holdings in so-called patrilineal groups pass into the hands of uterine kin and affines. Among the Orokaiva the departures from a patrilineal norm are so frequent that it is unusual for any man to hold precisely the same blocks as his father who was *enda mama* before him. Nor do clan boundaries and village boundaries remain unchanged for any length of time. In themselves, such departures from patrilineal ideology do not in the least reduce the usefulness of a descent model for the explanation of Orokaiva land tenure, providing that we can plausibly regard all departures from the patrilineal rule as random responses to the vicissitudes of life. In the past, some New Guinea ethnographers have proceeded from this assumption, whereas others (e.g. Lawrence 1967) were willing to recognise structural regularities in the transfer of land to persons other than agnates:

> The potential social relationships which can be deduced from titles to land are of great theoretical importance. They represent an interlocking system of rights and obligations which can reinforce purely biological relationships (those of kinship and descent) within the security circle. (Lawrence 1967:114)

The first question that needs to be resolved, in the case of the Orokaiva, is whether there is really a *rule* enjoining a man to leave his land to his sons (if he has any). I found the rule to be much more ambiguous. If a man has sons, he is expected to leave them *at least half* his land, but he is free to dispose of the other half to others — sisters, daughters, adopted children, for example. Thus a degree of freedom of disposition *is built into the Orokaiva system.* The many cases of non-patrilineal inheritance quoted by Rimoldi, and others I could add, are therefore not exceptions to a rule but the operation of a rule clearly stated by informants. In this discussion, I shall first show on a purely empirical basis that some land transfers are explained by a principle of descent and others on the principle of what Lawrence calls reinforcement of relationships within the security circle. Next, I shall investigate how far the transactional model developed above can provide a principle of higher generality which will sufficiently explain *all* land transfers, patrilineal and other. In the present section I shall concentrate on transfers within the patrilineage.

We have seen earlier in this discussion that the obligation to 'look after' a plot of land formally arises out of an arrangement between an individual (a newly born child) and an ancestor. In practice, however, the ultimate responsibility falls on the head of the extended family, the 'father of the ground' (*enda mama*). This *enda mama* inherits his title from his father or elder brother who died before him. If he has sisters, younger brothers, children or grandchildren, all these will regard him as *enda mama.* Thus, the death of an individual will not affect the performance of the obligation to ancestors living on the land, as the *enda mama* will either discharge these obligations himself or appoint some other occupier to carry them out.

Politically, the *enda mama* acts as leader of his group both externally and internally. In external disputes he champions members of his group against the claims of outsiders. This role is an exceedingly important one and many examples are given where a young man who had a perfectly valid claim to land could not take possession of it because he had nobody to 'speak for him'. (His father was dead.) Internally, in conflicts between members of the extended family, the word of the *enda mama* is final. Nobody outside the family can intervene, nor can juniors overrule the *enda mama*. In theory, a man who will not accept the decision of the *enda mama* has no option but to leave the village and forfeit his patrimony.

Economically, the *enda mama* is theoretically in full control of all products of the soil and of all resources owned by his family. He also has full control over the allocation of land to family members and others, with the proviso that his sons, if any, should get at least 'half' of the land when he dies.

In summary, the religious, political and economic attributes of the extended family enable us to describe it undoubtedly as a corporate group. It has to be recognised, however, that the parcels of land controlled by this corporation vary considerably from generation to generation. A corporation will shed parcels which are permanently vested in other lineages, and will obtain new parcels from uterine kin and others. Plant (n.d.), Belshaw (1951), Crocombe and Hogbin (1963) have all treated this land corporation as comprising a 'lineage', so that it may seem idiosyncratic that I am calling it an 'extended family'. My reason for changing the description is that I was unable to find any case of an extended family lacking an *enda mama*. There are, of course, lineages comprising more than one extended family, but in such cases one finds more than one *enda mama*. Crocombe and Hogbin, faced with this phenomenon, added the term 'sub-lineage' to their pyramid of segmentary patrilineal groupings, but their small sample contains no case of a 'sub-lineage' comprising more than one extended family. In these circumstances we may well delay discussion of the range of control of the *enda mama* until we examine patrilineal ideology in Chapter X.

We notice, however, an apparent conflict between patrilineal ideology and practice. According to the ideology, an Orokaiva patrimony is passed on from an *enda mama* to his successor; there is no rule for splitting up the patrimony between the sons of a deceased *enda mama*. How does it come about, then, that every extended family has its own *enda mama*? The process is easy to describe. It is customary for an *enda mama* to allocate land to all married men of his extended family on a more or less permanent basis. He has the right to change these allocations when special circumstances arise but changes do not occur often. As the *enda mama* becomes older, and less able to make his own gardens, he tends to distribute more and more plots, either to his sons or to other persons of his choice. Though the patrimony remains undivided in theory, in practice it is being divided. In this subdivision, the rights of brothers are supposed to be equal regardless of seniority.

When the older brother dies, the position of *enda mama* passes to the younger brother. The sons of the elder brother then retain no rights of succession and will depend for their well-being on the new *enda mama*, their uncle, who often adopts them if they are young. If the younger brother dies, and there are no other brothers left, the younger brother's eldest son becomes *enda mama*. The custom in such cases seems to be that the portion of the original patrimony set aside for the elder brother should go to the sons of the elder brother; the portion set aside for the younger brother should go to the sons of the latter. Theoretically the eldest son of the younger brother would be *enda mama* over the entire original patrimony but in practice a gradual splitting up would be inevitable. Orokaiva do not easily accept the authority of their cousins or adoptive brothers.

In any case, there are no strong eonomic or political reasons to prevent the splitting of the patrimony. Nor are there religious reasons, because every married male is fully competent to carry out ritual in the garden he is cultivating. The Orokaiva do not have primogeniture in the sense intended by Raglan (1963:100); it is not in the *enda mama* that the spirits of the ancestors are reincarnated, but in all the individuals of the extended family. The *enda mama*, therefore, is not the sole channel of charisma, but rather a kind of revered manager. He usually contrives to keep the patrimony together through the respect and obedience that is due, in Orokaiva custom, to a father and elder brother. I know of several instances where this authority was challenged and found that, in practice, the sons of younger brothers were not cut out of the patrimony, but their share was cut out and the relationship was severed.

Informants were all agreed that at any time either the *enda mama* or the junior member of a land-holding corporation may opt out of the relationship: such a separation involves, first of all, the breaking down of a social relationship in which protection is exchanged for deference and obedience. Therefore such a breakdown involves a high cost for both partners. When I inquired into some breakdowns that actually happened at Sivepe, I was given two kinds of explanation: (*a*) the senior partner broke off the relationship because he was not obeyed; (*b*) the junior partner broke off the relationship because the senior 'did not look after the land properly'. The first kind of explanation suggests that the elder partner, not receiving obedience, no longer received any rewards from the relationship and therefore terminated it. The second kind of explanation is more obscure as I never could find out just *how* the seniors had failed to protect the land. I gather there had been bad harvests, that the juniors thought something was wrong with the land, or that the senior had done something to provoke sorcery which endangered all the land of his lineage. Whatever the details, the juniors felt that the cost of deference to their elder brother was no longer warranted, in view of the amount of 'protection' they received. There was no fear, in any of these cases, that such a separation would be followed by retribution, physical, magical or supernatural. As I showed in Chapter III, the Orokaiva accepts fraternal strife as a natural consequence of events in primal time.

When such separations occur within a three-generation extended family, they are regarded by the community as (minor) misfortunes. On the other hand, they are regarded as normal when they occur between first cousins in a four- or five-generation lineage. Implicit in such judgements is a notion that there is a lower and an upper limit to the useful size of corporate groups. The young man who loses land rights because he has nobody to 'speak for him', obviously needs incorporation in a group. The secure man in middle age who has his land interests cut out of the control of the *enda mama* obviously feels that the useful upper limit of the corporate group has been exceeded. We may express the transactions at the lower and upper limit of the useful size of groups in the following exchange cycles:

MODEL 13

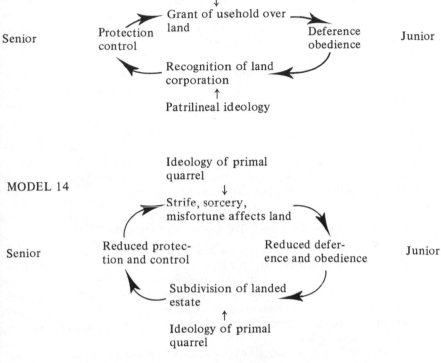

Patrilineal Ideology
↓
Grant of usehold over land

Senior

Protection control

Deference obedience

Junior

Recognition of land corporation
↑
Patrilineal ideology

MODEL 14

Ideology of primal quarrel
↓
Strife, sorcery, misfortune affects land

Senior

Reduced protection and control

Reduced deference and obedience

Junior

Subdivision of landed estate
↑
Ideology of primal quarrel

Models 13 and 14, when considered together, represent two phases of the history of a family. In the first phase a man who has separated out, aided by his sons, establishes his own landed estate. Gradually, he adds to his estate in various ways (conquest, inheritance from maternal relatives, etc.) and he adds to the number of adherents to whom he is *enda mama*. Before two generations have elapsed, the estate thus established will probably be subdivided again. The process of incorporation and subdivision repeats itself *ad infinitum*, and may be expressed in the following cycle:

MODEL 15

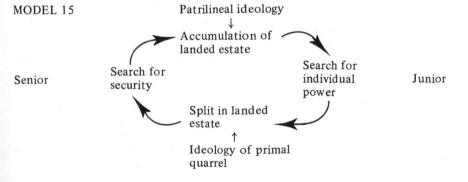

Patrilineal ideology
↓
Accumulation of landed estate

Senior

Search for security

Search for individual power

Junior

Split in landed estate
↑
Ideology of primal quarrel

Previous research such as that of Rimoldi (1966) has shown clearly enough that the Orokaiva patrilineage is not *in practice* an enduring corporate group. The model I am proposing here goes further: it states a rule according to which patrimonies are fragmented and the fragments constituted into new units. It follows from this rule that neither lineage membership nor the principle of patrifiliation (cf. Barnes 1962, 1967) suffices to account for the inheritance of landed estates.

The basic condition for inheritance is that there should be a continuing filial or quasi-filial relation, usually based on co-residence and filial services, thus inducing the *enda mama* to make an appropriate response and continue the protection of the real or fictive junior, as symbolised by the transfer of land, often in gradual steps during the *enda mama's* lifetime.

Having shown that patrifiliation is not a sufficient condition for land inheritance, we shall proceed in the next section to show that it is also not a necessary condition. This argument will be followed by an exposition of an alternative model based on the principle of exchange.

5.   Transfers of Land outside the Corporate Group

The land transfers so far discussed were conducted between agnates and largely prescribed by rules of inheritance. We have seen that there is some freedom of disposition, as the father is not obliged to transmit more than half of his land to his sons. His freedom is even greater if he has no resident sons or brothers. Even a man with many sons and brothers, and with only limited land holdings, is not prevented from making occasional land transfers, though these are more likely to be on only a temporary basis.

The extent of known transfers outside the rules of patrilineal succession has been recorded for the villages of Sivepe and Inonda. In Sivepe more than half of 104 parcels of land belonging to the Jegase clan have been so transferred (Rimoldi 1966:59) whereas only 15 out of 34 gardens investigated were planted by primary members of the right-holding lineage (*ibid.*: 70). In Inonda, the proportion was 20 out of 55 (Crocombe and Hogbin 1963:34). Recipients were sometimes members of the same clan but of a different lineage: sometimes they were members of another clan. The whole of the land now occupied by the Andiriha clan of Inonda was donated by the Tandai'undi of Seva in 1915, when they were affines.

Most of these transfers were made to sisters and daughters of the *enda mama* and, by implication, to the men who had married these women. They were most commonly full sisters and full daughters, but there are many cases involving classificatory and adoptive relationships. The making of such gifts depends partly on inclination; a man who greatly dislikes his son-in-law will not settle land on him. If the daughter marries outside a radius of about three miles from the home village, she usually receives no land. Many women who marry in a neighbouring village receive land close to the boundary. The popular explanation of such gifts is the deep love between a man and his sister (or his daughter). There is, however, another consideration which may have encouraged these transfers: the Orokaiva practised preferential patrilateral cross-cousin marriage, so that a village which allowed a woman to cultivate land, while married in an adjoining village, might receive land at a later date when that woman's daughter married, according to the rule, in her mother's home village. This kind of pattern is described by Hogbin (1967:24) for the Wogeo, who operate a system of land dowries in conjunction with second-degree patrilateral cross-cousin marriage.

Often land is granted, on a temporary or even life-long basis, to persons other than sisters or daughters. Land transfers may arise in a variety of social relationships which cannot be easily categorised. In Inonda, where the village domain is rather large, land is often lent by one lineage to another so that cultivation areas can be close together or contiguous. This is done because people like to work at not too great a distance from one another. In Sivepe, some land loans were made from a similar motive, mostly for rubber gardens. When migrants from Garombi[2] settled in Sivepe, several grants of land were made to them, both for taro and yam gardens. Such arrangements do not usually extend beyond the life time of the recipient although I do know of exceptions. If the gift endures, it signifies a close and permanent bond between families who may be unrelated by kinship.

From the viewpoint I have adopted in this work, two questions are of special interest in the analysis of land transfers: what social benefits are being exchanged between the partners; and what are the symbolic motives for using land as an object of mediation in these relationships? In order to approach these questions, I shall first cite some situations in which land transfers are of practical use and common occurrence:

1. Land transfers from wife's father to daughter's husband used to be very common, especially in the early years of marriage. A man was expected to help his wife's father with gardening and other tasks, and to stay with him for a year or so. During this period, the father-in-law gave the couple a garden for their own use. On occasion, this might be a garden to which the daughter had been granted a permanent usehold. This type of bride-service is very much on the decline today, as the payment of a substantial bridewealth in money acts as a substitute. I encountered the custom once or twice and found that the son-in-law regarded himself as the father-in-law's 'worker' or servant. We may therefore regard this type of land transfer as offering to the donor the satisfaction of seeing the receiver reduced in social status.

2. In the other types of cases I shall mention, transfers of land do not place recipients in a position of social inferiority. Certainly, in many cases harvest gifts are expected from the borrowers of land but these tend to be small in size and to lack any implications of status difference. For instance, many transfers are made by widowers. These men have a choice between attaching themselves to the family of a son, a daughter or a sister's son. In Sivepe, I found that each of these choices was made twice in a total of six cases with which I am familiar. In all the cases where an old man attached himself to a daughter or sister's son, he made transfers of land to those who looked after him. The choice he makes is prompted primarily by mutual affection but nonetheless his position is greatly strengthened by the knowledge that he has some tangible way of showing his gratitude, namely in the form of land. If he is unhappy with one relative and moves to another, some part of his inheritance will probably move with him.

3. Cripples and widows are often in a similar position. They may need a

man to take responsibility while their sons are still too young. This man will 'look after' their land in an economic, political and religious sense and will restore it to the son or sons when they come of age. But in the cases of which I have knowledge, some land is likely to stay with the protector, who often becomes an heir of the widow or cripple.

4.   In all the cases mentioned so far land is an object representing respectable status and exchangeable for services of a quasi-filial nature. The same applies to most instances I know of uxorilocal marriage. Here it was usually the wife's relatives who desired the husband to stay with them, whereas the latter had no pressing reasons to leave his home village. They were generous in their offers of land, and no sensible man would move without such inducement. After the eruption of Mount Lamington, the survivors of the Sangara tribe, greatly reduced in numbers, offered generous land portions, on a wholly permanent basis, to men who would marry uxorilocally. Widowers dependent on the care of their daughters will encourage uxorilocal marriage in the same way. (The frequency of uxorilocal marriage among the Orokaiva is between 5 and 10 per cent.) In these cases it is clear that land donors are motivated by the desire to attract the son-in-law, and that the son-in-law is motivated by pleasure at the status he will gain as symbolised by the land he is allowed to 'look after'.

5.   A very similar motivation may be found for the land transfers made in Sivepe in 1966–7 to families who had migrated from neighbouring Garombi. Seeking an increase in population, Sivepe leaders frequently encouraged dissident minorities in some neighbouring villages to join them. When the Garombi people came, a good deal of effort was made to obligate them and attract their friendship and loyalty. Two men gave useholds over gardens and one man gave a usehold over three yam gardens. It is likely that there were other transfers as well, just before I left the field and afterwards. One of the men who received a taro garden started using the donor's plant emblem when working in that garden, thus emphasising the closeness of the bond with the donor's family, as plant emblems are normally transmitted only by descent. Here the donors were motivated by a desire to attach the immigrants more closely to themselves, and the recipients gave friendship and loyalty in return. Here, as in uxorilocal residence, the migrants' willingness to settle in the village was itself treated as a benefit bestowed upon the local people by the migrants.

6.   As already mentioned, the transfer of land to sisters and daughters is very common. It is the rule that, in the absence of brothers and sons, sisters and daughters should inherit land in preference to second degree kin. I know of several instances where absent brothers and sons were overlooked in favour of sisters and daughters resident in the village. Even if brothers and sons are living in the village, some land may be transferred to females. This will occur especially if a daughter's or sister's husband is known to be short of gardening land. In addition, it may occur for the kind of reasons given by Lawrence in his discussion of land transfers among the Garia, i.e. the enhanced status gained by the mother's brother when he acquires a junior follower strongly dependent on him. Among the Orokaiva where the majority of people marry close to home, a man's generosity to his sister may yield him quite a number of loyal supporters if the sister happened to have many children.

7.   Land is sometimes made available by an individual *enda mama* for a

community purpose. Whenever a new village is built it is necessary for some individual to give garden land. Often several individuals give a piece each, but such a gift does not entitle the donor to decide just who should live on each house site, nor to control in detail what residents do with their housing sites. Trees planted by householders remain theirs in perpetuity. Such gifts to the community are not balanced by any specific reciprocal gifts or services, but the donors benefit by the contiguity of the village to their gardening land and perhaps, in a diffuse way, they benefit in social and religious status. Similar gifts have also been made in recent times for co-operative cash-cropping ventures, such as rice-growing in the late 1940s and a recent rubber co-operative in Sivepe. Here again, the total 'company' land was contributed by a number of people, some of whom shared out parcels to persons interested in planting rubber trees. In such cases, donors told me they acted for the good of the community, and everybody emphasised that the recipients incurred no obligation.

Let us now summarise briefly what social benefits are being exchanged between partners in land transactions. Frequent as they are, voluntary land transfers are always treated, in ideological statements, as departures from a regular and more secure patrilineal pattern. It is a though a maternal uncle or affine or distant agnate has voluntarily assumed the role of fictional father of the borrower. One receives a benefit which, in the 'normal' state of affairs, would be given only to a younger brother or son. I do not know of cases where long-term borrowing of land in itself sufficed to induce a man to change his clan affiliation, as seems to happen among the Garia. In one case I quoted, a man adopted the lender's plant emblem, thus emphasising the element of fictional fatherhood. Other informants regarded this as entirely proper and highly sympathetic behaviour, though totally voluntary. Harvest gifts, however, were not wholly voluntary but expected. So was a certain filial attitude of loyalty, obligatory avoidance of quarrels, and willingness to perform supportive services. Only in the case of a son-in-law performing bride service did such an obligation place the borrower in a servant-like position. On the contrary, in most of the cases I quoted it was the lender who felt the stronger need to attract the borrower and enter into a closer relationship with him. For instance, the donor would often have a strong desire for a reliable military and political alliance with the borrower. If supportive familial services were needed, as in the case of old men and widowers, these services were not provided in repayment for land, but in fulfilment of a kinship-determined social obligation. By making a gift of land, the donor was doing no more than express his quasi-paternal sentiments.

We may conclude that, strictly, land is hardly ever an 'object of exchange', in that one cannot suggest any specific major counter-gift or counter-service which could be used to reciprocate. Allegiance and protection, benefits which the land-borrower usually does furnish, cannot be bought with land. They may be given as a response to quasi-paternal support and the enhancement of economic, social and ritual status. Social benefits of this kind are regularly exchanged between non-agnates. In fact, it may be said that it is from social exchanges of this kind between non-agnates that Orokaiva society derives its cohesion or, to use Lawrence's phrase, maintains its security circle.

Why is land appropriate as a mediating object in such exchanges of social benefits between non-agnates? One might answer this question in a preliminary way by saying that land is the only valuable permanent economic asset the Orokaiva have at their disposal for the making of gifts to relatives and close kin. Such gifts, apart from their economic significance, buttress social relationships both inside and outside the clan. The recipient is induced to maintain or assume a filial attitude towards the donor, with all the political implications this may have; a requirement evident not only from the social responsibilities he is apt to accept but also from the magico-religious care he must take of the spirit (ancestor of the donor) resident on the land.

Land gifts made to non-agnates should be considered not solely from the viewpoint of sentiment, but also of their social consequence. When gifts are made to a sister or daughter, the husband or son or the recipient must subsequently, in regular daily practice, show increased allegiance to her family. The *enda mama* of that land has become, in some ways, similar to a true father. The recipient is made to feel, however gently, that he is a dependent. Furthermore, it is a situation which it behoves him to manipulate; his rights are always ultimately uncertain. He must try to tighten his hold over the land, and in the end he can do this only by making himself loved, indispensable and redoubtable in the eyes of his maternal family.

The key to the significance of land in mediating relationships of this type lies in the continuing doubt as to the permanence of the land transfer. At the outset it is often for a single growing season. Sometimes a man is told that he may keep the land as long as he resides in the village, or for his lifetime. But in practice his tenure depends on the course of his relationship with the donor. He may even be told that the land will be his permanently, though this is commonly only when he is the original owner's sister's or daughter's son. Such a promise of permanent occupancy, however, is never tantamount to ownership. In the next section we shall show that it remains hazardous and unwise to grow cash crops such as coffee on land given by the maternal family as long as fifty years previously, because even after this long interval claims can be made for the return of the land or of the proceeds from the crop. Thus a man has to pay very special respect to his maternal family and have regard to its wishes, if he desires continued enjoyment of the land. No other type of gift could do so much to ensure that he will feel a dual allegiance to both his paternal and maternal family.

We may summarise this relationship with the maternal family, for successful cases, in the following diagram. It will be noted that this diagram is basically similar to model 13, but there are significant differences in benefits exchanged: a maternal relative has no 'control' over the land-borrower, nor does the latter owe him any 'obedience'. Conversely, the land is not unconditionally available to further the best interests of the useholder's paternal family.

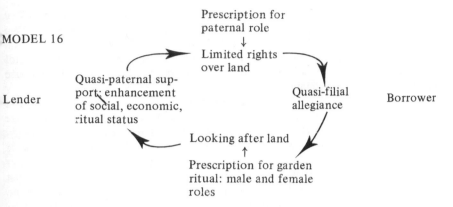

MODEL 16

6. *Case Study of Uterine Land Inheritance*

If a person resides at too great a distance to make gardens on his land, he commonly passes it on to a suitable kinsman to be 'looked after', which means the establishment of gardens on it at regular intervals and the performance of religious rites. After a decent interval (perhaps twenty years), the caretakers will begin to press for a permanent arrangement: does the owner intend to return or will he pass over his land permanently to a resident? It is possible to stall on such a decision for a long time, but even if the owner's rights have the strongest basis, viz. patrilineal inheritance, they gradually become more tenuous and the man who looks after the land increasingly becomes the real master. Theoretically, however, the right to patrimony land is never extinguished. At the same time, a land gift to a sister or daughter is often made on the basis that when the land passes to her male heir he will be able to keep it permanently for his descendants. The formal rules on this point are flagrantly contradictory. If we wish to understand the principles behind uterine land inheritance, our most useful course will be to consider how the system operates in a concrete case.

The data I shall discuss here were reported in Crocombe's and Hogbin's study of Inonda (1963) and supplemented in a brief study by myself. A leading man from Tandai'undi clan (Seva village) gave most of the present Inonda domain to a leading man of Andiriha clan. The Andiriha made various gifts at that time (1915) and also gave Tandai'undi two women in marriage. In the following generation Tandai'undi, according to the custom (of patrilateral cross-cousin marriage), gave two women in exchange to Andiriha, or to be precise, to the son of the donor of the original two women. It was then promised that the son of the elder of these two women would assume control and be permitted to pass on this land to his heirs.

In the 1950s several incidents occurred which emphasised the limitations of the rights of Andiriha. When some Tandai'undi were dismissed from a construction job (by a European overseer), they went to Inonda village where the foreman, an Andiriha, lived. They reminded the foreman that Inonda was 'their' land and that if he wanted to remain on it he had better get them their jobs back (Crocombe and Hogbin (1963: 72). As I have pointed out, a land borrower always has a duty to protect the interests of the lender and this protection was now demanded on pain of eviction. Around the same time, coffee was being introduced in Inonda as a cash crop, but none of this was planted on Tandai'undi land. Three men who had land derived from a different source planted coffee there in 1955 but the other families who had only Tandai'undi land had planted none as late as 1967. They feared that if they did, there would be trouble with the Tandai'undi.

There are many examples in other parts of Orokaiva territory to show that these fears were fully justified. To confine myself to Sivepe, where my data are most detailed, I found that although more than half the land was occupied by rights other than patrimony only two out of fourteen coffee gardens were established on such land. When I inquired into these two cases one grower explained to me in careful detail that he had nothing to fear because the mother's brother who gave him the land to 'look after' had absolutely no descendants, neither male nor female, nor any brothers and sisters. The other grower, who was occupying his wife's land, was in trouble already. His solution had been to plant a second coffee garden and to promise he would relinquish the first when the second began to bear. The other twelve growers all held the view that it is better to grow coffee on patrimony land.

I know of only one case where the coffee-growing occupiers ignored the views of the holders of patrimony rights. This was in Mumuni where after some years of fruitless disputes the holders of the patrimony began to raid the coffee gardens. When the victims of these thefts asked my advice, I had to tell them that a Government Court could probably do nothing for them as I knew they had no legal title to the land.[3]

Under traditional Orokaiva law, the holders of the patrimony probably have a valid claim to cash crops. These crops may be viewed as an unforseeable increment in the value of the land transferred, an extraordinary stroke of luck. In Orokaiva religious thought, there can be only one explanation for such a stroke of luck, namely that it was given by the spirits dwelling on the land. As far as the Tandai'undi were concerned, their link with the spiritual essence of the land was still unbroken. The Andiriha were only caretakers. A perpetual gift of the land to the Andiriha does not mean to the Tandai'undi what it would mean to Europeans. Rather than a gift that is made once for all, it is a gift that is continuing to be made in perpetuity. As the function of this gift is to mediate a social transaction, it presupposes that the social transaction continues in perpetuity. If the value of the gift increases dramatically through unforeseen causes, the donors may no longer consider it appropriate for mediating this relationship, unless the rewards from the relationship also increase.

We may express this notion in the following diagram which is a modification of model 16:

MODEL 17

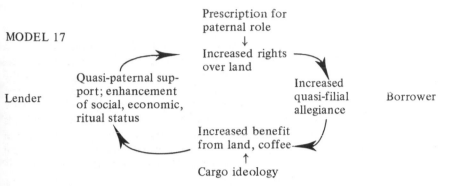

Prescription for
paternal role
↓
Increased rights
over land

Quasi-paternal support; enhancement of social, economic, ritual status

Increased quasi-filial allegiance

Lender   Borrower

Increased benefit
from land, coffee
↑
Cargo ideology

The argument of the Tandai'undi and other owners of coffee-producing land is that the production of coffee gives the occupiers increased rights over land so that they owe an increased quasi-filial allegiance which must be expressed in increased prestations. These may take the form of substantial gifts, a share of the crop, etc. The benefit the owners seek to obtain from the land is nearly always money.

It may seem far-fetched that my model shows 'cargo ideology' as the 'mythological charter' for this desire for money. It may even be argued that the desire for money requires no ideological explanation. Without entering upon this larger question, I would directly relate the significance given to money in Orokaiva ideology to what has been said in the previous chapter about Jesus Christ as a *dema* figure. It is He who is credited with the introduction of money into the world and this is regarded as perhaps His greatest blessing. Hence the pursuit of money is not despised by Orokaiva nor even viewed as morally neutral: to acquire money is to give evidence of having followed the precepts of the *dema*. If the mysteries of the *dema* were more fully revealed to the Orokaiva, they believe they would acquire a great deal more money.[4]

I would argue that the Orokaiva regard the coffee industry as a premonition of greater wealth and power that may later come as the result of the return of the ancestors. Until the coffee industry started, Orokaiva could earn money only by leaving their villages to work for white men. Suddenly it became possible to obtain equivalent amounts from the products of village soil. What stirred the imagination was that a man could go to his garden, pick the coffee and then, after a not too demanding ritual of processing, pour it into a bag and obtain money for it. This was not classified as work but as a kind of magic. *Work* (the Pidgin English word) referred exclusively to paid labour done for an employer. *Pure* referred more specifically to the traditional gardens. *Kapi* (coffee) was what one might compare to a 'money tree': it was the source of the benefits which enabled a village family to share in the 'new day'.

From the cases I observed at Mumuni and Sivepe I gathered that some modest proportion of the proceeds of the coffee garden (like a tithe) would not satisfy the owners of the land upon which coffee was grown by useholders. They seemed to want all, or nearly all, the cash that could be gathered from the bushes. It was because their claims were immoderate that I began to think of the influence of cargo ideology.

One might well regard such immoderate claims as the response to a breakdown in the social exchange relationship. According to model 17, increased rights over land should mediate an *increased* quasi-filial allegiance, implying an increased willingness to aid and share with maternal relatives. Such, however, was rarely in evidence. On the contrary, most coffee-growers, engrossed in the new task of growing coffee, tended to ease up on their family obligations, gave fewer feasts and were apt to neglect their maternal relatives. This was especially so because Church influence reduced the scope of initiation ceremonial which is one of the traditional key functions of the maternal family. Certainly the maternal family hardly shares at all, under normal circumstances, in the increased wealth generated by coffee-growing. Thus the uterine landowner feels relatively alienated from his affluent nephew.

In order to demonstrate the importance of quasi-filial allegiance as a factor in land transactions, I shall cite one case, again from Inonda, where coffee gardens are being run profitably on land over which the grower holds only 'permissive' rights. The three coffee gardens established in 1955, and still harvested in 1967, are on land owned by the Endehi'undi clan but relinquished after a defeat in war. It has been used by Andiriha of Inonda since 1915. When Inonda people started to grow coffee, Endehi'undi reclaimed this land. Inonda paid $32 in cash, as well as pigs, traditional valuables and taro, in other words, a very substantial consideration (Crocombe and Hogbin *ibid.*: 73) After a few years, as Andiriha continued to benefit from the coffee, it became obvious that Endehi'undi did not regard this consideration as a *sale* price as Andiriha hoped they would do. They saw it as no more than a proper display of quasi-filial allegiance, and expected this sort of gesture to be repeated, or to recover the land.

The Andiriha leader now invited a widower belonging to the Endehi'undi group to move into his household. The invitation was accepted and in 1967 the old man was still there. There was no further trouble over the coffee although Andiriha did not tempt fate by making further plantings. By Orokaiva legal concepts, the balance was restored. By a shrewd manoeuvre, the Andiriha leader had found a way to offer increased quasi-filial allegiance in such a way that the profit from the coffee gardens was not reduced too much.

Instances of this kind help us to understand what was involved in the Orokaiva system of residual or dual rights over land and dual allegiance owed by individuals to different families from which land useholds are derived. We have long tended to believe that the basic co-operating groups in primitive societies are *corporate* groups. The Orokaiva data presented here show a second possibility: namely a system by which individuals derive their land, and therefore their sustenance, from a cluster of corporate groups in only one of which they are a corporate member, although they maintain permanent exchange relationships with the others. These other corporations do not make them permanent gifts but leave them conditional upon the successful continuation of the relationship. The fact that a man holds land on such terms *forces* him to continue the relationship.

It is impossible, therefore, to say just what constitute 'residual' rights in land. In the example I analysed, it appears that a group's rights include rights to coffee when it lives in another village, but not when a member of that group stays in the house of one of the growers and is fed by that grower's wife. Perhaps the best definition of 'residual rights' would be 'benefits that are claimed when the social exchange relationship has broken down'. They are a sanction applied to punish the loosening of quasi-filial allegiance.

The case of Inonda is atypical as the entire village domain is held under an arrangement derived from the ideology of exchange. A more frequent pattern is for an individual to own some blocks of land in virtue of more or less permanent gifts. In neither case does this land mediate sacred and indissoluble bonds. In the case of patrilineal inheritance, the individual violates no supernaturally sanctioned rule if he cuts himself loose from his *enda mama* (and often keeps his land). In the case of land gifts, he may also cut himself loose if bonds of affection and expediency weigh less with him than the cost of satisfying his donor. If he should break with his donor, there is likely to be theft, intrigue, sorcery and perhaps violence and it is quite unpredictable who will eventually occupy the land.

If a man has only gift land at his disposal, he is in an insecure position in his relations with his exchange partners. This seems to be the case in Inonda. If a man has only patrimony land, we may assume that he has no close bonds outside his extended family and lineage, as such close bonds would probably have led to offers of land. Such a person has too narrow a base of social support in the community to count for much, and to counter effectively challenges to his position and property that will be made from time to time.

7.   Conclusion

It remains to be shown that the facts and analysis of land transactions illustrate the general principles set out at the beginning of this chapter. I have dealt with a series of social relationships in which one partner has a strong need to identify with the other, to maintain a stable and permanent bond and to obtain what the other has to give. This need was sometimes social, sometimes economic, sometimes emotional, sometimes religious. All these bonds depended heavily on land for their efficacy.

I have shown that a donor of land does not necessarily separate himself irrevocably from the land as such, but from the usehold of it and thus from the productivity of the land for a certain period. There are no return payments which can ordinarily compensate for the gift, the main purpose of which is to mediate a certain social relationship. The donor can never quite know in advance whether the gift will be efficacious, as the receiver of the land may not, in the end, make the social prestations for which the donor hopes. The receiver is usually someone from whom substantial social support, in one form or another, can be expected. The relationships arising in land transactions are therefore precisely those which my model was designed to interpret.

In the introduction to this chapter, I argued that a gift could be regarded as a 'mediating element', for the purpose of my analysis, only if there is identification between the donor and the mediating element. In the case of land, we have seen that the owner strongly identifies himself with the lineage spirits believed to be resident on the land. The land is a part of him, just as his ancestors are a part of him. By transferring the land to another person he causes that other person in turn to identify himself with the land. He is thus magically imbued with the spirit of the donor and (ideally) compelled to behave as though he owed the owner quasi-filial allegiance. This is a magical action of precisely the kind I envisaged in the introduction to this chapter.

Finally, a transfer of land may be maintained indefinitely as long as, in the donor's view, it has 'virtue', i.e. as long as it mediates the kind of relationship the donor desires. But when the relationship breaks up, for one reason or another, the owner desires to have his land returned to him. This is why 'residual rights' on cash cropping land are so awkward. The modern age, the desire for money, the commitment of productive effort outside the range of the security circle all tend to disrupt the relationships envisaged by the lender of land. Meanwhile, modern political, judicial and administrative institutions have taken over many of the functions of the old-time alliances which were bolstered by land gifts.

I have explained in detail why traditionally the Orokaiva considered land to have 'virtue' as a mediating element in their most intimate alliances. In particular it mediates the bonds between husband and wife, spirits and living, paternal, junior—senior agnates and maternal family, and between an indefinite category of close friends.

Land may also act as a mediating element in a negative exchange between a sorcerer and a person who has aroused the anger of that sorcerer, as happens when the former blights the crops of the latter by placing a curse on the land. In many situations of this sort, events which we would class as metaphysical, physiological or climatological are explained as arising out of social exchange. Such beliefs tend to increase the importance attached to the maintenance of satisfactory social exchange relations because the averting of misfortune in the metaphysical, physiological and climatological realms is made conditional upon successful social relations.

The prosperity and opulence of the land thus becomes a measure of its owner's moral and spiritual wellbeing and the amity with which he is regarded by his fellow men. A good man is a good gardener: a good gardener is a good man. This equation is not arrived at by the Orokaiva with the aid of some Frazerian notion of contagion, but on the assumption that the good man has good exchange relations: therefore nobody would wish to harm his garden; therefore the garden must necessarily be in perfect condition. In this as in many other instances exchange is used as the *explicans* of what might well be explained in many other ways. It is because of such gratuitous use of exchange as *explicans* that I am inclined to regard it as a key concept in Orokaiva philosophy.

REFERENCES

1.   I am using the term 'transcendental' in the sense of Schutz 1967 who demonstrates the transcendental expenses arising in social relationships.

2.   For the location of Garombi, see Fig. 10.

3.   These growers held certificates of title issued by the Higaturu Local Government Council, but these certificates have no legal force. I shall discuss in the next section of this chapter the pressures by which the Orokaiva are gradually being induced to establish sole titles.

4.   Money as the means of salvation is a theme of many millennial cults, as is argued in detail by Burridge 1969 (*passim*, but see especially pp. 41—6).

CHAPTER VI

TARO

1. Introduction

It has already been pointed out (Chapter II) that taro is the staple food of the Orokaiva and that most of the taro produced is consumed directly by the producing household (over 90 per cent in all villages surveyed). Nonetheless, taro is the most ubiquitous of all Orokaiva objects of exchange: most households give some of it away every day and it is part of the conventional set of gifts that change hands on virtually every ceremonial occasion.

It is the purpose of this chapter to show that taro has all the characteristics of an object of mediation in the sense in which the term was used in the discussion on land. In particular, man identifies himself with taro, there is a series of myths which validate this identification, and these myths indicate the special significance of taro gifts. A wide range of social relations are mediated through taro gifts. Their main purpose is usually the mediating of social relations rather than the setting up of a claim for a specific return gift. In this respect again taro and land gifts resemble one another.

In his discussion of 'Reciprocity and Food', Sahlins (1965: 170—4) takes very

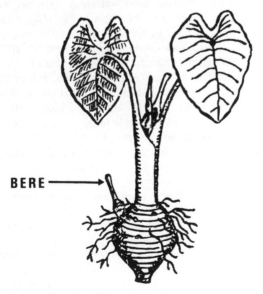

Fig. 7.   *Colocasia esculenta* (taro).

111

much the same view of gifts of staple foods as I shall present here. He writes:

> The character of the goods exchanged seems to have an independent effect on the character of exchange. Staple foodstuffs cannot always be handled just like anything else. Food is life-giving, urgent, ordinarily symbolic of hearth and home, if not of mother. (*ibid.* 170)

I am wholly in agreement with this, except that I do not see why we should confine this argument to staple foods. Many other gifts objects have a similar symbolic quality and are 'socially not quite like anything else'. The essential point, however, is that Sahlins clearly recognises that the symbolic quality with which an object is invested helps to determine how it is used as a gift:

> From this several characteristic qualities of food transfers appear to follow. Food dealings are a delicate barometer, a ritual statement as it were, of social relations, and food is thus employed instrumentally as a starting, a sustaining, or a destroying mechanism of sociability. (*ibid.*)

The present chapter elaborates these ideas, as applied to taro gifts among the Orokaiva. With the aid of some recorded myths, I shall try to show just how taro is conceptualised, in what precise sense it is symbolic of 'hearth and home', and specifically, in what sense it is symbolic of 'mother'. Secondly, I shall distinguish between two specific ritual statements that can be made with the aid of taro and show that these are indeed concerned with the starting and the sustaining of social relations. I shall show on the basis of mythological and ritual data that the two statements may be viewed as standing in a binary opposition: a masculine gift of raw taro inaugurates relations whereas a feminine gift of cooked taro maintains them.

Taro has a special position in the Orokaiva exchange system in that it symbolises commensality. Persons who exchange taro are either in fact or symbolically commensal. Thus taro exchanges are an almost infallible index of intimacy: once two persons have established a certain degree of intimacy, taro exchanges inevitably follow. The same cannot be said for any other object of mediation, not even pigmeat (which is exchanged only in certain specific circumstances) or coconut and areca (which are given, as a matter of custom, to even very casual acquaintances). I could put this more clearly perhaps by suggesting that the network of intimate associations maintained by any individual Orokaiva coincides with that individual's taro exchange network.

In the second part of the present chapter I shall refer to a somewhat detailed, statistically based, study of taro exchange networks. This study aims at answering the following questions: what role do taro exchanges play in the strengthening of existing intimate bonds based on exchange? What role do they play in widening the range of objects exchanged between partners, i.e. in making an already close social relationship even more intimate?

It is obvious that taro exchanges cannot make any essential change in the relationship of members of the same corporate group. By definition, this relationship is already determined by the rules of incorporation. Thus, two brothers do not become more intimate by exchanging taro. On the other hand, if the taro is a feminine object of mediation, it may strengthen the relationship between the wives of two brothers, i.e. between persons whose existing intimate bond is based on marriage exchange. Similarly, when married siblings of opposite sex reside in the same village, taro exchanged between their households would tend to strengthen the relationship between a sister and her brother's wife, and between her brother and her husband. Again among the Orokaiva where corporate groups are rather small, the kinship bonds between distant agnates would carry no implication of intimacy. Intimacy could in such cases be maintained only if the kinship bond were strengthened by fairly frequent exchange transactions for which taro would be a most appropriate object of mediation. In all these instances, taro exchanges mediate an extension of intimacy beyond the narrow confines of the corporate group.

So far we have restricted our discussion of exchange to the mediation of dyadic relations between partners. But if the Orokaiva exchange system is to solve the problem of the smallness of corporate groups, dyadic relations alone would clearly be of limited utility. As evidence presented in this chapter will show, the most intimate relationships are mediated by rather frequent gifts of taro, as well as a variety of other kinds of social interaction. There is a limit to the number of such relationships that any individual can maintain. The maintenance of such intimacy between a cluster of three households would require each household to carry on very frequent exchange with two others. While this is manageable, it could not be extended to the whole of a village such as Sivepe, with twenty-two exchanging households. Nobody can maintain twenty-one intimate associations all at the same time.

This kind of problem may be attacked by the setting up of a variety of corporate groupings on a basis other than kinship, and the study of such groupings is one of the main subjects of political anthropology. The Orokaiva, however, do not have corporate groupings of this type (no secret societies, no age sets, no economic institutions whereby 'big men' can achieve clear ascendancy over others). Instead, Orokaiva developed a principle of cohesion which I would call the circuit of mediation. The simplest way in which twenty-two households can be joined in intimate association by a circuit of mediation would be if there were intimacy between households 1 and 2, 2 and 3, 3 and 4, and so on, the chain being closed by an intimate association between households 22 and 1. Households 1 and 3 might not maintain an intimate association, but they would share intimacy with 2 and this would serve to mediate relationships between them. In theory such circuits could be unlimited in length, though the system would be rather cumbersome and expensive if extended too far.

I shall show in this chapter that the Sivepe taro exchange system presents a striking instance of such a circuit of mediation. The demonstration of this point unfortunately requires some painstaking and perhaps unduly tedious statistical analysis, which is to be presented as a separate paper elsewhere; only the basic argument is set out here.

The analysis of taro exchanges provides us with a model of the Orokaiva exchange system. We may not, of course, assume *a priori* that a model applicable to taro exchanges is applicable to anything else. That needs to be established empirically. If the culture is fairly homogeneous and the empirical data are reasonably full, the model ought to be confirmable in other areas such as marriage rules and the political system. If such confirmation is forthcoming, our gain will be not only ethnographic but also theoretical: we shall have learnt that the analysis of mediating elements in exchange may provide the key to social structure in an exchange-oriented culture.

2.   *Taro Ancestors*

I shall begin the analysis of taro symbolism with one myth especially rich in content, which includes all of the five characters, some of whom, in one way or another, appear in all the myths. It also stands out by the clarity of its detail on the cultivation cycle. As I proceed, I shall discuss some variant myths which emphasise certain themes omitted in the main one or convey the same message in different codes.

The myth is part of the Totoima cycle. It has been reported, very incompletely, by Williams (1930: 155, 158–9, 276) who believed that 'the eating of Totoima's body is generally made to account for nothing more than differences of dialect'. On the other hand the informant who told me the myth in Sivepe volunteered the explanation that it was the story of the origin of taro cultivation. His version, the fullest of a number collected, did not mention the name Totoima, but it occurred in different versions of the same tale given to me by others in the Sasembata district.

1.   A husband slept with his wife. She became pregnant and gave birth to a male child. The husband came and asked: 'Woman, where does the boy come from?' 'I have just given birth to him.' 'Then he is mine to eat. Strike and sever him; when he is dead cut him up and cook him for me to eat,' he said.

(*Commentary*: These words are clearer if we remember that the narrator is thinking simultaneously of a woman giving birth to a child and a woman harvesting a taro. The Orokaiva believe that a growing taro has spirit life and that this spirit life is lodged in the leafy top. Therefore a taro does not die when it is harvested but the spirit life stays in it as long as the leafy top is not severed from the tuber. The act of cutting the top from the taro thus always bears a symbolic similarity to the act of killing. We shall see later that there is a crucial difference between gifts of taro with and without the tops.)

2.   The woman was very sad because she had to kill and cook her child. They slept together again and this time the woman gave birth to a female child which was treated in the same manner. Male twin children followed next. But when the man came to fetch these, he could not find them. The mother had taken them to a hiding-place where she covered them with a heap of weeds (*bivese*) by the root of a tree.

(*Commentary*: The word *bivese*, used in all versions of the tale, is a gardening term used to describe a heap of weeds left in a field after clearing. It was a woman's task to keep taro plants snugly protected after planting by using these weeds as a cover. The tale thus continues to unfold on two levels: the social and horticultural level. The twins are being treated in the manner of seed taro after planting.)

3.   On some pretext, the mother returned to the field, nursed the children and covered them over again. When she came home, her husband said: 'Wife, what did you do with my child that was in your belly?' 'Husband I threw my

child into the water because it was bad,' she replied. 'I am going to collect cabbage.'

(*Commentary*: The reference to the water is the first of a series of apparent lies which always hide a symbolic truth. In this case it is easy to see the meaning, as several myths exist linking the origin of the taro with water. In one myth a woman was prodding the ground with a digging stick. She found water there (and this was the origin of water); later taro grew in that spot. In another myth a boy and girl who were siblings were washed away in a flood on a coconut tree. At the place where they finally landed they discovered taro. Taro, being identified with a human child, is thought of a growing in the water of the womb. The growth of the taro plant requires a very great deal of water and heavy rain so that the growing plant actually lives in a watery environment, which thus resembles a womb. In this sense, her statement is true.)

4.   'I am going to collect cabbage.' Having said this she climbed a cabbage tree. As she looked down and saw the place where she had put her children, she began to weep. When she returned to the ground, her husband said: 'Wife why did I see you cry when you climbed to collect cabbage?' 'When I went to collect the cabbage the sap squirted into my eyes and I rubbed them,' she said. 'You are lying,' he said.

5.   When the children were fully grown, she took them to the mountain far away. She told them their history; 'therefore, I must leave you behind and you must stay,' she said. When she joined her husband again, he asked: 'Why did you stay away so late?' 'As soon as I had done my work and planted my seed (*bere kovitie*), I started on my way home,' she said. 'Woman, you are telling lies,' he replied. When the man understood what his wife had been saying, he went away.

(*Commentary*: When a taro is fully grown it begins to grow shoots on the side of the main rhizome. It is then the duty of the woman to take cuttings from the plant. Strictly speaking these cuttings (Orokaiva: *bere*) are tops of corm-bearing bases of petioles (*Vide* Barrau 1965). These cuttings[1] are taken to a new garden being established, usually, at some distance from the old one. When the husband heard his wife saying this, he understood at once that she had been hiding the offspring she said she had thrown into the 'water'. He could not know, however, that his wife had had twins and this became his undoing.)

6.   The two children, all by themselves, made a garden, ate their food and kept alive. The man went to where the two children were staying. The female sibling (*du ate*) had gone to collect taro while the male sibling (*du bite*) was lying asleep with his chest turned upwards in the shelter (*gaga*). It was there that the man found him, understood at once he was his child and cut out his heart and intestines. He ate these, leaving the rest of the body behind for the next day.

(*Commentary*: I do not know whether the narrator of the myth made a mistake when he said at the beginning that the hidden children were 'male twins'. There is no doubt whatever that at the stage the story has now reached they are siblings of opposite sex. While we cannot rule out the possibility of a narrator's mistake, my informant was an unusually reliable one and it is quite possible that there was an actual change of sex. This will become clearer later when we analyse the significance of male and female roles in this tale. The horticultural reference in this passage is to ordinary harvesting routine. The woman digs the taro and places them in a *gaga* or shelter where they stay until she takes them home. The brother is clearly identified with taro growing in the field.)

7.   The story tells in more detail than is relevant here how the sister learned what had happened, how a magician from Managalasi brought the brother back to life by giving him the heart and intestines of a wallaby, how this man married the sister and how the young man killed his father when the latter returned to complete his meal. He cut his father into many pieces which were shared out among men whose descendants became the various population groups in the Northern District, as discussed in Chapter III.

The myth takes us through two complete cultivation cycles from the planting of the *bere*, the covering over with weeds to protect them from the sun, the gradual growth of the plants under the care of the woman, to the shifting of a new *bere* to a new garden, and finally the growing of these new *bere* to maturity I was given no explanation as to why the myth contains two cultivation cycles rather than one, but it becomes clearer if we regard the myth, on the horticultural level, as symbolising the domestication of what was at one time a wild plant. At this level, the myth starts with the finding of wild taro and the transplanting of the *bere* of that taro to a garden clearing. When these *bere* grow to maturity, new *bere* are taken from them and these in turn are transplanted The products of this second planting are regarded as properly domesticated taro

One may well wonder why the second cultivation cycle was introduced into the myth at all. Direct inquiry did not produce wholly satisfactory answers. People no longer eat taro that grows in the bush, I was told, because it does not taste sweet, it is small, it hurts the mouth. Nobody transplants wild taro *bere* to cultivated gardens nowadays; this was done only in the times of the ancestors. Informants' attitudes to this question were often of this kind when we were discussing the jungle. It was above all a place where the ghosts (*sovai*) lived and therefore dangerous. Wild pigs, especially, often harbour ghosts. If plants or animals are domesticated, it is the dispelling of ghostly essences that is the objective of the practices followed. I shall show this in more detail when discussing the domestication of pigs. Taking into account this fear and suspicion of the bush, it is understandable that a seed taken from the bush is not regarded as domesticated just because it has grown to maturity in a garden. A plant grown from a bush seed is regarded as still being contaminated by *sovai* influence. It is only the second harvest that can be regarded as wholly belonging to the domesticated domain.

We have already met the same idea when discussing the taboo on taro-growing on a dead man's land. This taro is effectively contaminated in the same way as bush taro. It is not eaten by those whom it endangers. The next crop planted is still dangerous, and it is only the second planting after the previous owner's death that is free from taboo.

This discussion has already developed one of the main themes of the myth, namely the opposition between bush and garden, the wild and the sown, the dwelling place of spirits and the cultivated domain from which they are carefully banished. If we now turn to the message transmitted by the myth at the social level, we find a similar opposition, namely that between Totoima and his wife. Totoima who kills his own children, using his tusks as he does so, has partly a pig nature, partly a human nature, and these aspects are only partly differentiated. He ravages taro lying in the *gaga* in the manner of a wild pig. The wild taro *bere* planted by the woman in the beginning of the myth are fitly equated with his 'children' because Totoima's realm is the bush; bush taro are the children he might be expected to engender. The garden, however, is his wife's realm. It is she who nurses taro to maturity and who nurtures her family. She too has a dual nature, as she nurtures Totoima and also conspires to kill him. This second aspect is found in numerous myths concerning Totoima's wife. In the present version not only the wife but also the daughter is involved in conspiracy.

The taro are her children, and it is right that Totoima should eat them. She feeds them to him. However, she places restrictions on Totoima's appetite. The *bere* of the domestic taro must be preserved for planting. Hence it is the woman's duty to withhold these from her husband. Woman's two aspects — nurture and domestication — are crucial in the ritual statements made through gifts of taro.

Here we encounter again the dichotomy in sex roles to which I referred in the previous chapter. The male tends to be concerned with the killing of enemies and wild animals, the driving out of ghosts, the felling of bush before a garden can be made. On the other hand, the female is identified with the cultivation of taro. The *dema* of the taro are regularly called upon in drum songs performed at harvest time:

> Bako jape teijo jape bako
> Punduga kovari terijo jape bako, etc.

'Taro-being, ancestress, come to our aid, ancestress, taro-being; with the *punduga* harvesting help us, ancestress, taro-being', etc., where *punduga* is a variety of taro and the song continues with lines similar to the second one, invoking a great number of taro varieties, one after the other.

Taro, clearly, is a feminine plant. The first taro plant is found by a married woman in several myths I have recorded, though in others it was found by a brother and sister travelling together. One may well ask why it is, if taro is a feminine plant, that in this myth (and in others) we find its origin associated with two siblings of opposite sex (*du*), and why in particular it was the male sibling who was lying in the *gaga* while the female one was in the field. Those who like to impute laziness to the Orokaiva male may say that this scene is only too typical, but one cannot seriously believe this myth to indulge in caricature. In my explanation I shall anticipate an argument developed at greater length in Chapter VIII. It is a male sex role to clear a garden and give it to a woman; it is a female sex role to grow taro and give it to a man. These gifts are complementary and mediate the relationship between man and woman. The Orokaiva will classify a garden as a feminine thing 'because it is given to the woman' and a harvested taro as a masculine thing 'because it is given to the man'. This is why the taro lying in the *gaga* was a male sibling.

Evidence presented in the course of this chapter will show that Orokaiva regard taro as having a dual nature: while in the earth, they are identified with the woman who nurtures them and who regards them and nurses them as her children. When harvested they are victims to be killed, cut up and cooked and finally eaten. In this role of victims they are male, because the male is the killer and the male is also the most illustrious victim of the killer — the victim whose name and spirit is adopted by the killer. This theme, widely reported among headhunters, is strongly emphasised in Orokaiva culture, as Williams recognised. In the myth discussed here, and in several others, these complementary male and female aspects of the taro are indicated by the presence of a pair of *dema,* probably always siblings of opposite sex, and clearly marked as such in the present myth.

In addition to father, mother and twins, the myth contains a fifth character, the man from Managalasi, whose peculiarly male role is the hunting of animals. The marriage between him and Totoima's daughter lays down the Orokaiva principle that taro is a female product given to a man whereas meat is a male product given to a woman. In a number of myths I collected on the origin of marriage, that institution is set up by the male hero's action of bringing home meat to a woman instead of eating it in the bush, as was customary before marriage existed.

If female nature, in its pure state, is found in the taro garden and male nature, in its pure state, in the jungle, then it follows that human beings, being born of a man and a woman, have a mixed nature. In Totoima this dual nature is imperfectly developed (for he eats taro in the manner of a wild pig); similarly it is, at first, imperfectly developed in his son who does not hunt and has a purely taro nature. It is only when the man from Managalase has replaced the son's taro entrails with animal entrails that the latter has the power to defeat his father. He is then superior to his father because he has a fully human nature which is symbolised for instance by his manner of killing, with a club rather than the teeth (tusks), as did Totoima.

The analysis of this myth has enabled us to understand more precisely the sense in which it may be said that taro is, as Sahlins put it, symbolic of 'mother'. The Orokaiva do speak of taro as 'our mother' and the ideas they have in mind when they do so have been explained above. Taro is two things: it is a gift from a woman to her husband, and it is the offspring of the woman's womb inasmuch as she is identified with the taro goddess. The woman gives most of the taro-children she collects in the garden to her husband and others of her household, but she may extend this munificence by giving taro to others, i.e. by acting towards others as a quasi-wife or as though they were part of her household. Gifts of taro always have this intimate and deeply personal character as though the receiver was made part of the donor's household. The woman bears herself proudly, being pleased at having grown and cooked the food well; her attitude is formal and ceremonious, thus emphasising the importance of the gift and her respect for the recipient; at the same time she shows a certain solicitude, as though the recipient must be very hungry and very much in need of this meal.

3.   Taro as Mediator of Social Relations

Gifts of taro may mediate either the establishment or perpetuation of a social relationship. But the ritual context of the gifts differs considerably. By far the most frequent type are gifts which maintain relationships; these are made by every Sivepe household every day. In the twenty-eight days for which I took records of taro gifts made in Sivepe village, the number of gifts made and received averaged 2.5 daily, ranging from a minimum of 1.3 averaged by the household least involved in the exchange system, to a maximum of 4.1 averaged by the household that made and received the most frequent gifts during the period. Allowing for variations in size, age and personality characteristics in the various households, these figures present a fairly homogeneous picture of customary exchanges.

Most of the gifts were made within the village, though a small proportion went to relatives and good friends who visited the village or who were visited by members of the Sivepe community. The usual practice was for the woman to bring home with her from the garden not only the taro her household was to eat that night and the next morning, but also taro to be used for giving away. When the recipient was of the same village, the taro would be cooked and presented ready to eat. The presentation was hardly ever made by the husband and most frequently by the children who were sent over with the cooked food and gave it to the named recipient without any ceremony. When there was any ceremony about the gift at all, the housewife was the proper person to make the presentation.

If I inquired who was the donor of the food I was often given the name of the woman, but sometimes the name of her husband, especially if the recipient was one of the husband's close kinsmen. There was always the notion that the gift served to maintain a specific relationship which would be involving either the husband or the wife. Strictly speaking, by far the greater proportion of the gifts were thus made to consanguines rather than affines. But it is better to regard the household as an integrated unit in its relations with other households, as the spouses undoubtedly mostly discuss together to whom food should be given. Essentially, taro gifts mediate relationships between households rather than individuals.

The size of the gifts was constant and seemed to be approximately what one person would eat for a meal. If a household made a gift of several meals to another household, this would be described to me as several gifts, with specification of the names of individual recipients. Here again, there was a contrast between the strict form of the gift and its overall significance. Strictly it was food given by one person in household A to one person in household B. When the family sat down to eat, the person who received the gift taro would share it out to others in the household. Therefore one may say that the gift was, in its general effect, from one household to another, but in strict form, it was emphasised that the social relationship between households A and B was mediated by one person in each household whose relationship was especially close. Thus, I might be told that 'X' sent taro to his brother 'Y'. In fact, X's wife would give the taro to one of her children who would take it probably to Y's wife. Y's wife would give it to Y, saying it came from X. Y would then give everyone a piece of it. A single gift would thus mediate quite a number of bonds.

As the gifts were very frequent, it seems a hopeless enterprise to specify on what occasions they were made; at first I thought taro gifts were made without any reason. Nonetheless, it is useful to discuss briefly a series of instances when taro gifts are considered appropriate. Let us first list a few of the more formal occasions when the housewife herself would make the presentation:

1.   The recipient's household was receiving a guest from a different village, or a family member returning after a period of absence. In such a case, the guest would invariably be specified as the recipient of the gift. Informants would also say that they were 'helping' the host household.

2.   A woman in the recipient's household had just had a baby. In such a case the woman herself was forbidden to go to her garden (*post partum* taboo) so she had to be helped by others who would bring her food.

3.   After any death in a household, food would be brought by women from a number of households, again because death places a taboo upon the garden of the bereaved family.

There were also certain stereotyped situations where people felt they must make gifts of taro, but where no special ceremony was necessary. Here the food was often sent through the donor's children:

4.   The recipient had performed some service for the donor's household during the day. The gift in such cases was not really a payment for services rendered, though sometimes it was explained to me that so-and-so was sent some food because he had been unable to do his garden that day: he had spent the day helping the donor. Such an explanation was always unsatisfactory because the man's wife had usually gone to the garden. Also, it would be very wrong to suppose that there was something like a free labour market and that a day's work could be purchased for a meal. It is better to assume that the two households were on an intimate footing, were in the habit of sending each other food occasionally, and that such gifts never signified more than a confirmation of the warm feelings existing between them. When a man had just been helping the donor household, such an affirmation of warm feelings would be especially appropriate.

5.   The recipient was too old to grow for himself all the food he needed. In such a case he or she rarely moved into the household of a younger couple. There are actually a number of strict rules which make such an arrangement most uncomfortable for Orokaiva. For instance, spouses are not allowed to quarrel in the presence of a parent or an affine. Until an elderly person becomes very sick, he or she lives in a separate house, but cooked food is sent to that house regularly by one or more women who look after the old person.

6.   Food was also sent, as a matter of common obligation, to the house of a person who was sick or disabled.

These cases by no means exhaust the occasions when taro gifts were made. There were, in addition, certain households with which relations were so close that food was sent over several times a week, even in the absence of any particular reason. One might say that such households lived in a state of semi-commensality. Though they each ate in or in front of their own houses, they tended to spend the evenings together sitting and chatting around the same fire. In the mornings they would sit together before going to their gardens.

The proper form in which to present taro in all the cases discussed so far was without the taro tops, cut up, cooked and ready for eating. These gifts signified no more than a simple extension of commensality from the mostly nuclear household to other households with which the bonds were intimate. Their function was to maintain existing social relationships. Nobody maintained relations of this sort with every household in the village; in the twenty-eight days for which I kept tally, the number of partnerships of individual households varied from three to fourteen out of a total of twenty-two households surveyed. This means that the households with the smallest networks had only three exchange partners during the survey period, out of a possible total of twenty-one, and the households with the largest network still failed to exchange with seven of the available households. The average number of exchange partners for the sample was 8.5. If the survey period had been longer, no doubt this average would have been higher, but even when critical events occurred (there was one death and one important visitor in the survey period) food contributions were not sent by *all* households, nor even by all households belonging to the same clan. Each household had its own private network, partly determined by close consanguineal and affinal ties but partly also by idiosyncratic considerations.

Taro gifts made to establish new relationships were of a different kind. In speaking of a 'new' relationship, I do not mean only those cases where gifts were made to persons hitherto unknown. Such cases were rare indeed. It may be justified, however, to speak of 'new' relationships when the nature of a relationship was changed dramatically, made significantly more intimate, as the result of a ceremony where gifts were made. Such a change would occur when one village invited another to a feast, thus terminating old hostilities and placing the relationship on a new footing. Similarly, a dramatic change in relationship would occur as the result of a wedding ceremony when two kinship groups, whatever their previous relation, would begin to regard each other as affines. On a smaller scale, some relationships are intimate only at the time of actual contact. An example would be guest friendships and trading partnerships. Here the intimacy has to be re-established on every one of the infrequent occasions when one partner visits the other. Even if there has been no conflict whatever, Orokaiva always ritually assume that a long-absent friend has become a stranger and the relationship must be restored. As far as I know, Orokaiva do not carry this notion as far as the Maori, who greet a long-absent friend as though they were still heavily in mourning for his death.

Taro is always given by the hosts when such a 'new' relationship is established. But in such cases the taro is uncooked, and still has the top attached to it. I was told that taro, in that form, still contained a spirit and was 'alive'. The ceremonial way of giving such taro is in the form of a pyramid-like mound, the tubers facing outwards, the tops facing inwards. On the top of the mound, a few taro are placed with the tops facing upwards. The mounds should be built on a *gaga*. It will be noticed that the position of the taro on the *gaga* is precisely the same as the position in which Totoima's son lay ('with his chest turned upwards') when his father attacked him.

If we compare this type of gift with the type considered previously, we notice several reversals of the symbolism:

Taro given for	*Maintaining relationships*	*Starting relationships*
Parts of plant given	tuber only	entire plant
State of preparation	cooked	raw
Donor's sex	female	male
Ancestral twin with which gift is identified	female sibling	male sibling

The giver of a feast is always a male. Taro is hardly ever the only gift made on a ceremonial occasion, as pigs, *hambo* etc. must also be presented. Nonetheless, taro is essential as a mediating element in the starting of a 'new' relationship.

What is the significance of taro gifts in this context? Sahlins' suggestion that staple food when used as a gift object is symbolic of hearth, home and mother seem less cogent here than in the case of gifts of cooked food discussed earlier. In previous chapters I have presented a method for interpreting actions aimed at the establishment of social relations. I suggested that some objects are believed to have a special potency in attracting partners and that this potency is believed to be due to the presence of the donor's spirit in the gift object and the transfer of that spirit to the recipient through the mediation of the object. The questions are these: why, and in what circumstances, can a *male* use taro for the mediation of social exchange? What is the mythical and philosophic charter for such mediation? What is the distinctive power of feast taro to compel the recipient to respond to the donor's wishes?

The spirit substance transferred by the *male* when he gives taro at a feast is derived from his ancestors who are present in the land and in the tops of the taro. Just which ancestors are thought to be present it is hard to say, but they include the dead of the lineage who have used the land and they also undoubtedly include the spirit of the original *dema,* Totoima. It is believed that only certain varieties of taro are capable of successfully transmitting spirit in this way. These are known as feasting taro (*pondo ba*). I obtained a list of them, but this list was not very instructive. It contained virtually all the taro varieties growing in the informant's garden, though I was able to identify a few grown varieties which were specifically stated to be unsuitable for feast taro. Only a small minority of plants growing in the gardens belong to these varieties.

Males can use taro for the mediation of social exchange only if they are feasting varieties and if they are displayed, complete with tops, in such a way that they may symbolically represent Totoima's son: lying on a *gaga* with their chests turned upwards. What message does this symbolism convey? Totoima's son appears in the myth in two apparently contradictory roles: that of victim (eaten by his father) and of victor (killer of his father). So much is indisputable fact. It is easy to see what the gift of a feasting taro might mean if we take this symbolism to its logical conclusion. The message would be: 'You may eat me now; I shall kill you later.' No informant actually explained this meaning to me and this interpretation is therefore no more than conjecture. It accurately represents, however, the actual traditional relationship between feasting partners. A man who gives a feast deprives and humbles himself; every one of his gifts is symbolically a sacrifice of himself. His feasting partner is, in a symbolic sense, his enemy with whom he is now becoming reconciled. In order to effect this reconciliation, he sacrifices himself symbolically in the form of his feast taro. But as the myth states, this sacrifice is not a final death. After the feast is over, the feast-giver is more spiritually potent than ever, having obtained the assistance of his own ancestral spirits. He is thus able to overcome his enemies.

Although these ideas are all in some way implicit in gifts of feasting taro, their threatening aspects are kept very much in the background, as the ostensible purpose of the occasion is to establish amity. If the gift represents a display, in very pacific form, of the donor's power, it also offers an opportunity for communion as the recipient consumes food imbued with the spirit of the donor and the donor's spirit thus becomes, as it were, part of him.

At this point we may summarise in a more formal manner the results of our analysis. The insight we have obtained into the meaning of taro gifts suggests that part of the Totoima myth may be represented by the following exchange cycle:

MODEL 18

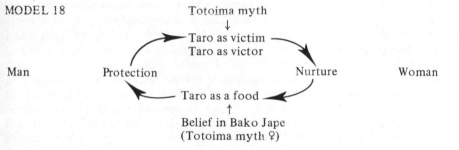

This diagram does not represent the transaction between Totoima and his son (which has already been analysed in model 5) but rather the transaction between the taro woman (Totoima's daughter) and the man from Managalase. Here the man acted as protector while the woman provided nurture. The man from Managalase is primarily a hunter. He arrives on the scene with a wallaby slung over his arm. When he finds Totoima's son with his innards missing, he replaces these with the innards of the wallaby, thus enabling the son to kill his father. Clearly the meaning is that man, while having nothing but taro inside him, becomes necessarily the victim of the wild pig (Totoima), but when he has meat inside him he becomes strong and able to kill the wild pig. Thus man, by his concern with hunting and the provision of meat, becomes a protector to his wife.

The Managalase is a neighbouring district where the main crop is yam, not taro, though a variety of inferior taro (*pijama*) is grown in small bush clearings. The Managalase magician is therefore in an intermediate position between Totoima and his son. Unlike Totoima he recognises the technology and domestication of taro, but inadequately as he is mainly a hunter. Such, at least, is the Orokaiva view of Managalase.

Taro, for the Orokaiva, is symbolic of strength; it is preferred to other staples because it is believed to build stronger men. The success of an Orokaiva feast is measured principally by the amount of taro that changes hands. It is significant that in the fighting between Orokaiva and Managalase, the former were most often the agressors and the latter the victims of cannibal raids, inroads on hunting territories and the like. Thus the Orokaiva regard themselves as stronger than Managalase (certainly they are more numerous as their fertile land can support a far denser population), which served to show the superiority of taro over yam.

The taro myth discussed above may therefore be recognised as a charter for two contrasting types of taro gift made by Orokaiva. Woman provides cooked taro domestically but man, in providing the raw feasting taro, employs taro as a symbol of fighting strength. Heaped up in the manner of sacrificial victims, they are given to guests, not so much to express commensality as to display and offer for consumption the competitive strength of the donating group.

4. *A Survey of Taro Gifts*

One special interest that taro gifts hold for the field anthropologist is their great frequency which opens the possibility of statistical analysis of a fairly large number of gifts of a fairly homogeneous kind. Twenty-two households were visited daily (or almost daily) providing a record of taro gifts made over twenty-eight days from 31 January to 10 March, 1967. Informants were asked to whom they had sent presents during that day and from whom they had received presents. The survey provided useful incidental information about visitors who had been in the village during the day without my knowledge, and about gifts of objects other than taro. For the purpose of analysis I ignored gifts made to persons not resident in the village, as these were scattered over a great many villages and the survey period was not long enough to establish statistical regularities. Waddell reported that 40 per cent of taro gifts were made to persons outside the village (Sivepe), 10 per cent to villages within one mile of Sivepe, 14 per cent to villages situated between one and two miles from Sivepe, 9 per cent to more distant villages and 6 per cent to expatriate centres. (1968: 218). The statistics compiled by Waddell, however, are in terms of weight rather than the number of gifts. A gift of cooked taro made within a village was for one meal only (averaging perhaps 5 lbs.) while a gift of raw taro made to visitors from other villages or at feasts was more likely to weigh at least 25 lbs. Thus the number of gifts made to persons other than villagers was less than 10 per cent of the total.

As I intend to draw some significant conclusions from the statistics of intra-village taro gifts, it is relevant to describe briefly some difficulties I had in collecting these statistics. The fact that households were asked to report on gifts received as well as gifts made provided an effective check, as ideally all items should have been mentioned twice, once by the donor household and once by the recipient household. People very often forgot to tell me of some of the gifts received and made. Some people were most likely to forget what they had received; others would forget what they had given. If my study had been biased towards psychological anthropology, the frequency of these types of memory lapses among individuals might have given me a basis for establishing a typology of exchange partners. I soon found that nobody claimed gifts they had not actually made or received

From the first day of the survey it became obvious that my questions, simple though they seemed, contained an unexpected ambiguity: should the informant include gifts to persons of the same household? It would have been easy enough to lay down a rule that this kind of gift should be excluded from the survey and nor mentioned by informants, but I decided that it was not for me to start defining to the Orokaiva what was meant by a phrase like *ba ikari* 'to give taro'. Evidently food given to household members was, in certain circumstances, regarded as a gift. I recorded a total of 265 such 'transactions' from fourteen households during the survey period. Among those who mentioned such 'transactions' were some of my most helpful informants. At the beginning of the survey, household members were only sporadically mentioned but the number of mentions increased as the survey proceeded, until a pattern emerged.[2] A gift of food from wife to husband was never mentioned. A gift to a household member other than a natural or adopted child of one or both of the marriage partners was always included. Married daughters and sons old enough to live in a bachelor's house were always included. What confused informants most was how to regard gifts to younger sons and daughters.

Some parents included their children if they were old enough to be of school age. Others included the boys if they had gone through the 'birthday' ceremony which nowadays takes the place of initiation and included the boys if they had been through puberty seclusion. Others again did not include their dependent children at all. There was no uniform pattern. I ascribe the confusion to two factors: first, it used to be customary for children to start working in the garden at a very early age, doing whatever was within their capacity and making some contribution to the household economy. Boys would be given their own small garden plots at an early age and their sisters would fulfil some feminine tasks (planting, harvesting) in these plots. When schooling became general in the district, the children ceased making that kind of contribution. Secondly, school 'lunches' were mostly taken by the children every morning and eaten on the school grounds. These lunches were identical in form to the intra-village taro gifts: they were a meal of cooked taro cooked by the mother and taken out of the home.

Intra-household taro gifts were reported to me in too inconsistent a fashion to permit statistical analysis, but they were interesting as they revealed the household to be, in itself, a minuscule exchange system. This system was intact to a greater extent in Hohorita, where schooling ends at grade 3, than in Sivepe where adolescents are mostly at school rather than in the garden. At Hohorita adolescents grew and (if they were females) harvested vegetable food, gave this to their mothers, and their mothers fed and looked after them. The same principle applied in Sivepe to adults living with their adult and married children, brothers or sisters. Even very old men and women do what gardening they can to make a contribution. The record shows, in the case of some of these old people, that they made hardly any contribution at all during the survey period. As this was a period when taro was becoming scarce, their small gardens were exhausted, but a few months later some of them would again have crops of their own.

Most of the older people who thus depended on gifts for their sustenance were not fed by one household only, though usually one household bore most of the burden. However, wherever there was a helpless old person, there were always at least two regularly contributing households in addition to the one to which that person was attached. We must distinguish, among the Orokaiva, between co-residence and commensality, notions which the Orokaiva themselves clearly do not regard as synonymous. Persons who are co-resident are always, in practice, at least in part commensal, they are not necessarily wholly so. Not only old people but also bachelors and young women, single or married, receive gifts of taro from other households of which they are the specific recipients. Food they receive in their own residence may therefore be classed as a gift if they have not supplied raw food to the housewife on the same day.

To what extent is there a notion that food gifts should be balanced as between donor and recipient? According to the statistics, perfect balance is uncommon and occurs most often where exchanges are somewhat infrequent. In Table VI/1, I classified households according to the degree of balance in all intra-village taro gifts made to persons resident in other households. The code number 0 indicates perfect balance in the total number of gifts sent and received; the code number 6 indicates an imbalance greater than the proportion 75:25. Intermediate code numbers indicate a lesser amount of imbalance. At first sight, Tables VI/1 and VI/2 suggest that little importance is attached to balance in food gifts. In more than half the households, the total imbalance exceeds the proportion 60:40. Nor does there seem to be an ideological charter enjoining a person who has received a food gift to return that gift in the near future. The donor says he expects no return gift. If one asks him why he has made the gift he never mentions services or gifts received in the past for which he may be reciprocating. He will say, 'because that man is my wife's father's sister's son' or whatever the kinship relation may be.

A more careful look at the figures, however, makes one wonder whether such indifference to balance is the whole story. Some informants stated that though the donor expects no return gift, the recipient often likes to make one. Some families are more punctilious than others in this respect. The most punctilious of all was the leading family of Seho (H5, H12, H13, H14, H20, H21). They all had an imbalance smaller than the proportion 55:45. Only one other household in the sample achieved this low score.

In most of the households where there is an extreme inbalance, the explanation is that the household contains aged people who require help, or that the household is deeply involved in giving help to aged people. This factor accounts for the inbalance in households 1, 2, 3, 6, 7, 10, 18, 18a, and 19. The imbalance in households 8 and 9 is explained by the fact that householder 8 was helping householder 9 to build a house. Householders 5, 15, and 17 were immigrants from Garombi who gave more than they received, probably because of an anxiety to become accepted and build up good relations in their new place of residence.

Finally, the notion of balance is implicit in the timing of many of the taro gifts. It was a very common practice indeed to make a return gift on the same day as a gift of taro had been received, or on the day immediately following. Though informants told me they were under absolutely no obligation to respond so urgently or to respond at all, the record shows that in practice they frequently did so. We must therefore conclude that the Orokaiva do have some notions which lead them to reciprocate taro gifts, even though there is no rule enjoining immediate balanced exchange.

I would suggest that the Orokaiva proceed from a notion that taro is a

TABLE VI/1

SIVEPE: TARO TRANSACTIONS BY HOUSEHOLD

Household Code No.	Total Transactions	Sent	Received	No. of Partners	Degree of Imbalance*
1	58	40	18	9	4
2	37	1	36	6	6
3	41	26	15	9	3
4	57	35	22	9	3
5	101	54	47	14	1
6	70	45	25	4	3
7	87	24	63	12	5
8	56	33	23	3	2
9	71	40	31	6	2
10	58	21	35	5	3
11	68	36	32	10	1
12	117	59	58	8	1
13	85	44	41	7	1
14	101	52	49	7	1
15	60	34	26	11	2
16	60	37	23	13	3
17	79	50	29	14	3
18	62	9	53	10	6
18a	48	37	11	10	6
19	81	54	27	9	4
20	84	46	38	12	1
21	82	41	41	8	0

* Code: 0 = larger donor gives exactly 50% of gifts;
1 = larger donor gives 50–55%; 2 = larger donor gives 55–60%;
3 = larger donor gives 60–65%; 4 = larger donor gives 65–70%;
5 = larger donor gives 70–75%; 6 = larger donor gives over 75%.

mediating element in the perpetuation of social relations. Within a village, social relations of some sort exist between almost all the members. In my enquiries in Sivepe I came across only one instance of two men, both resident in Sivepe, who denied having or ever having had social relations of any sort with each other. There may have been one or two more instances I did not detect, but they would be very rare. Social relations between households in a village may range from very distant (when no taro gifts are exchanged) to very intimate (when taro gifts may be made four or more times per week). Many households have social relations which are close but not intimate, symbolised by taro gifts made a few times per month. The frequency of taro gifts is of course not the only way of symbolising intimacy, though it is the sign I found the easiest to quantify. It was my impression that those households which maintained the most frequent informal association with one another were also those who made each other the most frequent taro gifts. These were the households who were deeply dependent on one another in sentiment, in economic tasks, in political support. They would tend to side with one another in village disputes. Thus, taro gifts were a ritual statement in which one household expressed its desire for close association with another.

Now, on this level of association, mutuality and reciprocity are obviously essential if the association is to be established on an equal footing. The return gift should therefore not be considered principally as an obligation (arising from a 'norm of reciprocity') but as a ritual statement reciprocating the desire to maintain a close association. Here the question of the frequency of gifts is closely connected with the question of how intimate either side wishes the association to be. An increase of the frequency of gifts means a desire for a more intimate association. The recipient may wish to keep the association within certain limits. The Garombi migrants who gave more than they received seemed to be constantly trying to build up new alliances and were welcomed more warmly by some of the old residents than by others.

Failure to make a return gift of course does not always 'mean' that one is not interested in maintaining social relations of the closeness envisaged by the other party. There are many circumstances when people are not immediately in a position to make return gifts. In such cases I would not say that the recipient remains entirely without obligation, but rather that the obligation is delayed indefinitely. Thus a man may say he is giving food to his father or other senior relative because of some benefits received in the past. (He was himself fed by the senior person in his youth; he was helped with his bride-price, etc.) Or else a man will say that when his hosts visit his own village, he will then reciprocate. In fact guests customarily press their hosts to make an early return visit and hosts sometimes feel some obligation to do so. It is a pleasurable obligation no doubt, but it is clear that the purpose of such a journey is not to get one's taro back but to maintain the association.

It follows from this discussion that the households to which the most frequent taro gifts are made are those with which the greatest intimacy is desired. If the recipients, though fully capable of making equally frequent return gifts, reciprocate too half-heartedly, the donor household will probably reduce its gifts to the level acceptable to its partner. If the recipients are not capable of making equally frequent returns, the frequent gifts will continue, and the taro ledger will remain unbalanced. Thus, irrespective of the degree of balance, we may regard high frequency of taro gifts as a generally reliable index of intimacy of association. I am leaving out of consideration here the question, raised by Sahlins (1965), of whether degree of balance is determined by kinship distance. Exchanges of taro have a social as well as an economic aspect. Where the social aspect is uppermost (i.e. where the exchanges are not primarily based on need), they tend to be close and balanced, as long as both partners are satisfied with the prevailing frequency of interaction. Where the economic aspect is uppermost (i.e. where one partner is for some reason unable to harvest his own taro), no *social* importance is attached to imbalance and Sahlins' generalisation would probably hold for the Orokaiva of Sivepe.

5.   Clusters and Chains, Two Patterns of Intimacy

How can taro gifts mediate close associations among larger groups than dyads of exchange partners? This involves a complex sociological problem that cannot be solved in the framework of the present study: why do men tend to give disproportionate attention to a very small number of their closest associates and much less attention to a larger group who are still close and trusted friends? A principle of allocation clearly operates here: intimate relationships demand more time and energy than can be devoted to the entire circle of close friends. But it is by no means clear what is the role of intimates as distinct from other valued friends. This hierarchy of association, whatever its explanation, is very evident among Orokaiva, not only in the way in which individuals spend their leisure time and compose their co-operative groups, but also in their allocation of taro gifts among their exchange partners.

In Sivepe the number of exchange partners maintained by a household varies from three to fourteen, with an average of 8.5. The first (i.e. most frequent) partner is involved in an average of 38 per cent of all taro transactions, the second partner in 24 per cent, the third in 12 per cent while the other partnerships account for only 26 per cent of all transactions. It is clear that the first and second partners are in a very privileged position in comparison with the others.

A second way of describing the pattern of intimacy would be to assume that there is some community norm whereby a certain degree of intimacy is expressed by a specific frequency of interaction. My impressions, supported by the statistical data and some generalisations offered by informants, is that each household has a few preferential partners to whom it gives or from whom it receives taro at least twice a week, but often far more frequently. In this sense every household in my sample had at least two preferential partnerships. Ten households out of twenty-two had a third, five households a fourth and one (the Seho clan leader) had five preferential partnerships.

The data show that where households are linked by primary kinship, they mostly set up a 'preferential' taro partnership. Only 30 per cent of preferential partnerships, however, fall in this category. The rest can be accounted for only if land transactions, political considerations, and the total past history of personal relationships and transactions are taken into consideration.

For statistical reasons alone it would seem that preferential partnerships are worth some detailed investigation. They clearly add substantially to the number of intimates on whom an individual can count for support over and above those who can be depended on purely by virtue of membership of the same corporate group. In addition preferential partnerships are of crucial importance as a basis for close co-operation between sets of persons larger than the exchanging dyad.

In Fig. 8, all preferential partnerships in Sivepe are shown in sociographic form. A distinction has been made in the sociogram according to the extent to which social preference is mutual. Households A and B may be said to stand in a 'closest mutual relationship' (marked by a hard line), if B is a first or second partner to A and A is a first or second partner to B. If none, or only one of these conditions are satisfied, the relationship is shown by a wavy line.

Though a full analysis of taro gift patterns has to await separate publication,

TABLE VI/2

SIVEPE: TARO TRANSACTIONS BETWEEN PREFERENTIAL PARTNERS

Household Code No.	First Partner	Sent	Received	Second Partner	Sent	Received	Third Partner	Sent	Received
1	H17	7	11	H2	16	0	H5	4	3
2	H1	0	17	H3	0	11	H17	1	4
3	H2	12	0	H17	4	4	H4	2	5
4	H5	15	12	H3	5	2	H7	6	0
5	H4	12	14	H6	11	7	H21	11	6
6	H7	33	12	H5	7	11	H4	2	2
7	H6	14	30	H19	5	11	H4	0	6
8	H9	13	16	H10	18	7	H7	2	0
9	H8	15	15	H10	16	7	H13	4	2
10	H8	7	17	H9	7	12	H11	3	4
11	H12	10	11	H20	18	4	H18	6	2
12	H13	17	19	H14	15	19	H11	12	10
13	H14	21	17	H12	19	16	H9	2	3
14	H13	16	21	H12	17	16	H15	6	8
15	H14	8	6	H16	6	7	H12	3	5
16	H17	8	6	H15	7	6	H7	7	0
17	H1	11	5	H16	6	8	H18	7	3
18	H18a	0	15	H17	3	7	H11	3	6
18a	H18	15	0	H19	8	4	H17	3	3
19	H7	24	5	H18a	4	8	H12	5	6
20	H21	28	19	H11	4	8	H5	4	4
21	H20	22	20	H5	6	11	H11	4	1

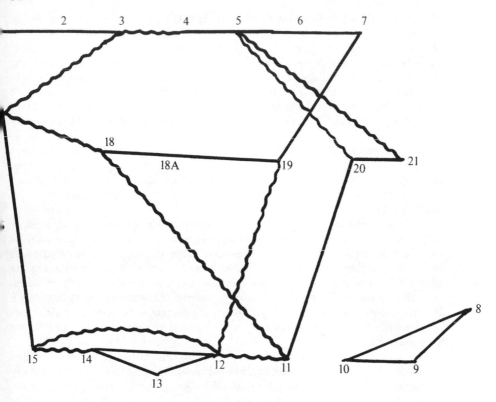

Fig. 8.   Taro gifts in Sivepe: sociogram of preferential partnerships. Households are
numbered as in Fig. 9 (see p. 202). Straight lines indicate closest mutual
relationships, while wavy lines indicate other preferential partnerships.

some generalities are given here, related to our general argument. Taro gifts were
used especially to mediate relationships between neighbours, close kin, exchange
partners, and with certain persons of special status such as leaders, magicians,
and the like. The Garombi immigrants used the system somewhat differently
from the old residents, as the former were more actively seeking new
partnerships, especially with the more influential old residents.

Graph analysis shows two chief patterns: the cluster and the circuit. From the
viewpoint of the quality of social relationships, the cluster is obviously to be
preferred, as it provides intimate one-degree links between all members of the
community. No doubt the Orokaiva's traditional predilection for small villages
of six households or so arose from the comfortable feeling that all households
could then be intimate with each other. We find several clusters among Sivepe
inhabitants, especially among Seho and Sorovi households, but if preferential
partnerships did not exist except inside these clusters, the result would be a
division of the village into very loosely connected cliques.

In fact, we find a second connecting principle which I have called the circuit,
as it resembles the Hamilton circuit familiar in graph theory. A circuit of *n*
households (H1, H2, H3 . . . , Hn) is defined as a set in which H2 has a

'closest mutual relationship' with H1 and H3; H3 with H2 and H4 and so on. Closure of the circuit is achieved if Hn has a 'closest mutual relationship' with $H(n-1)$ and H1. The largest such circuit, or near-circuit, connects the great majority of households of all clans and may thus be considered a unifying principle for the village as a whole. The second, much more strongly constructed, links eleven households of the Jegase-Sorovi clans, but includes not a single Seho household. Even though this circuit of ten households contains two flaws (wavy instead of hard lines), it is most improbable that it would turn up by chance.

How circuits are generated in time becomes clear from a study of the recent immigrants from Garombi. Householder 17, before leaving Garombi, had no particularly close links in Sivepe; yet our survey shows him as having two preferential partnerships with old-time Sivepe residents, one Jegase and one Seho (H18 and H16 respectively).

A curious feature is the almost uniform practice of choosing immediate neighbours as preferential partners. It would be too simple, however, to suppose that there is a rule whereby one must have these specially frequent exchanges with one's neighbours. Certainly I never found a trace of such a rule. On the other hand there are quite complex considerations in the choice of house sites, such that there is the maximum correspondence between physical and social distance from others in the village. When social relations between neighbours become bad, one of them is liable to shift his house elsewhere, so he can be close to an intimate.

The circuit corresponds remarkably well to the Orokaiva system of clan formation. Thus the Jegase 'clan' in Sivepe is actually constituted by four totally unrelated groups, three of which migrated to Sivepe since the beginning of the century and which gradually grew into a single clan by a process of fusion (See Chapter X). They now occupy six houses and ancillary buildings on the Jegase-Sorovi circuit, and three houses which form a chain attached to that circuit, i.e. a total of nine houses. Each 'lineage' forms a short chain of its own, and the chains are mostly linked together by uterine bonds. Now it is precisely these uterine bonds which brought about the fusion of the groups of migrants into a single clan. Yet this clan was still far more fragmented than Seho. Therefore, there was not much incentive to clustering, which requires far greater intimacy than existed among the Jegase.

It is precisely the lack of intimacy between small social chains that produced the Sivepe circuits. As we have seen, these circuits are mathematical models built after the reality of residence and taro exchange patterns. It is characteristic of a circuit that no two households share the same 'closest mutual relationships'. Thus H2 and H3 have a 'closest mutual relationship' but H3 does not share the 'closest mutual relationship' between H2 and H1. It is in this respect that a chain is quite unlike a 'minimal cluster'. The chain arrangement has two practical consequences: if H1 falls out with H3, H2 will mediate; and if H1 and H3 wish to co-operate, H2 will normally be a party to the arrangements as these tend to be made in front of his house, in his hearing and probably in his presence. The structure provides for the possibility that H3 may draw in H4, H4 may draw in H5 and so forth. Actual cases of such political action will obviously tend to be less tidy but lateral communication by means of intermediaries was a pattern to be frequently observed.

The topographical position of a house was therefore at the same time a fixed position in the taro exchange network and in the network of alliances. One could almost tell from where a person lived what that person would do. When fierce arguments and hot abuse rang through the night as two households held a cutting dispute with each other, those households were likely to live at opposite ends of the village, either at far ends of the chain or at opposite ends of a wider and looser chain of associations which comprised the village as a whole.

The Seho clusters and the Jegase–Sorovi chain were at opposite sides of the village, but were linked to each other by two connecting chains, consisting largely of people who lived at the outer ends of the elongated village rectangle. One of these connecting chains was formed by men who came from Soroputa and who married wives from the Seho clan. (H5, H20-H21, H11, H12.) The other connecting chain consisted of Seho and Sorovi householders whose distinguishing feature was that they maintained rather wide taro exchange networks, had peaceful natures and tried to keep on friendly terms with almost everyone. (H14, H15, H16, H17). The links shown on the sociogram between the Jegase-Sorovi chain and the Seho people are of great interest as they show the degree of closeness between the two main clan formations (Jegase and Seho). Judging from the taro exchange network, these relations are not critically remote but on the other hand not so close that the two sides are in any danger of losing their separate identity.

Leadership in the two clans differed in a manner that is clearly recognisable on the graph. Seho had an aristocratic type of New Guinean 'big man' leadership, the leader (H12) having hardly any real intimates except primary kin who were rather numerous. These primary kin, however, between them, had intimate links with nearly everybody in the village. The leader had preferential partnerships and close connections with a few but not all the Garombi immigrants, using his close contacts as middlemen. The Jegase sociometric star (H5) had a far wider exchange network, including all the Garombi families, and almost nightly there were large gatherings in his *arara*. On the other hand, his primary kin links were far fewer; he depended on the systematic fostering of new associations for his challenge to the Seho leadership. Thus cluster and circuit, the two types of association found in Sivepe, each had its own characteristic form of leadership.

6. *Structural Implications*

We have found that gifts of cooked taro are essentially a woman's gift, and that these gifts, if made continuously at short intervals, are a ritual statement of the maintenance of intimacy between pairs of households. The exchange may be stated formally in the following diagram:

MODEL 19

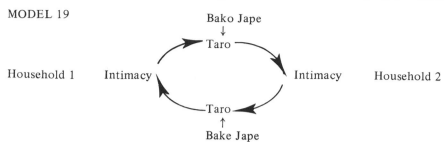

How can an exchange model of this sort establish enduring solidarity in a village containing as many as twenty-two households? In a small cluster of households solidarity can be established by the device of every member exchanging with the required frequency with every other member.

But when there are twenty-two households, the same pattern could be maintained only if twenty-one 'closest mutual relationships' were kept up by each household. This is manifestly impossible as the relationships require, not only regular gifts of taro, but also close and frequent association.

Several devices for increasing the range of a solidarity network have been explored in Lévi-Strauss' theoretical study of marriage exchange (1949). They may be classified as various forms of direct and generalised exchange. Theoretically, any of these devices might have been used to cope with the problems of taro exchange. There might have been a rule delaying the return of gifts, or even forbidding the acceptance of taro gifts from those to whom one had given taro. But these devices would have made an exchange network of twenty-two households theoretically feasible. None of them is, in fact, found among the Orokaiva. Instead we found the pattern I called a chain.

The problem which a circuit-like structure attempts to solve is that of establishing or maintaining amity and solidarity between two parties (A and B) who are not linked by bonds of any special intimacy. The procedure followed is that A and B use one or more persons to mediate between them. In the simplest case, where A and B are separated by only one link in the chain, they share the same intimate associate who can act as mediator. If they do not share an intimate, i.e. if they are separated by two or more links in the chain, an accommodation may be reached through a series of mediators who act vicariously on behalf of the principal parties. The arrangement, in its simplest form, is shown in Model 20 which may, of course, be extended indefinitely by inserting intermediate exchange cycles. In practice, this model would be utilised rarely between neighbours living only two houses away from each other. It is, however, a pervasive pattern of Orokaiva social life. It is regularly employed in the making of requests by someone who is not an intimate. A refusal always offends. But if a request is made through a mediator both sides may pretend it has never been made. At least, no hard words are spoken. There is a customary blank, expressionless style which is used for the transmitting of requests — symbolic gestures of neutrality. The mediator avoids all risks of endangering his own alliances while still making what effort he can to satisfy the party seeking the benefit. If the mediator's intervention is successful, this undoubtedly increases his standing and creates an obligation on the part of the beneficiary.

MODEL 20

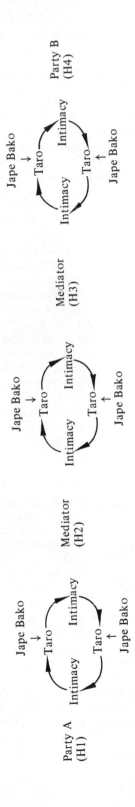

In dealings between different villages, the use of a chain of mediators is extremely common. A will approach a fellow-villager B, who has connections in the other village; B will go to the other village and see C, his closest contact. C will then most likely go to D, one of the intimates of the person E with whom A desires to deal, and D will look for E. During the ensuing conversation, A and E will say very little, and it is the intermediaries who do most of the talking.

The intimate associate, often a neighbour, is thus extremely valuable, as he opens up a vista of alliances to which his partner has no easy access. A man's effective social network is therefore much wider than any network he could personally maintain by direct exchanges. Most of his effective alliances are vicarious and can be reached only through intermediaries.

The social network maintained by a sizeable circuit is therefore very considerable. It is greater than any solidarity group the Orokaiva could build up by maintaining their patrilineage bonds or by exclusively exploiting any other principle of kin group solidarity. The significance of gifts of cooked taro is that they maintain the intimate bonds needed to retain vicarious access to this network. Cooked taro mediates not only the exchange of intimate attachment, but also the exchange access to *alter's* private network of alliances.

If a village formed a perfect cluster, this kind of exchange could not happen, as all members share exclusively each other's most intimate alliances. Where a circuit structure prevails, a man's partner always has an intimate relationship he does not share, so that the man is dependent on his partner for access to that partner's distinctive exchange network. A society whose solidarity depends heavily on direct immediate exchange may have a rather wide network of alliances as long as it has strong institutional patterns of mediation. The importance of these patterns in Orokaiva society cannot, of course, be gauged by reference to taro exchanges alone, but it is now possible to inquire to what extent the model I have constructed on the basis of taro exchange applies in other areas of Orokaiva culture.

Clearly this model, if transposed to the level of marriage exchange, would include elements of both direct and generalised exchange. The cluster resembles direct exchange: the maintenance of relationships within the system depends entirely on benefits received from all households included in the system. On the other hand the chain has the circular form characteristic of generalised exchange. It includes households who receive no direct benefits from one another except the vicarious one of joint membership in the system. In some respects the chain, of course, differs fundamentally from a system of generalised exchange: the taro travels in both directions around the circle. But I have emphasised that taro is not strictly an object of exchange but of mediation. If there is a need to establish intimate social exchange between remote members of a chain, this will not be, as a general rule, for the exchange of identical benefits. Thus the benefits travelling in each direction along the chain may differ and may not belong to the same sphere of exchange.

While relationships within a cluster are very intimate, those within a large chain may require delicate diplomacy. Yet a chain does not, in my experience, contain members who are actively hostile to one another. The exchange of cooked taro has to to with the maintenance of friendly relations, and collapses if serious conflict arises. The management of serious conflict requires different objects of mediation, such as pig meat, which will be discussed in the next chapter.

REFERENCES

1   The propagation of the taro plant (*colocasia esculenta*) is illustrated in Fig. 7.

2   Waddell's survey excluded gifts to household members. This may explain informants' initial hesitance in mentioning them.

CHAPTER VII

PIGS

1. *Introduction*

While taro exchanges serve to maintain the basic social network used in transactions, the pig is the most common object of mediation in critical situations. Unlike taro, pig is not consumed as part of the ordinary diet, but is commonly described as a 'feasting food'. As feasts are held only to mark a crisis in social relations, it will be our task to investigate what makes pig meat specially suitable as a feasting food. One may, at the outset, answer this question with a remark about the physiological properties of pig meat: as the Orokaiva diet normally includes little first-class protein, any meal at which meat is served may be expected to have a specially invigorating and exhilarating effect. But in the present inquiry it does not suffice to give physiological explanations: our problem is to discover how the exhilarating experience of eating meat becomes symbolic and how it is magically utilised in the managing of social crises.

Pig meat is used both for the restoration of good relations after a quarrel or estrangement and for the establishment of new social relations. As such it serves a function in widening the social network. This function is hinted at in the basic pig myth about Totoima to which reference has been made earlier. When Totoima was killed, the joints cut from his body were distributed far and wide and caused all those groups who shared in it to multiply rapidly. This sharing may thus be regarded as a kind of communion which implies both social relations and the conferment of a blessing. Both these themes are strongly present in all ceremonies where pig meat is shared.

But there is a second theme as well: there is in every gift of pig meat the notion of a reparation, either for past services rendered or for past injuries suffered, even though these injuries on some occasions may amount to no more than the lapsing of social contact. The Totoima of the myth, of course, was guilty of many murders and his death was an occasion for dispelling many grievances. Thus the gift of pig meat implies not only a communion but also an expiation.

In treating pig as an object of mediation in exchange, I shall need to demonstrate specifically that in certain respects a gift of pig resembles a sacrifice. It must be shown that the offerer identifies with the pig that is given away or sacrificed, and that there is a belief in the 'virtue' or magical power of the sacrifice both in establishing a social link between sacrificer and human beneficiary and in strengthening the spiritual state of the sacrificer himself.

The data show that pig sacrifices may be regarded equally well as rites of communion and as rites of expiation. The key to their significance, however, lies neither in communion nor in expiation, as they are essentially magical devices to bring about a transformation in social relations with a partner.[1]

While this partner may on occasion be a close kinsman who is given a feast for some special reason, he often has a rather distant position in the exchange network of the donor, with whom commensality occurs only on rare occasions. Not only do feasts tend to extend in this way the range of individual social networks but they are especially apt to extend the range of social relations existing between villages. Feasts are often given by one village to another, thus leading to the establishment of at least one partnership between each household of the host village and each household of the guest village.

The explanation of pig sacrifices requires an elaboration of my model of exchange. The models used so far may be called *transactional*. One may distinguish between positive transactional cycles (in which the two sides exchange benefits mediated by gifts) and negative transactional cycles (in which the two sides exchange sanctions mediated by penalties). In addition one may construct *temporal* cycles, which may show the alternation between friendship and anger, offence and repentance, mortification and forgiveness. A violation of the exchange code will shift a relationship from a positive into a negative transactional cycle, while a reconciliation feast will restore positive reciprocity. The value of pig sacrifices lies in their power to set a relationship upon a course of positive exchanges where, previous to the sacrifice, the two sides were engaged in a mutually injurious exchange of sanctions.

This implies an assumption about the nature of social relations: namely that they cannot be described as intrinsically positive or negative. One cannot divide the Orokaiva social universe into concentric circles distinguishing between permanently friendly and permanently hostile groups. The most one may do (if one has data over a sufficient period) is to show that in the association between villages A and B the cycles of negative reciprocity have been relatively short while between villages A and C they have been relatively long. In this sense one may call B a 'friendly' and C a 'hostile' village, and it may be expected that inter-village feasts, in which pig sacrifices figure, will be more frequent between A and B than between A and C.

This conceptualisation is not based on my own private theory of sociality, but on the Orokaiva expressed belief that strife is a 'natural', i.e. *dema* established consequence of social relations. This belief implies that any relationship will tend to alternate between positive and negative cycles, primary kin relationships not excepted. In *original time*, we find only positive cycles of reciprocity; strife periodically engenders negative cycles, while pig sacrifices lead to the periodic restoration of positive reciprocity.

2. The Wild Pig: Marauder

To the Orokaiva the wild pig is above all a troublesome enemy, as it attacks taro crops in gardens and is liable to kill an unwary hunter. It lives in the jungle where it is believed that ghosts (*sovai*) may enter its body. A pig inhabited by a *sovai* is especially dangerous and harmful to man. The ontology of the pig is explained in a series of myths of which the following, recorded by Williams, states its message most clearly:

A man and a pig (apparently a pig in form but really a man) were up a tree together after fruit . . . the man gave the pig a push and he fell down . . . helpless. Another man came along with a dog . . . the Man-pig cried, 'Hold your dog or he may bite me.' He then asked this new man to build him a house . . . this done he asked for food . . . and an arrangement was reached by which this man always sent taro, etc. from the village to the Pig-man's house . . . and in return received a brought real pig. But the man grew lazy, and once sent his son with the taro. This so annoyed the pig that he tried to kill the boy . . . but he made his escape back to the village . . . After this the Pig-man thought the villagers would want to kill him . . . so he took to the bush (Notebooks 1923, W. 56).

This myth is concerned with the question why man and pig are differentiated species with separate assigned domains.[2] The pig-man of the myth (like Totoima discussed in an earlier chapter) is clearly neither fully man nor fully pig, but has an intermediate position. The assumption appears to be that in primeval time the present discontinuity between the species man and pig did not yet exist. The myth describes how this discontinuity came about and distinguishes two stages. At the outset there was no differentiation at all, a state symbolised in the myth by the image of pigs being able to climb trees. But even then they were less capable of arboreal life than man; man pushed the pig from the tree, thus inaugurating the first state of differentiation. An exchange relationship was now established whereby each partner offered the other the products of his own capacities. But there was an asymmetry in this relationship, as man offered a house and taro, whereas pig was able to offer only his own offspring. This state of equilibrium may be expressed by the following diagram:

MODEL 21

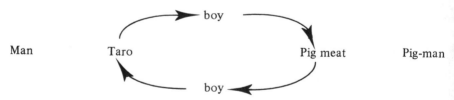

Except for the friendly intervention of the boy, this diagram represents the pattern of exchange that persists to the present day, as wild pigs take man's taro and man takes the pigs from the bush. But man defaulted in this exchange, omitting to send taro. Man thus set in motion the usual process of breaking a relationship. He sent the boy but the response of his neglect was not pig meat; it was anger and an attempt to kill the boy. The boy now ceased to visit pig-man: the social relationship between man and pig-man ceased and thus pig-man, bereft of social relationship, ceased to be 'man' at all but became fully pig. From that time on pig (no longer pig-man) kept to the bush and the exchange between man and pig was no longer friendly but hostile. Pig still takes man's taro but it is no longer given to him; he steals it from the gardens. Similarly, man still takes pigs, but he hunts for them in the bush.

The separation of man and pig leads immediately to the division of the world into two separate realms: the human world, comprising villages and gardens, and the wild world, *ariri,* the bush, where everything is dangerous and inimical to man, and where the ghosts (*sovai*) have their abode. The area friendly to man is thus reduced to a small space, whereas the area hostile to man is an infinite expanse. Thus man is forever at strife with all but a small circumscribed portion of the universe. The myth of pig-man restates in another idiom the message of the primal theft of the piece of string.

3. Domestication of Pigs: Husbandry

Separate though the worlds of bush and human habitation may be, Orokaiva still view them as linked by an exchange relationship. One side of this transaction has already been described in detail by Williams (1930:267ff.). A man becomes a *sovai* at death. As such he enters into various animals. An important class of *sovai* (though not all *sovai*) can be recognised by the abnormal appearance or behaviour of the animals into which they have entered. They are greatly feared and are thought responsible for a great variety of misfortunes. Thus if a man fears the supernatural dangers of the bush, he does not regard these as generated by anything inherent in nature, but as introduced by dead hunters and killers who retain their human wilfulness while deprived of human bonds.

In certain special circumstances bush creatures may re-enter the protected confines of human society. The most important example of such a reverse transaction between bush and village is furnished by the domestication of pigs. There is, of course, no zoological difference between wild and domestic pigs, both being scientifically known as *sus papuensis* and known in the vernacular as *o ohu.* The myths explaining the domestication of pigs are all very simple. In one of them the first pig ever killed by man was a sow marauding the taro gardens. After killing her, men heard a mournful song by the root of a tree. It was sung by her piglets who were thirsting for their mother's milk. The piglets were taken to the village and became the first domestic pigs. The piglets' song, of course, is still known.

The breed has continued until today, being constantly replenished by foundlings from the bush. As boars are castrated, sows mate in the bush. In the bush around Sivepe some wild boars must still exist, though these are probably the offspring of tame sows who have escaped to the bush.

The domestication of piglets is a complicated task which I once saw performed at Inonda. When a piglet was found in the bush it was given for rearing to an old woman who was an expert at domestication. She made a medicine by chewing together betelnut, *hingi* (a peppery leaf) and *arifa* root (in Sivepe *akore* root would have been used). She spat this medicine into all body apertures: mouth, eyes, ears, nose, rectum, genitals. A few hours later she carried the piglet to a creek, washed it and placed it in a string bag (*eti*) in the same way as a baby. Five days afterwards, the piglet could be seen walking through the village on a leash, held by its 'mother'. After two or three weeks, it was regarded as domesticated.

The medicine was intended to seal the piglet from *sovai* who might otherwise enter it. As a bush animal, the piglet was considered impure, dangerous, and liable to spirit entry. The Orokaiva believe that it is *sovai* contamination which distinguishes wild pigs from domestic ones. Once the spirits have been effectively expelled, the piglet *thereby* becomes domesticated. This means that it obeys the calls of its mother. It learns to forage in disused gardens but keeps away from growing taro. The piglet will not stray too far into the bush but comes home every night to be fed, and goes to sleep under the house.

Yet some danger of *sovai* contamination always remains. It may happen that a village pig stays away in the bush and does not return when its mother calls. The mother keeps on calling it from day to day, still hoping that it will return, but after a fortnight or a month it is accepted that the pig has gone wild. Or else it does return when the mother calls but returns to the bush as soon as it is fed. In all such cases people say that the spirits took the pig away and did not send it back.

These facts suggest an exchange cycle arising out of the following four notions: (1) A man turns into a *sovai* upon death. (2) *Sovai* entering pigs maraud gardens and attack humans. (3) A pig is domesticated by the driving out of the *sovai*. (4) Meat from the domesticated pig provides man with the *ivo* (strength) he needs for hunting pig. (This *ivo* makes man a dangerous *sovai* after death.) This cycle may be expressed as follows:

MODEL 22

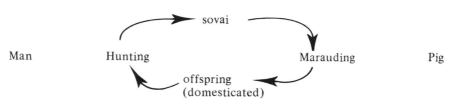

Man   Hunting   Marauding   Pig

Live domesticated pigs are not used a great deal for the mediation of social exchange. Certainly the rearing of pigs enters widely into the exchange of prestations between the sexes, for it is a task women customarily perform for close kinsmen (husbands, brothers, sons). In addition it is not infrequent for piglets to be given to relatives and friends from different villages whose wives then rear them 'for the owner'. Salisbury (1962) noted a similar custom among the Siane, but here the purpose was somewhat different. The Siane have feasts at which 150–200 pigs are slaughtered. Here the recalling of lent pigs is an essential prerequisite for the holding of a feast and, indeed, feasts on this scale would be impossible unless the task of rearing was distributed among several villages. Orokaiva feasts involve far fewer pigs (seven, at a Hohorita feast, seemed normal). Admittedly, lending pigs for rearing does have an obvious economic advantage, similar to the one suggested by Salisbury: once the owner has lent a piglet to a man from another village, he finds it easier to resist demands that will be made from time to time by relatives who 'urgently' need a pig for purposes too compelling to ignore.

Basically, however, this institution is just another way of mediating social exchange. By lending a man a piglet one starts a partnership. The partner does not usually return the pig he has reared but instead gives a piglet which will in turn be reared by the original donor. One might say that the offspring of the donated pig returns to its 'mother's' village. In this way the institution of pig-lending becomes a simulation, on a minor scale, of the customs of marriage exchange, where a reciprocating pair of groups send back and forth a female marriage partner at intervals of one generation.

This assimilation of domesticated pigs to human members of exchanging social groups is emphasised by much customary behaviour towards these pigs. This behaviour goes beyond co-residence in the same house and the use of kinship terms of reference, but extends to strict taboos of wide range prohibiting the eating of domestic pigs by their rearers.

4.   *Wild Pigs as Victims*

Williams (1930) describes in detail the techniques that are, or were, used for the hunting of pigs: the use of spears, pig-traps, and the collective burning of *kunai* grass to drive pigs towards their pursuers. I myself witnessed such a burn, in which three villages participated as owners of the burnt-over land (Inonda, Urio, Musou) as well as some hunters from Ajoro. The myths explaining the origin of the various techniques of hunting and of cooking the meat do not enlighten us greatly in the study of exchange, except to confirm a point already made in a previous chapter: the *dema* figure who is remembered as having 'given' a certain technique to mankind, is invariably described in the myth as the first *victim* of that technique. The ritual of killing is a very simple one: it consists in calling out one's clan name before striking the fatal blow. This is supposed to give the hunter the strength (*ivo*) he needs in order to kill. Both killer and victim are thus symbolically identified with a primal ancestor.

The killer of a wild pig is not bound by the same ritual restrictions as the killer of either a man or a domestic pig. Williams states that he found no rule prohibiting a man from eating his personal quarry. Nonetheless, I found that in practice the meat of the wild pig virtually always serves some purpose of exchange-sale, barter or the mediating of social relations. The two wild pigs killed by Inonda men during the hunt to which I have already referred will serve as an example.

Killer A presented his pig to his mother's brother who lives in Ajoro. Killer B presented his quarry to killer A, who is B's brother's wife's brother. A distributed most of the joints to men and women from Inonda (including B), and to two Ajoro men who had returned from the hunt empty-handed, but kept one joint. A's mother's brother kept part of the animal he had been given but distributed the rest of it to his Inonda relatives, including A., as well as several affines. In the end everyone in Inonda had received some meat, but sometimes this meat had gone through several hands. For instance, A's sister did not receive meat from the animal her brother had killed, but from the animal her brother received as a present. Her brother gave several joints to B and it was from one of these joints A's sister was able to eat, because B gave it to his own brother who was A's sister's husband.

After this set of circuitous transactions the fires were lit. I noticed that only some of the meat was boiled but that most of it was smoked for later use, In fact only a fraction of the two slaughtered pigs was eaten that night. The smoked meat was kept for a variety of transactions. In line with the modern trend, these included sale at the market, but there were also traditional prestations, e.g. a gift to a man who had lent an ornament for a recent ceremony. I was told that meat is sometimes kept for 'months' so it can be offered at a feast or used to discharge an obligation. The housewife smokes the meat over the fire every day so that, after a while, it becomes very 'strong'; the 'stronger' it is, the better.

While the economic motivation in the final disposal of the joints is plain enough, it is less easy to understand the elaborate exchanges immediately following the killing. There are no taboos that could explain why these exchanges were made. One might, of course, account for the whole series of gifts in the same way as I accounted for the taro gifts made between close associates: as a means of maintaining a quasi-commensal kind of social relationship. But such an explanation obscures an important difference between gifts of taro and pig meat, namely that gift taro is usually only a small part of the harvest, whereas it appears to be regular practice (even though not supported by taboo) to give away *all* the meat of a pig one has killed. There is a strong, empirically demonstrated, preference for eating pork that has been *given* rather than pork that has been personally killed.

The essential difference between taro and pork, as perceived by the Orokaiva, has already been discussed in a previous chapter. The difference is that taro is regarded as a staple food to keep men alive, whereas pork is regarded as a food of special power enabling men to succeed in tasks of great difficulty, in which success is always precarious. Pork has a special power or *ivo*. The reality of this belief is obvious from field observation. Meat-eating arouses in the Orokaiva a mood of extraordinary festivity and gaiety. After meat, he shows an exuberance and excitement Westerners display only when they have drunk a good deal or are 'turned on' by mild drugs. While one can think of biochemical causes for the Orokaiva behaviour, they explain this excitement themselves by referring to the *ivo* or spiritual qualities of meat.

These beliefs do not, in themselves, explain why it is considered better for meat to be given rather than consumed by the killer. They do, however, carry us back to the myth — already considered in detail — by which Orokaiva explain the origin of human *ivo*. *Ivo* was personified in Pig-man Totoima until his son slew him and cut his body into pieces. These joints, shared out among men, made the people multiply so that men are now spread throughout the world. The important point to note in this myth is that *ivo* did not come from the mere eating of the meat, but from the sharing out, following by the eating. If *ivo* is to be attained, it has to be through the re-enactment of the myth, which means not only the eating but also the sharing out. This sharing out is always done by cutting a pig into the very same joints as those into which the dead Totoima was dissected. Hence pork — whether derived from a wild or a domesticated pig — is magically most effective if it is a gift.

5. *Domesticated Pig as Victim*

Pig meat provided at the more important ceremonies of the Orokaiva comes far more frequently from domesticated than from wild pig. One reason for this is obviously practical: the more important ceremonies require very intricate planning in many spheres. The meat supply, which is a crucial requirement for such ceremonies, cannot be left to chance, though wild pork can usually serve to add lustre to a feast or to economise on domestic pig. Informants told me that for most ceremonial purposes, wild and domestic pig are interchangeable. In general, therefore, one may say that pigs are reared in order to provide a bigger and more dependable supply of pork. I was unable to discover any instance of a rule requiring *only* wild pig to be used for any kind of ceremony and declaring domesticated pig to be unsuitable. On the other hand certain ceremonial gifts of pigs are made between affines, where a rule stipulates that the pig *must* have been reared by a particular person – the bridegroom's sister or the bride's mother. Such instances have to be carefully studied, as they indicate that the value of the meat transferred in the transaction may sometimes be derived partly from the labour expended by particular persons who reared the animals.

We have already pointed out that some rudimentary sacrificial notions enter into a hunter's action towards his quarry, but it is only the killing of domestic pigs that can be described as *sacrifice* in the full conventional sense of the term. Williams (1930: 61) applies this term to the slaughter of pigs but provides no analysis of the sacrificial process. Such analysis is not altogether straightforward, as the anthropological study of sacrifice has hitherto remained confined to the application of two models: one derived from Robertson Smith after the analogy of Christian *communion,* and the other derived from Mauss, (1968: 193–307) whose chief inspiration seems to have been the doctrine of *piaculum* among the Brâhmanas (viz. Mauss 1968: 352–4). The wide applicability of Robertson Smith's model has recently been well argued by Stanner (1960–3) and Bellah (1964), while Mauss' model has been enshrined by such brilliant ethnographic applications as Evans-Pritchard's study of *Nuer Religion* (1956).

These two models have a great deal in common, but differ in final destination of the victim and the postulated aim of the sacrifice. As Evans-Pritchard has pointed out (1956: 275), the aim may be to keep the god away or get rid of him (as in Nuer piacular sacrifice), or to establish union or fellowship with him (as in Christian communion, and in Australian *intichiuma*).

Neither model appears to be very appropriate to Orokaiva sacrifice, as it is not clear at all just who the god is to whom the sacrifice is being made. The only divine agency that seems to appear in pig sacrifices, including the major feasts, are spirits, loosely described as belonging to the 'ancestors'. These do not appear to be specific personalised ancestors but seem to be identified with the demigod, or *dema* who instituted the feast, as well as with other *dema* who introduced the various products used at the feast as gifts, ornaments and the like, as well as with clan and lineage ancestors who are responsible for the well-being of the land. A big feast seems to involve the whole pantheon. If this were all, one could classify Orokaiva sacrifice as aiming definitely at communion, as the ritual preceding the feast and during the feast quite clearly has the effect of drawing the divine beings down into the village, and making them enter the persons of the celebrants who behave as though they are possessed by these spirits.

But in addition one must often regard the sacrifices as being made, in a very real sense, to the guests. There are of course pig sacrifices where communion with the god is the only or predominant purpose. For instance, it is customary to sacrifice a pig when new taro fields are prepared for planting and the flesh is shared between the men of the local clan group. Here the purpose is no doubt to bring about an identification of the men with the original ancestor who first successfully cultivated that land, and at the same time no doubt with *dema* figures who instituted agriculture. But most sacrifices have to do with social relations that are either being entered into or that are being restored after a period of hostility. In all such cases the sacrificed pig serves as a gift object to the persons whose friendship is being sought. These persons may be clansmen, uterine kin, affines, bond-friends, trading partners, or persons who have rendered important ritual services.

An exhaustive list of examples of such sacrifices, very often involving only one pig and a rather minor ceremony, cannot be given. If a person has broken off social relations with a close relative in anger, by showing this relative his plant emblem, then relations can be restored only if the angry man is persuaded to 'throw his plant emblem away'. If he does this, the person to whom the plant emblem has been shown will sacrifice a pig. Again, if a man feels that he has neglected a fellow clansman for an unduly long time, he will end the estrangement by offering up a pig. A pig may be sacrificed to mark any reconciliation after a quarrel. The sacrificer in such a case appears to admit his own guilt and to restore a wrong done to the other person. Very often such a reconciliation follows a misfortune attributed to sorcery. The medicine man will determine, if the sufferer does not already know, who has caused the sorcery to be performed. It is then considered highly important to arrange a reconciliation with the person responsible for the sorcery. This person is not infrequently a close relative, such as a father's sister or mother's sister. The sufferer will offer up a pig if the dangerous relative is willing to forgive and forget. Sacrifices are also required when a person has violated a taboo, e.g. quarrelled in the presence of a cross-cousin or affine. In all such cases a feast will be held at which the wronged person receives the sacrificial beast.

The same pattern may be found in the larger ceremonies. I shall show in a later chapter that the various prestations rendered between affines can be viewed as propitiatory gifts made to allay anger at the wrong done by the other party. This is certainly true for the gifts made on various occasions by the husband, the husband's sister, etc. to the wife's relatives. Feasts given on the occasion of peace-making, or on other occasions where whole villages are invited can likewise be shown to have as their prime purpose the ending of strife. In all such cases the sacrifice of pigs is preliminary to their utilisation for the mediation of social exchange.

This pattern does not appear quite consistent with the communion model of sacrifice. Not only is there no rule that the offerers of the sacrifice should eat of the victim; on the contrary, we shall see that they are strictly forbidden to eat of it. The guests carry all the meat away with them and distribute it among their own group. One almost feels that the expiatory model might be applicable: the offerers of the sacrifice define themselves as offenders, they expiate their wrong-doing by sacrifice, the flesh of the victim becomes taboo to them.

The contradiction disappears if we regard communion with the god not purely as the ultimate end of sacrifice but also (and simultaneously) as the means to the mediation of a social relationship. I am suggesting that the Orokaiva believe that the killing and offering of a pig is not *in itself* sufficient to initiate or restore a social relationship: it is also necessary to make the offering in a properly ritual manner. The ritual involves the establishment of communion with divine beings. One might say with equal truth that the purpose of communion is expiation and that the purpose of expiation is communion. The transaction may be expressed in the following diagram:

MODEL 23

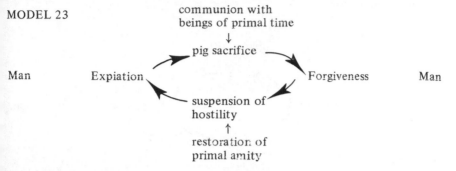

In this model the object of exchange is clearly expiation. Expiation is mediated by a ritual feast through which all participants identify themselves with beings of primal time and therefore with a period when strife had not become established. This identification is established in the first place by the offender's group which makes the sacrifice. It induces the offended party to participate in the feast and thereby signal its willingness, at least in principle, to suspend hostilities. The purpose of identification is therefore the expiation of offences.

In order to account for the rule that the meat is carried away by the offended party and that it is taboo to the offenders, we need to construct a second diagram, as follows:

MODEL 24

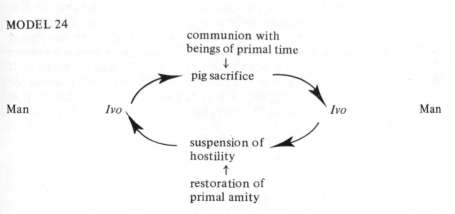

In this model the object of exchange is *ivo* which each group confers upon the other. The exchange is mediated by a pig sacrifice which, according to the Totoima myth, effectively bestows *ivo* upon the guests, *provided* that they carry the meat away with them, and also upon the hosts, *provided* that the guests remove the debilitating influence of any deleterious magic they may have directed at the hosts at an earlier time. One may say here that the purpose of sacrifice is a communion, as the obtaining of *ivo* is ultimately dependent upon an effective identification of man with the power-conferring ancestors.

Models 23 and 24 may be reduced to a single one which shows the essence of the whole transaction:

MODEL 25

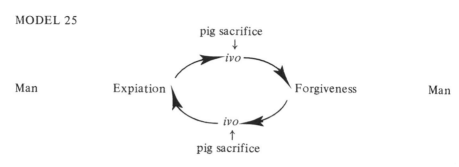

This model, which is on a more abstract level than the previous two, states that two parties standing in a relation of social opposition can establish or restore friendly association with one another through the *mediation* of *ivo* (the source of *ivo* being the pig sacrifices). This is the essential equation of social exchange. *Ivo* cannot be obtained by the offerers of sacrifice acting alone, but it is necessary and sufficient for efficacy if two parties participate, one in the role of offerer and another in the role of recipient. The roles of 'offender' and 'offended' are ritual roles in which the actual amount of guilt or shame felt varies widely according to circumstances. The assumption of such roles is made necessary because strife has a continuously debilitating effect on man's *ivo*. Like many other peoples (viz. Monica Wilson 1952: 99–112; 1959: 161, 165, 217; Burridge 1969), the Orokaiva believe that 'anger in the heart' weakens the man who feels it. But the Orokaiva emphasise even more the obligation of the offender to assuage that anger, however caused. Actual misfortunes are mostly explained by anger existing in someone else's heart. The guilty person is deemed to be he who, after being made aware of this anger, does nothing to remove it. If the angry person uses sorcery or does some other harm it is not he but the victim of retribution who should feel guilty. The oozing away of *ivo* as a result of strife can be reversed by the holding of pig-feasts at which the host goes through a ritual which contains elements of both communion and expiation, but which essentially serves the mediation of social exchange.

I shall now test the usefulness of this model by using it to account for some empirical facts related to Orokaiva pig sacrifice. I shall discuss, because of the relative wealth of available material, the sacrifices made at inter-village feasts at the time of the main harvest. I shall also show how gifts made between affines may be interpreted with the help of the model.

6. *Expiation and Communion in Feasting*

The decision to hold a feast might arise in two ways. First, there might be an urgent need to offer the feast to a specific outside group, e.g. to make peace, or return a feast to which the group had been invited. Secondly, there might be a desire to raise the prestige and potency of the group, to initiate a new age set. In that case, the village elders might well take the decision to hold a feast before they had determined precisely who would be the guests. Usually, a number of motives were present simultaneously: the feast would strengthen the prestige of the leader who gave it, and of that leader's village; it would build up alliances and allay hostilities, while at the same time some young people would be initiated and any other minor pending ceremonial duties discharged.

In 1967, all three villages I studied were involved in feasting. Inonda's feast was in return for the invitation from Sewa the previous year. Sivepe was inaugurating feasting relations with Togahou, a traditionally hostile village with which Sivepe desired friendly relations. Hohorita had held two feasts in the previous year and had received return invitations. The Sivepe feast of 1967 and the Hohorita feasts of 1966 provide an interesting example of the diverse arguments by which people may be induced to hold them. In the case of Sivepe, two generations had passed since the last war with Togahou. The abductions of that time had led to legitimate affinal relations and some reasonably peaceful marriage arrangements, but relationships had remained rather cool. The sickness of an old Sivepe woman married in Togahou led to a series of massive visits and to a desire on both sides to open feasting relations so as to bury old hostilities.

In Hohorita I was given the explanation that the feast in 1966 was held because 'feasts are what brings food', in other words feasts magically increase the yield of the gardens. Informants considered some of the important benefits of the feast to be that the first-born had been ritually blessed, that rain-making ritual had been performed, etc. But an analysis of the recent history of Hohorita made evident the presence of other motives. The village had been established in 1957, the inhabitants being the survivors of the Sangara tribe, which had lost over 90 per cent of its members during the Mount Lamington eruption. The establishment of the village had been followed by years of economic stringency, but at last by 1966 the economic effects of the disaster had been wholly dissipated, coffee trees had begun to bear, and the prime problem of the Sangara survivors became the establishment of friendly relations with surrounding villages. This was not easy, as the Sangara had been powerful warriors greatly feared by the rest of the Orokaiva. I found plenty of evidence that the Sangara are still far from popular.[3]

Sangara informants told me that they did not know which villages they would invite as guests at the time it was decided to hold the feast. The custom is, so I was told, for a prominent man to announce that he desires to give a feast. This man thereby assumes responsibility for a substantial part of the provisions that will be necessary. He must have wealth, but he must also have ceremonial knowledge and diplomatic expertise. Such a feast leader is called a *pondo kiari embo* – a feast expert.[4] Once this man has made the announcement the men present at the meeting will decide among themselves which village will be invited. It turned out that the first village chosen by Hohorita declined but a second village (Koipa) accepted. Although my Sangara informants did not overtly state to me that the purpose of this first post-eruption feast was to make peace or build up good relations with neighbouring groups, this was quite definitely the effect. We may conclude that feasts are normally decided upon for a combination of religious and political motives.

The first plans for a feast are laid at least one year in advance, as it involves extra plantings of taro as well as economising on pigs. By the end of December, the feast taro ought to have finished flowering and the tubers ought to have formed. It is only then that the chances of an abundant harvest can be reasonably assessed. The feast-giver stealthily tours the village gardens to see whether the taro are 'ready', collecting tubers in gardens where tubers have formed and collecting flowers in those gardens which are lagging behind. He hides these specimens in his house. If his examination has been successful, he calls a meeting attended by all the men of the village (but not the women) at which the assembled people formally acknowledge that they are planning a feast. The leader will display the taro and the flowers he has collected, thus demonstrating visibly whose gardens will and will not be able to contribute food to the feast. The meeting decides who will be invited to the feast. The men share the meat of an animal, traditionally a pig, but nowadays often a rooster.

This ritual is clearly intended to remove obstacles that might prevent harmonious social relations from being established at the feast. I have already discussed[5] a myth which contained a charter for this custom of examining the gardens: it told the story of a food shortage which caused a quarrel and concluded with the enunciation by a *dema* of a rule that feasts should in future be held only in times of abundance. It is not sufficient, of course, for the people to say and to believe that there will be abundance. Abundance must be established ritually so as to be placed beyond human dispute.

The pig sacrifice at this meeting serves to remove any latent hostility between the men of the group, so that all will be united and co-operate unreservedly towards the success of the feast. Though the *pondo kiari embo* tends to be a man of much influence in the village, he does not normally have any authority over resources held by any extended family other than his own. It is only for the specific purpose of feast-giving that he is given such authority, and it is limited in time from the meeting just described until the day of the feast itself. The meeting thus temporarily changes the authority structure of the village. The growing taro crop and the available pigs become, at least ideally, the corporate property of the village, whereas normally they are family property. The *pondo kiari embo* becomes, at least formally and ritually, the controller of this property. The unit of the group of offerers of the sacrifice is a necessary condition for the success of the rituals that follow.

The same principle underlies one detail of the ritual taro display to which I have not yet made reference. At the meeting 'special betelnuts' (I do not know just what medicine is used on them) are distributed by the feast-giver to be shared, after the meeting, between the men and their wives. The men are to ask their wives whether the taro are ready. This is a ritual question, as the men go to the garden daily, but it is the women who are supposed to have charge of growing taro and — in a ritual sense — the men therefore do not know. After receiving an answer to this question, the husband will share the 'special' betelnut with his wife. While the enacting of this ritual would make even the most slow-witted of women aware of what is afoot, the women should still supposedly remain ignorant of the plan to hold a feast. Informants readily admit that this ignorance is a fiction. The significance of the shared betelnut is to provide against the anger a wife might feel when the taro harvest over which she has ritual control is incontinently appropriated by her husband. The sharing of a fruit, especially a twin fruit, is a frequent practice when two people wish to establish or restore specially close bonds with one another. It constitutes a mutual pledge of friendship by agreeing to have a feast and take all the taro; they are re-establishing it by the betelnut-sharing. Thus we meet again the theme of the removal of conflict and the promoting of communion that dominates the feasting institution.

After the meeting, an invitation is sent to the chosen village. This takes the form of a small preliminary gift of betelnut and food, symbolic of the bounty to come later. The sending of this gift is called *sope ikari*. The men begin to build the feast house, a special structure which looks quite different from modern houses, but seems to correspond in almost every respect to the design of ordinary pre-contact Orokaiva houses. A style of carving used on the posts of modern feast houses seems to derive from the taro cult prevalent in the Northern District shortly after 1914 (see Chinnery and Haddon 1917, Williams 1928). The house is normally ready about a month before the feast. The ritual task of drawing down the spirits to dwell in the house and possess the offerers of sacrifice now begins. There is an all-night dance in which only initiated men participate, and at which bullroarers and flutes are used to draw the spirits. (For these instruments see Chinnery and Beaver 1915, Williams 1930: 195.) Though informants claimed that this ritual was now abandoned, I know it was enacted at Urarituru, two miles from Sivepe, in 1967. In some villages this dance is repeated (as Williams also notes, 1930: 230) from time to time before the feast, while it is also general practice to sit in front of the feast house at night and sing feast chants, which I heard one evening at Inonda. Each chant dealt either in forthright direct language or more symbolically with one of the objects necessary for a feast: meat, taro, various other vegetables and fruits, clothes, ornaments, betelnut, etc., telling them all to be plentiful. Another chant was addressed to the smoke arising from the fire inside the feast-house, telling it to draw to the village an abundance of guests. As these chants proceed at night, people busy themselves by bringing in food for the feast, preparing ceremonial clothing, and ornaments to be worn by the hosts.

The main effect of these preparations is to induce in the offerers of sacrifice a psychological identification with the *dema* of primeval time. Very little agricultural work is done in this part of the year except harvesting so that virtually all productive energy goes into ceremonial preparations. Those who are to play the role of visitors must likewise prepare, as they are usually called upon to dance, and so need to make or renovate the same paraphernalia and rehearse their dances. The change of identity that occurs when people wear ceremonial dress is strongly emphasised. Everybody must act as though this dress actually makes the wearer unrecognisable. Informants variously explain that the wearer is a wallaby, a flower, one of a number of species of birds perhaps, or an *embahi* — a spirit. Williams has described how initiands are expected to show fear of the *embahi* at initiation and be mystified by the disguise. Initiation, indeed, is the ritual whereby young people learn the dual identity of men: the everyday people one sees about the village, and the ancestral spirits which may at any time transform these familiar people into beings of primal time. The curious nasal sound of the feasting songs emphasises this new identity.

It is emphasised even more strongly by the curious symbolism of the ritual death of the feast-giver. Once the food is collected and heaped up on a platform in the village, a message is sent to the guests. This message takes the form (in Hohorita) of a report that X (the giver of the feast) has a big sickness, and that 'he died last night' or that he 'will die today' or 'will die tomorrow'. The message is made to sound realistic: 'a tree was cut and hit him on the head; he is nearly dead.' One informant told me that he was at first actually deceived by it.

The effect of the message is to oblige the guests to interrupt whatever they are doing and come at once, as they would in the case of a death. But it also has a clear symbolic significance in that it equates the feast-giver with the victims to be immolated at the feast. This notion is found in other Papuan cultures, e.g. the Kiwai, who told Landtman that men actually die shortly after they have given a feast (1927: Ch. XXIV). A feast, in any event, signifies the entrance to the world of death and the ancestors.

At a feast two totally different types of food distribution take place. Cooked vegetables and meat are handed to the guests by the women of the host group in front of their private houses, and raw vegetables and meat are hurled at the guests by the men standing on platforms in the public area of the village. The women serving the meal behave with the ordinary propriety of Papuan hostesses, whereas the men, though actually rather careful in apportioning the tied heaps of taro and the joints of pig meat in accordance with the prominence of each group and group leader, put on prankish, irresponsible, abandoned, even insulting acts, and start meat fights at which the blood runs over the bodies of the recipients.

The pigs used to be slaughtered ceremonially, 'a number of pigs being set in a row and struck simultaneously' with a spear (Williams 1930:61). They are butchered on a platform, the joints being invariably the same as those into which the body of Totoima was cut up. The giver of the feast enacts a ritual for the first-born sons of each family, passing them under his legs and then allowing them to eat of the heart and innards of at least one pig which are placed, still dripping with blood, inside the feast house. It is stipulated that the pig from which these parts are taken has to be killed by a 'father or brother' of the first-born and that the organs have to be extracted by the killer. This ritual, performed in Hohorita in 1966, is a fairly precise re-enactment of Totoima's murder of his son. It emphasises the identification of the feast-givers with Totoima. Although this ritual does not directly involve the guests, it can be performed only in the presence of guests, a curious fact that is adequately explained by the theoretical argument I presented above (Section 5).

The evidence given in the last few pages indicates that Orokaiva pig sacrifice is a form of communion with primeval beings. Certainly the men, after a ceremonial preparation of several months, have reached a psychological state of identification with the ancestors at the moment of sacrifice. There are no professional sacrificers among the Orokaiva, but all the men involved in the feast have, by the ritual exercises preceding the feast, developed *rapport* with the sacred world. Prior to sacrifice, the pigs are offered up to the clan ancestor by the calling out of the clan name. The fact that they are killed (or sacrificed) at all distinguishes the feast from an ordinary economic transaction, where the pig would serve as 'payment' for some gift previously received or a service rendered.

The sacrifice undoubtedly transforms the nature of the victim, as the meat, after the analogy of the body of Totoima, is divided among all the guests, who will 'greatly multiply' by the *ivo* the meat confers after this simple sacrament.

After the sacrifice the group who offered it becomes irrevocably separated from the victim. The composition of the group to whom consumption of the sacrificed pig is forbidden is as follows: the pig's 'mother' and 'father', their siblings, their parents, their parents' siblings, and their children. Infringement of the taboo is said to lead to the death of one of the sons of the pig's 'mother'. I was told that the taboo lapses once a woman's daughters have themselves given birth to children. We may safely deduce from this last limitation of the range of the taboo that it serves to protect the woman's power of child-bearing. The taboo does not reach to the third generation: it does not include the grandparents of the pig-rearers. Nor does it include parallel or cross-cousins. These rules emphasise the position of the pig as a member of the family group. The sacrificer of a pig is identified with Totoima precisely in that both killed their own children.

The membership of host and guest groups is defined mainly by residence: one village invites another. It also occurs, in multi-clan villages, that the two groups comprise only some of the local clan groups of the host and guest village. I did not note cases of two-clan villages where this happened, but it does occur in four-clan villages such as Hohorita and Sasembata. Some close relatives of the hosts, though not resident in the host village, may decide to attend and may make a food contribution. The guest group that is invited usually matches the host group approximately in strength. If there is a wide disprepancy in numbers there is a tendency for several closely-linked villages to join together as hosts or to be invited together as guests.

Relationships between hosts and guests are cultivated on both the collective and the family level. The Orokaiva have no large houses for guests, so that each family of guests is accommodated with a family of hosts. If two villages have never feasted together partnerships are arranged at a preliminary meeting, always making allowance for previously existing relationships. Once partnerships are established they become a standing reciprocal arrangement, inherited by the children of the original partners. A good part of the planning of a feast consists of amassing suitable gifts to be made to one's visiting partner. It is he who must, above all, be impressed by his host and overwhelmed with generosity. On the collective level, guests are expected to dance for their hosts and to carry out rain-making and crop-promoting rituals.

When I asked why the help of guest sorcerers was necessary to ensure increase of the food supply, I was told that if taro grows poorly in a garden it is assumed that an enemy is using *puripuri* (a form of magic) against this garden, thus stopping the taro from flourishing. When a whole village has poor results, it is believed that someone has used medicine against *all* the gardens. According to his reasoning, the task of the friendly magicians at a feast is to remove their own previous black magic from the gardens. As shown in previous chapters, the assumption is always that parties meeting at a feast have been living in something like imperfect harmony. This implies that there may have been sorcery.

The harvest feast is, therefore, an occasion when the community acts as a corporate group to meet a magical danger which transcends the individual. A crop failure at Hohorita would be explained as resulting from sorcery inflicted upon the people collectively by a sorcerer from one of the traditionally hostile villages near which the Sangara have been forced to live since the eruption. The sickness of a Sivepe woman resident in Togahou would be ascribed to an unknown Togahou sorcerer in whom the old anger against Sivepe still rankled. It might have been almost anyone. Both these types of trouble were met by the collective catharsis of a feast, as everybody had been involved in the wars that caused the hostility.

Yet it is clear, from the evidence presented here, that a feast does not serve to set up warm and affective relationships between collectivities: the host and guest communities, as such, do not actually eat together or converse with each other closely. Strictly, they do not even sacrifice to each other. Certainly, some significant bonds are established, but these are entirely between the sets of individual partners. It is they who sacrifice, offer hospitality and make opulent gifts to each other. It is they who come to know each other in the intimacy of their homes. In some cases the host has never met his guest before the feast was planned. In other cases, host and guest are kinsmen or traditional guest-friends. A partnership which starts at a feast may be ephemeral but if the partners feel attracted towards each other, it may be perpetuated and even become a hereditary guest-friendship. Moreover, feasts may generate love affairs and may make strangers into affines.

It is in the individual friendships established in the host and guest villages that we find the best hope of future peace. Though strife between individuals is always likely to recur, it is the inter-village friendship links that may prevent this strife from spreading and becoming collective. Any explanation of Orokaiva pig sacrifice has to take account of the fact that many of the vital transactions, sacred as well as secular, are between individuals, not collectivities. The rites give a good deal of evidence for both communion and expiation, but their concrete end product is a set of dyadic relationships restored or established between individuals and their households. Certainly religious ideas enter into the transaction between the offerer and the beneficiary of the sacrifice, but these ideas serve principally to give the act of sacrifice the deep significance that is attached to the human bond: the sacrificer is possessed by his ancestor as he kills his own pig-child. This is powerful magic indeed with which to obligate the partner who receives the flesh of the victim.

7. *A Model of Pig Sacrifice*

While the evidence presented above is consistent with model 25, that model does not account for all the facts under consideration. If we take a synchronic view of the transaction between host and guest, it is clear that both gain *ivo* from the feast. The guest gains *ivo* as he distributes the pig meat he has received to members of his family and perhaps some other members of his local group. The host gains *ivo* as the deleterious influences that previously caused disease, crop failure, etc. have been dispelled. We do not, however, obtain any explanation from the model as to why the pig sacrifice was a necessary preliminary to the obtaining of *ivo*.

The evidence presented in the previous section shows that we are in fact concerned not with one exchange cycle (i.e. model 25) but with two. The second cycle represents the exchange of sanctions which preceded the feast. Though our data with regard to both the Togahou-Sivepe and the Sangara-Koipa (Isivita) wars are rather fragmentary, we do know that there were a number of raids, the last of which are still known to informants today and date back no more than 60 years. Each side is reported to have raided the other; there were killings; there was cannibalism; women were abducted. Sangara admits having abducted Isivita women but denies that any of its own women were abducted; abductions between Sivepe and Togahou can be shown to have been mutual. The last killings were too long ago for me to be sure which side had made the last raid and which side had, in the finish, a favourable tally of killings. Sivepe and Hohorita both claimed to have come out on the winning side, but I had no opportunity to check the evidence with Togahou and Isivita. If we accept the Sivepe and Hohorita versions, both these villages were in the unpleasant position of having enemies who were still seeking revenge.

Due to the restraints of the *pax Australiana,* this revenge could not take the form of an armed raid, but sorcery was still a possible form of relaliation, as the Australian authorities could not easily detect this. Both Sivepe and Hohorita might therefore justifiably fear sorcery from their old enemies, supposing they wanted to even the scores. There is no evidence, to my knowledge, that either Togahou or Koipa had such ideas in mind, but whenever misfortunes happened to Sivepe people in Togahou, or to gardens in Hohorita, the thought of sorcery used by old enemies seemed reasonable to the Orokaiva. We may represent the exchange of sanctions, prior to the feasts, in the following diagram:

MODEL 26

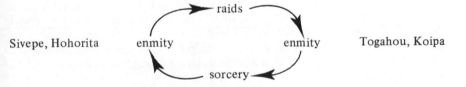

Sivepe, Hohorita   enmity   enmity   Togahou, Koipa

In order to account for pig sacrifice, we require both model 25 (showing the social exchange achieved by the feast) and model 26 (showing the circumstances which made Hohorita into an 'offender' and Koipa into an 'offended' party). In addition, we need to explain why the groups involved decided to adopt new objects of exchange in their social relationship. Until recently, the two sides exchanged enmity which they mediated by various penalties such as raids and sorcery. At the time of the feast, however, we find the same two parties exchanging expiation and forgiveness. It is possible to invoke a number of historical contingencies to explain this change. Informants liked to tell me that the change was due to the effect of the *iji eha*: the fact that everybody was baptised and moving into a new age when old enmities should be forgotten. I could not help noticing the connection between the reconciliation and the simultaneous fear of sorcery to which I have already referred. But perhaps neither historical explanation is necessary.

It seems clear from Williams' evidence and from the little I could reconstruct in 1966 that Orokaiva history had been one long sequence of hostilities and reconciliations. The reasons for the reconciliations were various: the legalising of marriages after abductions, the expediency of forming alliances with old enemies when faced with the threat of new enemies, a desire for peace after some Pyrrhic victories, and so on. On the level of myth we find the same message: the permanent state of *isoro* was interrupted by periodic feasts (see model 1). The series starts, according to myth, with a state of primordial peace. This is followed by *isoro, peka, isoro* in permanent alternation. We may represent the total pattern by the series of congruent ellipses drawn on parallel planes directly above one another (see Model 27).

I have presented transactions in historical time by a series of four transactions, the first and last of which are purely exchanges of penalties. Cycle 2 represents an agreement between two opponents to cease warfare and make peace (*peka*). This cycle would normally start with a message, sent by the original aggressor, that he is ready to make amends. This message would be followed by a visit from the other party to the aggressor, when the latter would promise to hold a feast. A customary practice at such a meeting was for the aggressor to plant a cordiline (*poponda*) in evidence of this promise. The aggressor would then arrange a pig sacrifice.

Cycle 3 would be marked by peace (*peka*). The victim of the original aggression would give a return feast which was probably obligatory. If the basic end of pig sacrifice were communion or expiation, no return feast would be necessary, but as we have found the basic end to be the establishment or restoration of social relations, on a basis of equality, there must be a balance of prestations. Each side must sacrifice pigs; each side must dance for the other; each side must dispel black magic from the gardens of the other. Each side must expiate past offences and each side must extend forgiveness. But the model shows that such reconciliation is not expected to be more than temporary although, of course, friendship between villages can sometimes be maintained for protracted periods and there is no rule against holding feasts before a quarrel has reached deadly proportions.

The model applies not only to inter-village relations but to all social relations in general, consanguineal and affinal relations included. Quarrels between consanguines differ only in their relatively greater reluctance to resort to an exchange of penalties and greater readiness to settle a quarrel before it has gone too far. But here a great deal is said to depend on the type of kin relationship holding between the quarrelling parties. A father or mother will rarely use sorcery or other harmful measures against his or her children. Certainly they will not do so until they have, in the course of the quarrel, broken off social relations by showing their plant emblem. Usually a quarrel does not go beyond the breaking off of relations, but if further unpleasantness should occur and if the person who has caused anger is experiencing some misfortune, sorcery will at once be suspected. The same is true in case of conflict with the father's or the mother's brother, though the showing of the plant emblem does not, in such

MODEL 27

PRIMAL TIME

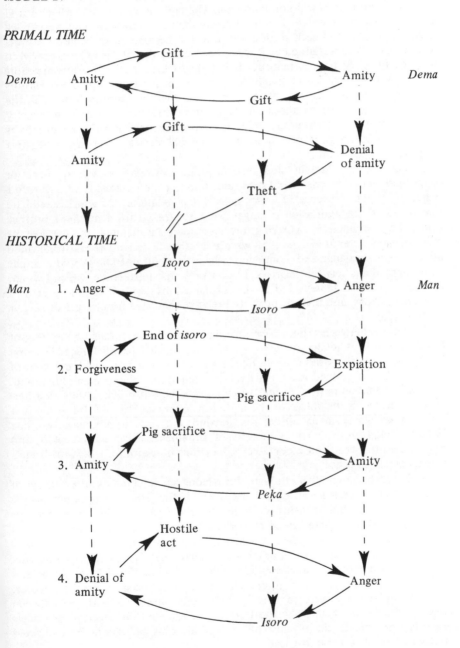

conflict, necessarily precede recourse to sorcery. It is believed, however, that such relatives will not usually carry their resentment too far. As soon as the afflicted person makes his apologies and shows himself ready to make a pig sacrifice, such sorcery will normally case. The same applies to the father's sister, though she has to be watched more carefully than the others, as she is very quick to resent neglect and seek retribution. She will be restrained, however, by the deep love she is expected to bear for her brother, so that she may be expected to agree fairly easily to a settlement. It is thought that mother's sisters are more dangerous as their bonds of family loyalty are much weaker. All these relatives may cause disease, failure of gardens, bad luck in hunting, etc. All the relationships give rise to the same type of positive and negative reciprocity cycles: if proper prestations are made from time to time, positive reciprocity is maintained, but neglect over a long period will create anger and a negative reciprocity cycle.[5]

In the case of certain close relationships, restraint in acts of negative reciprocity does not arise from any rules limiting the expression of anger, but rather from the existence of other close social relationships which would be threatened if the expression of anger went too far. Thus a mother's brother would be restrained in wreaking revenge upon his nephew by the risk of offending his sister if the revenge were excessive. It is hard to illustrate these principles of exchange with concrete evidence, as I do not know of any actual harm being done between relatives. I know only that misfortunes which I would ascribe to natural causes tend to be explained by sorcery on the part of a neglected relative, and that the neglected relative then asks for or receives a pig or other animal.

Prestations between affines have a similar explanation, though the pattern of hostile action and retaliation between affines is somewhat different. The first hostile action in the series tends to be the abduction of a woman for purposes of marriage. This is defined as a hostile act directed against the woman's kin group. The girl's parents look for her and show considerable fury when they find her, wreaking havoc in the village of the abductor. One may say that this is the first cycle of exchange in an affinal relationship and it is totally negative. The abductor's kin group offers a present of ornaments called *sovu hambo*, and promises a bridewealth of acceptable proportions in return for which the bride's parents depart in peace.

It should be noted that, though this second cycle contains an exchange of positive (rather than negative) objects of mediation, the bridegroom's people remain in the position of debtors, while the bride's parents continue to harbour their anger. All they have agreed to is the continued residence of the bride with the bridegroom's people, pending a satisfactory settlement. The third cycle is constituted by the payment of bridewealth, including pig sacrifices, on one side, and the transfer of the usual conjugal rights, including the right to the bride's offspring, by the bride's kin group. On the level of social exchange, however, there is still no exchange in benefits. The relationship remains one between creditor and debtor, as the bridewealth does not wipe out the anger of the bride's parents nor expiate the offence of abduction. This point will be explained further in the chapter on marriage.

It suffices to say at this stage that pig sacrifices made by the bridegroom and his family are a necessary part of the process of assuaging the affinal family's anger. However, such one-sided payments do not in themselves set up a social relationship between affines among the Orokaiva. During this whole first phase of the marriage, the strictest affinal taboos are maintained, prohibiting, for instance, commensality between son-in-law and parents-in-law and their close kin. For social relations to begin, it is necessary for the bride's mother to rear a pig for sacrifice to the bridegroom. Unless she does this the son-in-law feels too 'ashamed' of the humiliations he has been through and of the anger shown to him for social relations to be possible. This sacrifice, too, has therefore an element of expiation. After this sacrifice, the taboos are relaxed and the mother-in-law attends a feast at which she *pretends* to eat. Ruth Craig (1969:189), who describes a similar pattern among the Telefolmin of the New Guinea Highlands, comments cogently: 'The second transaction, the return payment, initiates the affinal relationship and emphasises its chief characteristic, friendly reciprocity . . . The relationship starts as one of equality.' It is thus clear that model 27 provides an explanation not only of inter-village feasts and consanguineal relations, but also of the establishment of affinal relationships. On the social plane pig-sacrifice establishes positive reciprocity, while on the magico-religious plane it generates *ivo* for the participants. Reciprocity and *ivo* are thus homologous notions on different levels of conceptualisation.

REFERENCES

1 Durkheim wrote that a sacrifice is composed of two essential elements: an act of communion and an act of oblation (1961: 384). He distinguished sharply between representative or commemorative rites and piacular rites, according to the prevailing mood. The former are performed in a state of confidence and joy, the latter in a state of sadness, arising out of misfortune, evil omens, sorrow or fear (*ibid.* 434–5). Evans-Pritchard (1956:275) made a somewhat similar distinction, though perhaps a less subjective one, between 'communion' (involving a desire to be close to God) and 'piaculum' (involving a desire to keep God away or get rid of him).

The phenomena described in this work, though aberrant from the viewpoint of the Durkeimian and Evans-Pritchard models, are fairly widespread in Melanesia. For instance, Lane, describing pig sacrifices on South Pentecost, points out (1) that sacrificer and sacrificed pig merge and share identity; (2) that the meaning of the offerings is 'clarified by reference to the way in which a special formal friendship is instituted between two men' (1965: 267). The Mae Enga sacrifice pigs to a ghost when that ghost is suspected of causing misfortunes. But half or more of the meat, sometimes all of it, goes to maternal kinsmen as the ghost is always considered to belong to the uterine line (Meggitt 1965*b*: 112–3). Elements of communion and piaculum are both present, but also a need to influence critical social relationships.

2 For a detailed discussion of myths related to the differentiation of species, see Lévi-Strauss 1964.

3 For details on the effect of the Mount Lamington eruption on the Sangara tribe and the founding and development of Hohorita, see Schwimmer 1969.

4 A fuller discussion on Orokaiva leadership will be found in Reay 1953, Schwimmer 1967.

5   This interpretation of Orokaiva sorcery appears to be largely supported by Lawrence and Meggitt who argue that in societies with 'stable social organisation' (among which they count the Orokaiva), sorcery accusations act 'both as an important medium for expressing enmity and as an excuse for initiating warfare, which is ultimately the most effective means of relieving feelings of aggression' (1965: 17). The authors appear to believe that sorcery can be explained along psychological lines as fulfilling a need for channelling aggression (*ibid*. 18). I find it hard to see how the specific facts of sorcery behaviour (and especially the transactional patterns described in these pages) can be explained in terms of universal needs. Sorcery is only one of many substitutes for physical aggression and all these substitutes, in one way or another, serve to maintain a relationship of negative reciprocity.

Accusations of sorcery probably have a cognitive as well as an effective 'function', for they imply an explanation of misfortunes for which no natural cause is known. Furthermore, such accusations turn misfortune into an object of mediation in (negative) social exchange. The assumption is made that the misfortune will continue until the relationship with the sorcerer is basically changed, either by his defeat or by reconciliation.

CHAPTER VIII

COCONUT AND BETELNUT

1. *Theoretical Intermezzo*

We have discussed throughout this work the belief that crises in social relations are resolved by magic. In the last chapter we showed explicitly that this is the view expressed in the Orokaiva folk model of exchange (model 25). There are two implications in this folk model: that magical power (*ivo*) is required to establish social relations and that social relations have the effect of generating *ivo* for those who establish them. The objection that may be advanced against this approach is its subjectivity. One may call it a phenomenological approach, as it is based on *ego*'s experience of *alter*'s world as transcendant (see Schutz 1967: 312–29). One may also call it the approach of Marcel Mauss (1966), who explained exchange by a magical construction he called *hau*. It may be argued that it has some resemblance with Sartre's philosophy (1960), where the opposition between *ego* and *alter* is transcended by a 'dialectical process' or 'praxis'. Here again no interdependence of *ego* and *alter* is deemed to exist prior to a course of action inaugurated by *ego* and serving to transcend the opposition.

Against all these theories, Lévi-Strauss has argued that exchange is logically prior to giving, receiving and giving in return. In his theory, unconscious mental structures not only determine that man should order his universe by means of systems of binary oppositions, but also that these oppositions should be transcended by syntheses. Exchange, and any form of communication, is a synthesis where things are perceived simultaneously from the viewpoint of self and other and destined by nature to pass from the one to the other. The situation that they *belong to* the one or the other arises out of initial relational characteristics (Lévi-Strauss 1966: xlvi).

The evidence quoted for these unconscious mental structures is mainly linguistic: the Papuans and Melanesians have only one word for sale and purchase, lending and borrowing, which shows that contradictions between these terms must be illusory. If we survey the Orokaiva data reported in previous chapters, we notice that in general objects of mediation are similarly 'destined by nature' to pass from one partner to another. Meat, for instance, is magically effective only or predominantly if it is received as a gift. One may say that pigs are a family's gift-children: they are part of the family but it is their destiny to be given away. From birth, they may be said to 'belong' to some exchange partner. In fact, in my whole discussion on mediation, I stressed that the donor must be identified with the object of mediation and that, for the exchange relation to be effective, the recipient should also identify with it. I pointed out that such identification could be achieved only if there is a starting mechanism, in the form of a mythical charter, which defines the object as having the magical qualities that will enable it to act as mediator.

It must be admitted, however, that this mythical charter is logically prior to the social relation *only in the view of the indigenous culture* and that its logical status is no higher than *hau, mana, ivo* or any other mystical concept of the type Lévi-Strauss rejects as 'verbose phenomenology'. How can we meet this criticism? If we are to follow Lévi-Strauss' prescription, we have to turn to the largely unconscious categories of Orokaiva 'symbolic thought', i.e. the basic binary oppositions discovered in the culture by structural analysis. We have already, from the preceding chapters, some idea what the basic Orokaiva oppositions would be. We have noticed, especially, the importance of the male and female principle: most other binary oppositions we have found are related to this. The bush is classified as belonging to the male, the garden to the female; the wild pig to the male, taro to the female. Gifts of raw food are male, of cooked food female. Killing is the province of the male, nurture of the female.

Now such oppositions belong to 'symbolic thought', as Lévi-Strauss uses the term, precisely because of the kind of evidence I have brought forward in preceding chapters: it is the symbolic exchange relations holding between male and female, bush and garden, pig and taro, etc., that give them the status of binary oppositions in the structural analysis of Orokaiva culture. The difference between Lévi-Strauss' approach and my own does not lie so much in his and my use of binary oppositions as in my use of an exchange model in which the magical aspect of mediation is emphasised. For instance, my model 22 contains two binary oppositions: Man as Hunter/Pig as Marauder; and *Sovai*/Domesticated Pig. Both of these could, I think, be accommodated as part of a 'structural analysis' of Orokaiva culture. When I connect these two binary oppositions with arrows showing an exchange transaction distinguishing partners and objects of exchange and elements of mediation, I am introducing a 'subjectivist' element which is alien to structural analysis. I am showing a concern for the study of transactions, dialectical process, praxis, or perhaps Mauss' concept of *hau*. From a structuralist viewpoint, my arrows are entirely unnecessary as the exchange process is a prior condition of binary oppositions and has no place on the level of the model except as a logical operator (usually the symbol: /).

Now one problem with structural analysis is always at what point one should stop. Certainly analysis may reveal a great deal about the workings of symbolism in culture as it reduces social relations to exchange, exchange to symbolic thought and finally, in Lévi-Strauss' *Mythologiques* (1964, 1966, 1968) symbolic thought to computer signals. As Simonis (1968: 311) has wisely pointed out, at the final stage we move from a science of man to the logic of aesthetic perception. I think we should stop at the point most expedient for our own investigation. It is not useful in a study of Orokaiva exchange to carry on the analysis until exchange is reduced to the status of a logical operator. On the other hand, if in the manner of the phenomenologists we 'bracket' the logical priority of exchange, we find ourselves in difficulties when the folk system itself contains the type of dialectical reasoning upon which Lévi-Strauss founds his own theory. This is the problem with which we shall be concerned in the present chapter.

We shall need to consider exchange from two points of view: first, as in the preceding chapters, we may consider it phenomenologically, from the viewpoint of the transactional polarity of the exchange partners; secondly, we may consider it from the viewpoint of symbolic thought, as something like the dialogue between *Yin* and *Yang*, as the product of Orokaiva intelligence reflecting upon affective experience.[1] It is this second approach which will be appropriate for much of our discussion about the remarkable Orokaiva myth of the coconut and the betelnut.

2. *The Minor Foods: Objects of Mediation and Paired Symbols*

Although this chapter will deal mainly with the coconut and betelnut, it will be useful first to set this couple into a wider ecological and cultural context. Coconut and betelnut have been chosen for detailed treatment out of a large number of minor foods of the Orokaiva, many of which have their special importance as objects of mediation. An interesting aspect of these minor foods is that Orokaiva symbolic thought arranges them in couples to which a male/female opposition is usually ascribed. Very often these plant couples are grown in close association with one another and it is claimed that they will not prosper unless they are planted together and that, in their wild state, they are also found together. The symbolic association of these pairs of plants may be based on any of a number of shared characteristics: the similar outward appearance of the fruit, a coincidence in the time of fruiting, a similarity in culinary use, in taste, in supposed physiological effects of the fruit when eaten. Sometimes the pair of plants are linked in ritual use and in a common myth.

Among examples of this pairing tendency that may be quoted are two varieties of breadfruit, called *oga* and *eumba*; two condiments important in initiation ritual: the *puga* nut and the salt vine *hoe*; the yam and a red fruit called *hamesi*. The coconut (*vu*) and betelnut or *areca* (*sa*) are similarly a pair of subsidiary foods between which there are important points of resemblance which led to their being paired together, and important points of difference which led one of them to be classified as male and the other as female.

Coconut and betelnut are planted together in villages and also in gardens. Both nuts are eaten raw, young coconuts for refreshment, *areca* for relaxation, and both are consumed between meals. Both nuts grow on palms. Both foods have notable (though different) biochemical effects on those who eat them. Both foods are standard gifts made to strangers who visit a village, a coconut being offered as refreshment immediately upon arrival while betelnut is chewed (along with *hingi* pepper and lime) during the conversation. The two nuts are also associated in ritual use. At mortuary feasts, the most important gift objects are large quantities of betelnuts and coconuts harvested from the palms of the deceased, while dry coconut and betelnut are strewn on graves by affines of the deceased. Finally, coconut and betelnut are associated in an important myth which I intend to discuss in detail.

In studying plant couples such as coconut and betelnut two aspects of exchange need to be considered: first, exchanges between persons in which the food products appear as objects of mediation and secondly, mythical exchanges between the male and female plant, where the two plants appear as exchange partners, while objects of mediation are not imaginary and magical, but have a real existence. I shall deal with these two aspects in turn.

3. *Coconut as an Object of Mediation*

Coconut has several culinary uses: it is eaten raw; soup is made of the flesh; the squeezed flesh produces coconut cream in which taro and delicacies such as river crabs may be cooked. Young coconuts are cut open at the top and used for a refreshing drink. Coconut is reserved for two kinds of everyday food gift: cooked dishes offered to guests and young coconut offered to visitors on arrival. Waddell's figures for coconut transactions are surprisingly low (less than 1 lb. per week disposed of in an average household). In Inonda, where the climate favours the coconut, there has been sporadic commercial exploitation of the nut.

Coconuts are also a feasting food. At ordinary harvest feasts and bridewealth payments they are seen on display platforms along with taro and other vegetables. Williams (1930: 44) reports that they used to be placed under a taboo when a large feast was pending. I have already mentioned that at mortuary feasts they are the principal object of mediation between the plant emblem group of the deceased and the village which has provided services to the deceased at the time of death (See Williams 1930: 223—6). I saw a variant of this ceremony at Hohorita in 1967. The plant emblem groups of the deceased couple provided massive gifts displayed on a platform: feast taro, tins of fish, cartons of flour, corned beef in tins, sugar-cane, pots of cooked vegetable food, small bags of salt, smoked meat, a dead pig suspended from a stick, rice, bread, an abundance of betelnut and carved taro suspended from horizontal poles placed above the platform, while at least 1000 lbs. of coconuts, strung to poles supporting each other diagonally, were seen everywhere among the other gifts.

Coconut is correctly believed to be a valuable adjunct to children's diet, as it provides first-class protein. The belief is explained by Orokaiva in a myth quoted by Williams (1928: 122) according to which the first child ever to eat a coconut grew miraculously overnight. Children do eat a good deal of it and it is also fed regularly to dogs and chickens. Orokaiva also regard the effects of coconuts on dogs as miraculous. As neither dogs nor children have any other substantial supply of first-class protein, the coconut relieves a very real diet deficiency. Whatever religious significance is given to the coconut is related to this.

Coconut oil is used as a cosmetic for hair and body, not only to enhance beauty but also for its magical efficacy. In a ritual performed over a man-slayer, a coconut was broken over his head as a purificatory and 'defensive' device in the sense that the fluid would drive away dangerous spirits (1930: 175). With the same end in view, the bodies of female initiands and certain ornaments worn at dances are rubbed with coconut oil (1930: 207). It would appear, in view of this evidence, that the coconut is in general identified with *ivo* communicated by the dead to the living. The coconuts of a dead leader are thought to contain his *ivo* in a form which is communicable, not to his kinsmen to whom these coconuts are taboo, but particularly to his affines. The quoted ritual uses of the coconut are all associated with some contact with the world of death, i.e. critical situations in which the living have been in contact with death and need the help of the dead to obtain *ivo*. While this *ivo* is communicated, through the mediation of coconut gifts, in a great variety of sometimes quite casual relationships, the most crucial communication occurs in the large-scale, highly structured mortuary feast where we may regard the archetypal exchange situation as occurring between brothers-in-law (*dambo*), one of whom is dead while the other is alive. The exchange cycle is as follows:

MODEL 28

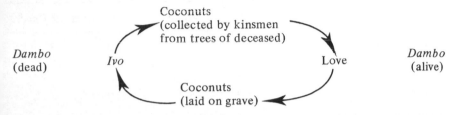

Dambo
(dead)   Ivo

Coconuts
(collected by kinsmen
from trees of deceased)

Love   Dambo
(alive)

Coconuts
(laid on grave)

4. Areca *as Object of Mediation*

Areca, a mildly narcotic fruit, is chewed with lime and pepper (*hingi*) when persons, often from different households, are sitting together to relax and talk. It is always offered when friendly visitors arrive from other villages. It is chewed by women as much as by men, though by Waddell's statistics men act more frequently as donors of *areca* in the exchange network (71 per cent of recorded cases). *Areca* is the only Sivepe food product of which, by Waddell's statistics, more than half the disposals are to other than village residents. Table VIII/1 summarises the number of transactions but does not show that Sivepe is an exporter of betelnut, while lime is imported. Much of this export is in barter but sales for money also occur.

When friends from the same village are sitting together betelnut is shared in much the same way as beer in our culture, i.e. people offer nuts to each other but expect to come out approximately even. At visits to another village, it is more common for the principal visitor to make a bulk donation. The hosts share out betelnut among their guests either by throwing a few nuts to each person or (on more formal occasions) by the principal host presenting the principal visitor with a large bunch, leaving the latter to share them out among his people. The visitors also hand a nut to anyone in the host group who has no nut to chew. The two principals will distribute some of the *areca* they have received to chosen persons within their own group.

Betelnut is treated as a valuable commodity. It is never given away in heaps like ordinary garden crops. Its value is undoubtedly associated with its narcotic properties. At social gatherings its main effect appears to be that it creates a relaxed and genial atmosphere, breaking down hostility otherwise likely to exist between groups. Its magical use is so widespread that its supposed effect is hard to determine from the evidence of medicines. Many medicines consist of *areca* chewed with some specific purpose, and as such it is applied in hunting magic, magic for drumming, and magic against a variety of diseases.

In ritual its role is often the same as coconut, e.g. at mortuary feasts. The exchange cycle shown in model 28 applies similarly to betelnut. Yet, just as its

TABLE VIII/1

'ARECA' TRANSACTIONS: SIVEPE AND INONDA

The following figures group together transactions involving *areca* nuts and
lime used for chewing with *areca*.

(*Source*: Waddell and Krinks, 1968: 180, 210, 218, 237, 265, 270, 272)

	Sivepe		*Inonda*	
	Acquired	*Disposed*	*Acquired*	*Disposed*
Total transactions (lbs.)	124	114	93	39
Distribution (%)				
within village	56%	44%	30%	57%
outside village	44%	56%	70%	43%
Non-monetary transactions (lbs.)	107	100	83?	38?
Monetary transactions (lbs.)	17	15	9.8	1.0
($)	3.70	3.00	2.06	0.20
Donors and recipients by sex:　Men	52%	71%	42%	36%
Women	48%	29%	58%	64%

biochemical action differs from that of the coconut (narcotic rather than nutritive), so its symbolic significance in magic and ritual also differs. A girl carries a bunch of betelnut at the ceremony concluding her seclusion after first menstruation. She also has betelnut to offer to a man at lovers' meetings.

The only betelnut myth recorded by Williams (1928: 123) emphasises the nut's aphrodisiac associations. The betel palm had a liaison with a village woman. Every night it bent over her house to visit her; every morning, as the birds woke, it bent back to stand once more as an immobile palm but left around her house a litter of small flowers. When the intrigue was discovered, the jealous husband cut down the palm. The lover cried as he fell: 'Now I am a man no longer but a mere betel palm; take these nuts and eat them.' This myth resembles the one collected by myself in that the hero was a male, although the *areca* palm is classified by Orokaiva as a female plant. The explanation of this remarkable discrepancy will be one of the main tasks of the present chapter.

The symbolic significance of the betelnut is not, however, exhausted by its role as a catalyst in sexual love. One may call it, more properly, a catalyst in any kind of social exchange. As such, it helps to restore amity between former enemies. Its narcotic action raises the spirits of both opponents to the sphere of primal time when no strife existed. In sexual love, according to Orokaiva, feminine sexuality is dangerous, even lethal, to man in certain circumstances, a notion which is reflected in a number of avoidances woman must practice in order to avoid polluting and ritually killing a man. In courtship, the woman must take the initiative; the man is represented as slow and reluctant, precisely because of the dangers he fears from contact with the female. By offering betelnut, woman overcomes this reluctance in man and draws him into the sexual exchange she desires.

5. *The Myth of Coconut and Betelnut*

Though we have now summarised the exchange cycles mediated by coconut and betelnut, we have not shown why these objects of mediation are considered to be efficacious in exchange. In past chapters we have explained efficacity in terms of indigenous philosophy. Indigenous logic generally relies on a myth in which a specific precept is either explicitly stated or implied. By giving this precept the status of an axiom, we can show by logical deduction that a thing (land, taro, pig, etc.) can have potency as an object of mediation in certain transactions.[2]

This kind of explanation of mediation draws on mythical sources much in the same way as Malinowski. Malinowski held that the 'function' of a myth is the charter it provides for customary rules. I can see no objection to this approach as long as we can be sure, from independent evidence, that charter and custom really coincide, which is not always the case, and as long as we check carefully how informants perform the logical deduction. If charter and custom do not coincide, we need to go beyond Malinowski's techniques of myth analysis and seek out the message by decoding the symbolic language of the myth. The betelnut myth already quoted provides an instance of discrepancy between myth and custom.[3] According to the myth it is the man who gives betelnut to the woman, whereas we know that in girls' initiation ritual and in courting custom, i.e. in the most structured betelnut presentations, the *woman* plays the role of donor and the plant is classified as feminine.

Such a discrepancy might easily be dismissed as too trivial for investigation but for the fact that it seems to be related to the disagreement between Mauss and Lévi-Strauss to which I referred earlier in this chapter. Mauss' theory of the gift would not easily explain this type of reversal, which would serve as a useful corroboration of Lévi-Strauss' contention that the 'contradiction' in the donor-recipient relationship may be illusory. I am not suggesting that his theory can be proved by empirical evidence, but only that it can be corroborated if we find evidence that Orokaiva informants do not treat exchange as purely magical, but recognise its synthetic character in their reasoning about myth, ritual and rules of behaviour.

The beginning of the myth to be discussed here is well-known; I was told it several times and Williams also recorded it (1928: 122). Here follows a summary of a version I collected on tape in the Orokaiva language: A beautiful girl, noted for her remarkable breasts, has the misfortune to kill all the young men with whom she sleeps. Her breasts prick and kill them. She warns them to sleep against her back but they never follow this advice. The girl's brother becomes concerned and tells her that he personally will choose her next sleeping partner. He chooses his own *dambo*, i.e. his wife's brother. He tells his *dambo*:

> Because mistakes were made other bachelors have died, but, my *dambo*, my true *dambo*, she is going to sleep; she is going up to bed. Therefore see that all is properly prepared and the bed is properly made for sleeping.

But this handsome young man, also, is pierced by the girl's breasts and killed. The brother buries his brother-in-law, then kills his sister and buries her beside the other grave.

After a mourning period the brother takes his wife to the two graves. They find a cocopalm in full bearing above the sister's grave. An *areca* palm has grown over the grave of the young man. Heaps of dry nuts are lying on the ground. That is how these two palms originated. He says:

> Wife, as we come close, we see coconut and *areca* growing where only grass grew before. Dry coconuts have fallen and are rotting away; dry *areca* nuts are growing shoots. It can be seen from my sister's grave that she was a creature of misfortune (*embavo*) and that the bachelors' deaths were her doing.
>
> The coconuts growing in the grave must stay there and the *areca* growing on *dambo's* grave must likewise stay. See to it.

The hero opens a dry coconut, then a budding coconut. Though he declares that he will die if he eats these nuts, his wife desires them, they are so delicious. He feeds them to the dog, expecting it to die, but it does not. He then declares:

> Wife, cocopalms are growing in my sister's grave, but the flower clusters on the stem have pointed sheaths (*peperuma*) which puncture the skin and make men die. It is always said that people die when that happens. The mass of sheaths will strike men with the sleep of death; when the sheaths have struck, men will die utterly. That was the cause of the girl's death. When I came here and saw coconut growing out of her grave and dry nuts fallen on the ground, I began to understand that my sister had killed the men I had carried to their graves and buried. . . .
>
> When a man has collected *areca*, he gives it back to a girl. When that girl has helped to fetch coconut, she in turn gives it to the man. It therefore belongs to the man. This being so, the coconut is a man but the *areca* is a girl; for this reason, girls give *areca*.

On the level of social structure, this myth is concerned with the Orokaiva institution of sister exchange marriage. Though such arrangements were not very frequent among the Orokaiva (I would estimate about 5 per cent of all marriages), sister exchange marriages are strongly idealised, as I have shown elsewhere. In this myth, a man arranges such an exchange marriage for his sister because he evidently believes it provides more protection against magical dangers than any other. When this ends in disaster, the brother feels entitled to assume there is no bachelor with whom his sister can sleep safely, as he explains in a passage not quoted here. He therefore kills her, but right through the story his *dambo* (wife's brother) continues to be regarded as husband of his sister. It is for him, rather than for any other man she has slept with and killed, that she grows coconuts. In fact it is the bond of love between the dead couple which gives the whole tale its meaning. The closeness of this bond is not explained psychologically by personal sentiments existing between the lovers, but structurally, by sister exchange marriage.

On the level of social exchange, the myth depends largely on rather complex and condensed ideological statements made by the hero. I have translated the crucial passages verbatim. In the full text, the brother comes back four or five times to the miracle that chiefly concerns him: the symbiosis of coconut and areca, dropping their fruits side by side and thus (as he implies rather than states) fertilising one another. Taking this symbiosis as a fact of nature, the hero uses it to explain several other mysterious facts: (*a*) why all the bachelors died; (*b*) the ritual uses of coconut and *areca*; (*c*) why the Orokaiva consider coconut masculine, *areca* feminine. To answer the first question, he refers to an easily verified fact: the *peperuma* of the coconut do look like a girl's breasts; they are very dangerous if one falls upon them with any force. His sister was clearly an *embavo*, a coconut spirit. In this way the deaths are, to Orokaiva thought, adequately accounted for.

The hero explains two types of ritual uses of coconut and *areca,* namely those related to mortuary feasts and those where the sex of the recipient of the nuts is opposite to that of the donor. The instruction that nobody should eat the nuts lying under the trees, on pain of death, constitutes a mythological charter for the taboo placed upon the cocopalms and *areca* palms owned by a person recently dead. An informant explained a further implication to me, which is not very clear from the version I quoted: namely that it is customary to place coconuts and *areca* nuts upon the grave of a dead affine. Thus it was the duty of the hero to place coconuts and *areca* nuts upon the grave of his brother-in-law; and the duty of his wife to do the same for the grave of her sister-in-law. In order to clarify these points, the myth tells of the wife's desire to eat the nuts and the hero's refusal to let her have them.

In a somewhat elliptical manner, the hero lists or implies three sets of rules concerning gifts of coconut and *areca,* where the sex of the recipient of the nuts is opposite to that of the donor. The sets are:

Areca	*Coconut*
1(*a*) The man fetches the nuts from the tree.	1(*b*) The woman *helps to fetch* the nuts from the tree.
2(*a*) The man gives the nuts to the woman.	2(*b*) The woman cooks the nuts for the man.
3(*a*) The girl offers nuts to her lover and carries an offering of nuts at initiation.	3(*b*) At a girl's initiation, a man prepares coconut oil which is used as a ritual cosmetic.

The first opposition is made quite explicit in the hero's speech, but is not free from casuistry. Men usually fetch not only *areca* but also coconuts from the high palms on which they grow. The woman may help by collecting coconuts once they have dropped to the ground, and by carrying them home. Very often, however, the coconuts are carried by men, who tie two nuts to a stalk, thus creating a huge effigy of a phallus. The feeble empirical basis of this opposition only serves to emphasise that we are here being taught an ideology which requires the opposition.

The hero's second opposition centres on the culinary use made of the nuts. *Areca*, in opposition to coconut, has no place in the kitchen. The fact that coconut is also often eaten raw would weaken the opposition, but this is suppressed. The third opposition is in fact the strongest, but it is stated in a rather elliptical manner. We are told that, in ritual, girls give *areca* to men, but the opposite statement is omitted, viz. that in the same initiatory context *men* (but never women) pour coconut oil over girls.

In the narrator's mind all these oppositions are probably subordinate to a philosophical question: why the Orokaiva consider coconut masculine, *areca* feminine. Numerous informants have confirmed this classification in conversations with me. In this story, however, it is not presented as a 'fact', but is deduced in a logical manner. The words used make it clear that we have to do with a logical deduction:

> *Ainge* embo amina ainge ena. Embo amina *ainge eto,* erevi u ra embo erevi u ra; te sa erevi meni kakara ra; — *ainge eto* ikena.

This passage, (translated above, p. 17) contains the notion of logical entailment three times: *because* the girl gives coconut to the man, it *therefore* belongs to the man. *Because* coconut belongs to a man, *therefore* coconut is masculine. *Because areca* is a girl, girls give *areca.* The problem, for those who do not know Orokaiva culture, is that every one of the conclusions appears to lack logical force. Furthermore, it will be noticed that, from a formal viewpoint, the narrator's argument proceeds quite differently for men and for girls. This difference also needs explanation.

When I heard this tale, I could not help arguing with my informant. I said: if the coconut grew out of the girl's grave and she later gave the coconut to a man, would it not follow then that the coconut is feminine? My informant received this argument with a tinge of pity. It proved to him, if any proof were needed, that white men are indeed quite incapable of abstract reasoning. It took him some time to understand what problem I could possibly be having. Finally he said: 'The girl intended these coconuts as gifts for a man; therefore, they must be masculine.' At that point I remembered I had heard this argument somewhere before: in Levi-Strauss' introduction to Marcel Mauss, *Sociologie et anthropologie.* If we produce something that is *intended to be given away*, it was called into being by a prior relationship between donor and recipient, and could not be utilised by the former without losing its predetermined nature.

We find the same line of thought elsewhere in Orokaiva culture: pigs cannot be eaten by those who reared them because they are, from the beginning, set apart as gift objects. The most striking and intimate instance may be found in a myth of a woman who has a detachable vagina. She pretends to her husband she has lost it: 'I dropped your vagina in the water.' The husband looks for it between the stones of the river: 'I am looking for my vagina.'

In all these cases the gift object partakes of the nature of the recipient. However, the narrator appears to follow a quite different line of reasoning when he says. 'Because *areca* is a girl, girls give *areca.*' There is an apparent contradiction here, resolved only when we recognise that two different types of gift must be distinguished — perhaps we are allowed to call them metaphoric and metonymic. If we call a coconut a man or a man a coconut, we are using a metaphor. Furthermore, if we proceed to call an *areca* 'a girl', we are setting up a metaphoric opposition (coconut/*areca*) which corresponds to the real opposition (man/woman). When Sperber (1968) speaks of 'code structures', he is principally referring to classificatory systems built up from such metaphoric oppositions. When I use the term 'metaphoric gift', I mean a gift about which we are told in a story, the message of the story being that gift and recipient are metaphorically identical. The point of the story is to establish the symbiosis of men and women, the use of the metaphor. An example of such a story would be the gift of sacred emblems to the infant Dionysus in Orphic myth. This story tells us how Dionysus received certain gifts (cone, bullroarer, golden apples, mirror, knuckle-bone, tuft of wool) which defined his nature. In the same way, in Orokaiva myth, men are given a coconut nature and women an areca nature.

Orokaiva informants offer what they regard as empirical evidence for this. Coconut may be recognised as a man because the palm germinates slowly and the fruit comes to maturity slowly ('it comes slowly'). Likewise, so I was told, the male is slow to be sexually aroused and to desire women. *Areca* may be recognised as a girl because it germinates and comes to maturity quickly — the fruit matures faster than the coconut. Likewise woman is quick to be sexually aroused and to feel desire for a man. In this analogy the botanical facts are evident but the psychological generalisations describe no more, perhaps, than Orokaiva role expectations.

We may clarify the myth and its philosophical message to a certain extent by an analysis on the level of exchange cycles. The fundamental cycle is obviously the following:

MODEL 29

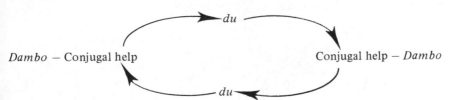

This is the model of sister exchange marriage where two men become brothers-in-law by each giving their sisters (*du*) to the other in marriage. If we now remember the identification between woman and betelnut (*sā*), and the social relationship which is considered normal between *dambo*, we may substitute as follows:

MODEL 30

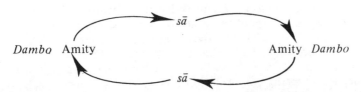

We thus derive the rather interesting conclusion that the sense of an exchange of betelnut between men is that they are symbolically exchanging sisters. This is a rather bold conclusion which is best left as a speculation to be explored in later enquiries. The same applies to a second conclusion that may be derived from the myth: that a man who gives a visitor coconut to drink is symbolically giving his own sexuality.

6. *Analysis of the Myth*[4]

As these implications of the model may arouse scepticism, a more analytical study of the myth seems desirable. One procedure which may lead to clarification is to compare the coconut/betelnut myth with the myth of Totoima discussed in previous chapters. The structural homology between the two myths is obvious enough. In the Totoima myth a *man wittingly* killed and *ate a son,* was transformed into *pig meat,* and distributed to mankind. He *did not intend* to make any gifts nor were any intended for him. In the coconut myth a *woman unwittingly* killed but *did not eat* a *spouse,* was transformed into *coconut,* distributed to mankind. She *intended* to make a gift and a return gift was intended for her.

We may isolate three distinctive features. On the ecological level we find an opposition between two types of symbiosis. The Totoima myth shows a predatory cycle: pig eats taro; man eats pig; thus strengthened, man causes more taro to grow. The coconut/betelnut myth shows the association of two plants always growing together, such that the presence of the one may be thought to stimulate the growth of the other. On the social level we find an opposition between the kin relationships holding between the principal participants. They may be represented as follows:

$$
\begin{array}{cc}
\textit{Totoima} & \textit{Coconut/betelnut} \\
\end{array}
$$

In the Totoima myth, the critical transaction was between the senior and junior generation, while in the coconut/betelnut myth it was between the male and female characters. Psychologically, the opposition was that in the Totoima myth the protagonists were motivated to kill and eat each other, while in the coconut/betelnut myth they were motivated by sexual love.

Both myths are concerned with exchange, viewed ecologically, socially and psychologically, but in the first myth exchange is diachronic, whereas in the second it is contemporaneous. Where exchange is diachronic, B cannot reach the fullness of prosperity without the death of A, a process symbolised ecologically by predation, on the social level by intergenerational competition and on the psychological level by the desire to kill the father. Where exchange is contemporaneous, B cannot reach the fullness of prosperity without the simultaneous prosperity of A, a process symbolised ecologically by plant associations, socially by the marriage relationship and psychologically by conjugal love.

Diachronic exchange is, on the ecological level, a familiar and empirically verifiable fact. On the social level, however, the competitive and negative aspect of the father-son relationship is suppressed by consciousness, among the Orokaiva as among ourselves, and is revealed only in dreams, myths and other messages from the unconscious. In contrast, synchronic exchange – as the love between spouses, the amity between affines – is overtly recognised and empirically verifiable on the social level. It is, however, purely imaginary on the ecological level, as plant associations, such as that of coconut and betelnut, *oga* and *eumba*, *puga* and *hoe*, yam and *hamesi*, are not necessarily found in nature but are generally brought about by man for magico-religious reasons. When man establishes these plant associations he is recreating on the ecological level the symbolic equivalents of the social relations on which his prosperity depends.

These social relations are, as we have seen, of two types. In sexual love we find the mystical and irrevocable unity of opposites where objects of mediation become, in the last analysis, irrelevant. But in other social exchanges we find a necessity for objects of mediation establishing a link between self and other. This relationship is exemplified in its purest form in model 29, the model of sister exchange, where a relationship between *dambo* is mediated by an exchange of sisters. But in models 28 and 30 we find important variants, where betelnut and coconut are substituted to mediate the exchange. Precisely because neither of these two products is of any great economic value, they are appropriate for serving as tokens of exchange, a signal of the potential existence of exchange, between any partners, though in the myth and in mortuary ritual this exchange takes place between the prototype-partners of the Orokaiva, the *dambo*. The rather bold suggestion I made at the end of the previous section therefore corresponds to a hidden reality, namely that gifts of coconut and betelnut are symbolic of sexual exchange. It is significant, in this regard, that sisters-in-law address each other by the term *bi*, which means penis.

REFERENCES

1   I am referring here to Radcliffe-Brown's discussion on Yin and Yang as an example of complementary opposition (1951) and to Lévi-Strauss' adoption of this example to present his theory concerning the real nature of totemism (Lévi-Strauss 1962T). Coconut and betelnut, in the myth discussed in the present chapter, may be seen as a further example of the same principle.

2   This type of logic, first developed by Gentzen in 1934, was adopted afterwards by Popper and has been shown to be the basis of primitive systems of thought (Jarvie 1964). It requires no investigation into the truth value of axioms. Gentzen called it 'natural deduction'.

3   Though Malinowski held (1926M) that 'myth serves principally to establish a sociological charter, or a retrospective moral pattern of behaviour, or the primeval supreme miracle of magic', he knew very well that the charter is occasionally 'flagrantly violated' by the actual norms of a society. He also recognised that where we find a fully institutionalised violation of a mythical charter, we should seek an explanation for the discrepancy. Malinowski even took initial steps towards such explanation: 'This violation always takes place when the local claims of an autochthonous clan . . . are overriden by an immigrant clan. Then a conflict of principles is created . . . ' (1926M; reprinted 1954: 117)

A very similar point was made by Lévi-Strauss in 'Legeste d'Asdiwal'. After pointing out that the institutions described in myths can be the very opposite of real institutions, he argues that any such discrepancy 'implies an admission that the social facts are marred by an insurmountable contradiction'. By investigating such contradictions, we may find means of 'reaching unconscious categories' (1961: 1110–1). This is precisely the strategy I have adopted in the present chapter.

4   I have followed a method demonstrated by Lévi-Strauss in *Le cru et le cuit* (1964). I have shown that the two myths discussed in this section are isomorphous; I have isolated their distinctive features and posited that they are interrelated. I found that in each myth three levels (botanical, social, physiological) were superimposed and that each level transmitted the same message. Between the two myths, there was an inversion of the codes and the message (1964: 205, 250–2).

CHAPTER IX

ORNAMENTS

1. *Introduction*

Exchanges mediated by ornaments may be studied in very much the same way as those mediated by coconut and betelnut. This means that (1) ornaments may serve as symbols of identity; (2) this symbolic quality attached to ornaments makes them suitable to serve as objects of mediation.

A symbol of identity, in the sense intended here, is an object which, if shown or given to another person, reveals the identity of its owner. A plant emblem is, in this sense, a symbol of identity, as anyone who sees it lying on the path knows the identity of the person who put it there. More specifically, the finder of the plant emblem knows that the person who dropped it is a member of a specific group which has the right to use this emblem and which is identified with it. Identity, in this instance,[1] is not defined as attached to an individual but rather as attached to a class, and the individual who uses the plant emblem is stating his membership of that class. Furthermore, identity in this sense must always have been *received from* someone. Membership in a plant emblem group is conferred by a father or mother. It is not a gift but an automatic result of filiation. As such it is symbolic of the system of rules governing co-operation within the corporate group.

An ornament may be ceremonially conferred upon a person who will henceforth regard it, in the same sense, as a symbol of identity. The ornament is then called an *otohu,* a term to be defined later. It is worn by its owner and those who see it recognise it as a symbol of its owner's moral integrity. It indicates that the owner has pledged to act in accordance with a historically established behaviour model. Therefore, in this instance again, identity is not defined as attached to an individual but rather as attached to a class of persons who follow this behaviour model. Furthermore, again, identity in this sense must always have been received from someone. It is not conferred necessarily by the wearer's father, but may come from any other male consanguine (or even affine) of the ascending generation. It is not conferred automatically; there is no rule saying that it should be conferred and it is not conferred upon everyone. The *otohu* is, in fact, always a gift. As such it is symbolic of a pledge made by the wearer that he regards himself as bound by the system of rules governing exchange between other corporate groups and his own.

Although it is usual for persons to own more than one ornament, I have not heard of any owning more than one *otohu.* The *otohu* is distinguished from other ornaments (*hambo*) by the addition of some special feature which constitutes its mark of identity. *Otohu* are not given away except in special ceremonial circumstances, but *hambo* are freely exchanged between partners. All the characteristics already described of such objects of mediation as land, taro and pigs probably apply equally to *hambo,* though my evidence on this point is far less complete, due to the very large number of magical substances that enter into the construction of *hambo*. They are not, however, symbols of identity.

On a functional level, one may regard the *otohu* after the analogy of a membership badge to some association or even a credit card. It indicates to others that they can safely carry on transactions with the bearer. On a structural level, the two types of identity symbol – the plant emblem or *hae* and the *otohu* – constitute, in combination and in their interrelation, the reality of the entire Orokaiva social system. This system is dominated by two principles: corporate groups bound to a system of rules governing their co-operation and a system of exchange between corporate groups on which they depend for vital benefits. The *hae* symbolises membership of the corporate group whereas the *otohu* symbolises participation in the system of exchange. There are several significant symbolic contrasts: the *hae* is a natural object (usually a plant), never given or lent to anyone, deposited as a sign to members of the corporate group that corporate rights have been used by the depositor, but never openly shown except to signal anger felt towards members of the corporate group and a resolve to break the relationship. In contrast the *otohu* is a cultural object, lent to relatives who are entitled to wear it, but otherwise never deposited or transferred, and always shown conspicuously by the owner when he contemplates transactions outside the corporate group.

While a *hae* is transmitted automatically, the conferring of the *otohu* is an important ceremony that will be discussed in detail in this chapter. This discussion will be followed by a summary of the available evidence on the use of *hambo* (other than *otohu*) as objects of mediation in social exchange.

2.   The Nature of Otohu Ornaments

Most ornaments are acquired by hunting, foraging, barter, purchase or inheritance. These may be regarded purely as decorations (*di* or *hambo*) and there are no restrictions on who may make or wear such ornaments, which are freely disposed of by barter or sale. The *otohu* is not distinguishable from other *hambo* except on the basis of specific knowledge of local practice. Some families have a particular shell which is their *otohu*, others may use a particular arrangement of hornbill beaks. Others again may have a special way of decorating armlets of white cuscus (*pauri*). There are many very beautiful and elaborate *hambo* which are not *otohu* and other much simpler ornaments which are *otohu*. Where large shells are *otohu* these are worn by themselves, on the chest or suspended on the side of the owner's betelnut bag. Other *otohu* are added to what would otherwise be an ordinary *hambo*: it is the addition of the *otohu* object which makes a *hambo* into an *otohu*.

In the earliest literature on the *otohu* it was regarded as an 'homicidal emblem'. Beaver (1920) reported that a man-slayer, having undergone some form of purification or exorcism, might at some convenient time receive his *otohu*. He gave two lists of objects that were supposedly so used, one for the coastal and central tribes (eight items) and one for the Wasida and trans-Kumusi tribes (twelve items), including in his list many *hambo* still in common use. Williams (1930) criticised this account on two grounds: some kinds of *otohu* were regularly conferred upon boys and girls at initiation before they had killed anyone, and most of the items listed by Beaver were in fact conferred on such occasions. While Williams did not rule out the use of homicidal emblems, he thought they should be called *esa* rather than *otohu* and provided a short list of such *esa*, i.e. ornaments given exclusively to man-slayers or to men who had slain a wild pig and presented it to the donor of the *esa*.

Williams reserves the term *otohu* for ritual objects used as symbols for ethical notions central to the Orokaiva world view. He thinks that the *otohu* is best understood in the context of boys' and girls' initiation, as conferment most often occurs at the conclusion of initiation ceremonies. In this chapter I shall first summarise Williams' description of the transfer of *otohu* in initiation, and proceed to add some new information which may lead to a clearer understanding of the nature of the *otohu*.

3. Williams' Account of the Conferment of Otohu

Orokaiva initiation ceremonies include four main rituals which are, as Williams reports, not always performed in the same order, but the one ceremony he witnessed occurred in the same order as those described to me by informants:

(1)   First, initiands are kept in seclusion for some months. Living in a separate house in semi-darkness, they are well-fed, kept warm with a fire, but must not wash. Williams rightly discounts Chinnery and Beaver's account (1915) that initiands are given detailed instruction of a moral nature at this stage. This was denied by my own informants who had themselves been initiated.

(2)   A nocturnal dance occurs during which spirits (*embahi*) appear from the bush, assail and frighten the initiands, but are driven off by the initiands' relatives. Chinnery and Beaver (1915) plausibly suggest that this ferocious scene serves the function of instilling 'absolute and lasting terror in the candidates', of obligating them to their relatives who saved them, and of inducing in them 'a receptive and chastened frame of mind' for the instruction that is to follow. The scene is graphically described by Williams.

(3)   The next morning initiands are, for the first time in their lives, dressed up in full dancing regalia, after which they make an impressive début at the village dancing ground. The ritual is known as *kogumbari*. It is performed by an expert whose main concern seems to be with the aesthetics of dressing up, and who lends the initiands feathers and ornaments from his own large store. He stands in no particular kin relationship to the initiand and may even be from a different village. (Fathers are excluded.)

(4)   If there is a presentation of *otohu* to initiates[2] this is not part of the initiation ritual as such, which occurs immediately after *kogumbari*. The dressed up initiates are 'shown to the people' and take part in a dance called *kuru*, which is described by Williams (1930: 188). The presentation follows this dance.

It begins with a series of speeches by old warriors (*aguma*) who recite their feats of war, their killing of victims. Initiates sit on a row of sticks laid on the ground ('lest through contact with the ground they run the risk of physical deformity'). The donor of the *otohu* (most often the father or mother's brother) then takes up a position behind the initiate while the *aguma*, standing in front of him, teases him by pretending to offer him the *otohu*. When the initiate stretches out to receive it, the *aguma* snatches it back again. It is tossed over the initiate's head to the man behind him, or to spectators or from one spectator to another. Williams reports:

> It is properly at this stage, while the initiate is waiting to receive his ornament, that the *aguma* lays upon him certain injunctions of an ethical character. These are always associated with the *otohu* and, as we shall see, they throw some light on the obscure meaning of the word. As he proffers and withdraws the ornament, the officiating *aguma* exhorts the candidate to refrain from thieving, from adultery, from quarrelling and from such lawless acts as killing a neighbour's dog. (1930: 191)

After describing the ceremony of presentation, Williams turns to the explanation of the word *otohu*. *Otohu*, he says, tend to be regarded as rather beautiful objects but embody a social distinction as well. The wearing of an *otohu* 'implies that the owner has paid a pig (if he acquired it in adulthood), or that it has been paid on his behalf, and thus the ornament has been formally and regularly acquired' (*ibid*. 203). Sometimes the *otohu* is acquired in return for the body of a man, rather than a pig, but Williams finds (unlike Beaver 1920)

> no very essential difference between the 'pig *otohu*' and the 'man *otohu*'. They are of the same nature, but one is bought with the body of a pig and the other with that of a human victim. . . .
> It would appear that the homicidal *otohu* or *esa* was less an *insigne* conferred, *honoris causa,* upon the man-killer as such, than an ordinary *otohu* purchased with the body of his victim. (*ibid.*)

Williams saw that his theory brought him into conflict not only with Beaver's explanation, but also with apparently obvious implications of the ritual of conferment. Why did the *aguma* always recite his own past killings? Does not this indicate an association between *otohu* and man-slaying?

Instead of elucidating this, Williams turns to interesting data on the usages of the word *otohu*. As an adjective, it means: well-behaved, decent, diligent, generous, respectable, set apart, holy. 'An *otohu* man was he who went about his work quietly, who returned from his garden with wood on his shoulder and set it down, then chewed his betel without "rowing".' There is a direct connection, Williams remarks, between the virtues subsumed under the word *otohu* and the injunctions laid upon the initiate by the *aguma*. He concludes that the possession of an *otohu* creates a social obligation, namely to behave in the manner called *otohu*. As for the derivation of the word, Williams has no suggestions to offer except one interesting point: the Baruga, southern neighbours of the Orokaiva, have a word *kortopo* which is used in the sense of *otohu* but *also* in the sense of *hae*.[3] He wonders whether the *otohu*, 'originally', might have been a clan emblem (*ibid*. 206). In addition he reports, but gives no significance to, the fact that the larger of the two flutes used at initiation ceremonies is called *otohu*. The sacred flutes are always played in pairs by two men facing one another. One of the pair (the *otohu*) is larger than the other, which is called *e* (= mother).

4. *Additional Data on* Otohu

Discouragement of initiation ritual by the Anglican mission and the consequent weakening of the institution greatly hampered me in obtaining the additional data needed to clarify Williams' account. Unable to attend any ceremonies, I had to depend almost entirely on interviews. Most adults still own *otohu*. The men usually receive them at initiation, the women either at initiation or, quite often, at the time of marriage. In about half the cases the father was the donor; in most other cases it was the mother's brother. One man who had been elected a member of the Higaturu Local Government Council, was honoured with an *otohu* by his wife's father.

With regard to initiation ritual, the seclusion of boys is no longer practised and the period of seclusion for girls tends to be much shorter than in earlier days. It is, however, rarely shorter than three weeks and sometimes still lasts for some months. The influence of the mission is given as the reason for the changes. When I asked why the modern custom for girls differs from that for boys, I was told that if girls were not secluded and subjected to the full ritual, they would be unable to control their menstrual flow; they would contaminate the village and sicken.

Kogumbari often occurs on the occasion of Christian festivals such as Easter, when the girls, fully dressed up, are 'shown to the people' during a dance on the mission ground. The white missionaries are unaware of the significance of the event. It appears that two ceremonies (puberty seclusion and initiation) to which adolescent girls used to be subjected have been reduced to one, which takes place upon the commencement of menstruation. *Otohu* are bestowed either then or upon marriage.

Boys receive their *otohu* at ceremonies which have become known as 'birthday parties', one of which is fully described by Crocombe (1966). The whole ceremony, including the conferral of *otohu,* usually occurs in a single weekend or at Christmas and a drinking party is sometimes given to the people by the father of the initiand. I never managed to attend one of these occasions but suspect that in many villages the ritual still involves the appearance of *embahi.* I have knowledge of one instance in a village close to Sivepe in 1967.

I was able to obtain additional data, relevant to the puzzle of the nature of the *otohu,* on two main topics: the role of the mother's brother and the role of the *aguma.* According to Orokaiva ideal norms, as stated to Williams (1930: 187) and myself, the mother's brother (*epe*) is the proper relative to perform initiation. This rule, like all others, is frequently broken, but it is worthy of mention that if there is no *epe* available to officiate, there is absolutely no preference for finding a uterine kinsman as a substitute: any other male consanguine is considered suitable, and in fact a father or father's brother often officiates. When Orokaiva informants were asked why mothers' brothers have this special relationship with their nephews, I was always told it is due to the love between the mother and her brother, in other words the *du* relationship. It is definitely not due to any special bond with the matrilineage or maternal patrilineage.

Bestowal of the *otohu* is only one of a series of ritual benefits customarily provided by the *epe.* These benefits take the form of medicines (*sivo*). A man receives certain essential medicines from his father (e.g. for hunting, for planting taro) but other medicines are acquired during adolescence from the person who performs initiation, i.e. ideally the *epe*. These medicines include: *ba kovari sivo*, a medicine applied to taro leaves when the tubers have filled out and are ready for harvest; *kakara sivo*, a medicine for success in sex; and *saruka*, medicines for killing enemies. Though these presentations are entirely separate from the gift of an *otohu* they do indicate what spiritual capacities a man normally derives from his *epe*; the fact that these include the capacity to kill enemies helps us to understand more easily why killing is so strongly emphasised in the ritual of the bestowal of *otohu*.

Nobody has the *right* to receive an *otohu* nor does anyone have an obligation to confer it. It depends in theory on the *epe's* appraisal of the worth of the young initiand and especially on how the latter has behaved towards his/her *epe*. Has the initiand been co-operative, obedient, well-behaved? The questions are rather similar to those asked by Father Christmas. But, like Father Christmas, the *epe* has a prior commitment: to part with his treasure to *someone*: it is in the nature of the *otohu* to be passed on from generation to generation, and ideally it is passed on in the matriline.

When I asked informants about the significance of *otohu*, their replies were in general very close to what Williams had reported: people respect their *otohu* as the concrete embodiment of the moral virtues they regard as most important in life. When I asked for the reasons for this respect, one informant answered: 'I received this *otohu* from my mother's brother who was a good man. My sister has a son now. I want to give this *otohu* to that boy when he has grown big. *That is what makes it otohu* (=holy).' We should note the emphasis the informant placed on the words 'I want to'. He invoked neither obligation nor 'custom' but rather a sense that his *otohu*, by virtue of its inner nature, was destined to be passed on to another initiate. My informant did not consider this a loss to himself, for he said: 'If I want another one, I can always make myself one.'

The second ritual actor about whom I obtained additional data was the *aguma*. The rite of tantalising the initiate before giving him his *otohu* continues; the term I was given for this rite among the Sangara was *otohu pasari*, the verb *pasari* being also used for catching fish. I was also told about the *aguma's* recital of his war deeds, but this information came from middle-aged men. When these men were initiated, there were still old warriors who could claim a respectable score of killings, but by now most of these old warriors must have died out among the Orokaiva. Profound changes in male initiation ritual have coincided with the dying out of the genuine old cannibals: one might say that one reason why the institution of initiation has been transformed is the absence of persons with the traditional qualifications of the *aguma*. One difference between the modern 'birthday party' and traditional initiation is the greatly reduced emphasis on killing as a capacity bestowed on the initiand.

Aguma were usually not from the same village as the initiands. They were generally invited from a village two or three miles distant. In Sivepe, villages such as Isoge and Kendata were quoted to me as suitable places from which to invite an *aguma*; for Hohorita initiations they might come from Bonge or Koipa. The total list of *aguma*-villages as given to me had a striking resemblance to another list which I had collected some time previously, namely the villages to which a person would go if he needed the services of a black magician, in other words, if he wished to apply *saruka* against a fellow villager who had injured him. When I pointed out this coincidence to informants they agreed that indeed they were always the same villages, but insisted there was no connection between *aguma* and *saruka embo*.

It is, however, the task of the anthropologist to explore such coincidences even if informants dismiss them as totally insignificant. In this exploration I was assisted by further facts, not noted by Williams, about the social exchange between the initiate and the *aguma*. Before the latter recites his war deeds, he will hand his limepot to the initiate. He then says something like: 'You are holding my limepot. Therefore promise not to beat your wife.' There are a good number of such vows the initiate must take. They no doubt vary a good deal from place to place, but generally cover a wide range of rules of social exchange, of the same type as are listed by Williams and by Chinnery and Beaver (1915: 76). Later, when the *aguma* offers the *otohu*, he does so *on condition* that the initiate keeps his vows. Persons who violate some rule of social behaviour are likely to be warned by fellow-villagers in terms such as: 'You had better be careful — you held the limepot.'

We thus find that *aguma* and sorcerer have something more in common than their provenance from the same set of villages. They are concerned with two interrelated aspects of social control: the *aguma* obtains certain pledges from a person and the sorcerer punishes that person if he breaks his pledges. It is significant that these guardians of moral values live in places which are on the fringe of the universe of friendly social relations maintained by any village. One may visualise this universe in widening concentric circles moving from friendly villages, to sorcery villages, to usually hostile villages. While the usually hostile villages tended to yield an occasional marriage partner obtained through abduction, the sorcery villages represent the outer limit of the area from which a person would ordinarily obtain wives, and therefore affinal and uterine kin.

It has often been remarked that guardians of moral values tend to be situated on the fringe of the social universe (e.g. see Gluckman 1965: 100—1). In view of what we already know of Orokaiva social relations (see model 20), we would expect that the initiand would normally have no direct significant social relations with his *aguma*. Usually his relations, if any, would be through one or more intermediaries. In the absence of such intermediaries, the initiand would see no reason why he should believe the *aguma's* recital of his war deeds nor his claims to greatness and why he should honour pledges made to a stranger. Williams shows that rude questioning of the *aguma's* authority, by young men in a position analogous to that of the initiand, was a regular part of the ritual (1930: 190). There is, however, a counterpart to these challenges which appears less clearly from Williams' account. I was told it was not enough for the *aguma* to protest his own war deeds; there must also be other war leaders present who will affirm that the *aguma* is speaking the truth. One gathers from Williams' account that there were two of these at the ceremony he attended (p. 189—90). He quotes one *aguma* as saying that these two intermediaries 'remembered his exploits better than he did himself'. The *aguma* then pretended to use these men as prompters. Whatever the two intermediaries were called upon to say or do, they would always add credibility to the words of the *aguma,* as their authority would not be questioned by the initiand.

The effect of this ritual would be to place the *aguma* in a very exalted position. The initiand would see that someone he regarded as an authority figure deferred humbly and showed his admiration to the *aguma.* The *aguma's* social distance thus increased the awe initiands felt before him and made the pledges all the more binding. We may express this transaction by the following exchange cycle:

MODEL 31

If the initiate should later break a pledge, the wronged person may call upon a sorcerer whose position I have suggested to be symbolically equivalent to that of the *aguma.* The Orokaiva never seems to use sorcery directly upon the person he wishes to punish, but always goes to a village on the periphery of his social universe, where he retains a sorcerer for a fee. Later on, when the victim of the sorcery (C) recognises the wrong he has done to the angered person (B), he will offer the latter some reparation. The latter will then ask the sorcerer (A) to cease pursuing the victim. We note that the exchange cycle thus set up is homologous with model 31:

MODEL 32

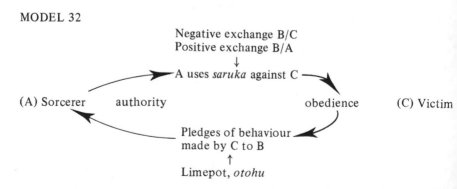

5. *The Message of the Sacred Flutes*

We are now in a position to analyse Williams' data on the *otohu*. Recent theoretical advances in anthropology help us to a fairly easy solution to the problem of the *otohu* by following up a clue Williams threw away as insignificant. Williams was actually very close to the solution I now propose. He recognised that the explanation of the *otohu* is to be found in the ritual of initiation. He also recognised that Chinnery's and Beaver's explanation of initiation, (viz. that it educates by showing initiands the terrifying power of the spirits), 'does not lay sufficient stress on the actual paraphernalia, viz. the bullroarers and flutes, which play a more important part in the ceremony than would appear' (1930: 195). Finally, Williams records (*ibid.*, 185) that in some localities such as Wasida, one of the duet of flutes is actually called *otohu* and the other *e* (= mother). Though this usage is only local, it nevertheless gives us a crucial insight into the significance of the word *otohu*.

Seeing that the Wasida people used the same word for the mental qualities known as *otohu* and the larger and lower-pitched of the pair of sacred flutes, it is useful to inquire whether some symbolic equivalence exists between these mental qualities and these objects. The question falls into two parts. First, we have to explain why there should be any association between a flute and a set of social virtues. Secondly, we have to explain why the flute called *otohu*, which is symbolically equivalent to a set of moral virtues, should be played in antiphony to another flute called *e*. As for the first question, Williams reports that these flutes are never seen but only heard by the uninitiated and that they are regarded as voices of the spirits or *embahi*. The initiated have seen the *embahi* and are allowed to see and play the sacred flutes. They have made the acquaintance of the world of primal ancestors who enunciated and established the moral rules of social behaviour. As children they were taught to obey these rules, but as initiates they have experienced a mystic unity with the deities who established them. The sacred flutes, being voices of the spirits, have communicated these rules in their spiritual essence. Now an *otohu embo* (a man of good character, ibid., p. 205) is a man who lives according to the message he has received from the sacred flutes. The connection between the flutes and the set of social virtues is therefore not difficult to establish.

Secondly, why should the flute called *otohu* be played in antiphony to a flute called *e*? To answer this question let us first recall that according to Williams' own evidence (*ibid.*, 185), the Orokaiva classify one of this pair of flutes – always the larger and lower-pitched one – as masculine and the other as feminine. If the latter is equated to 'mother', then what kinsman is associated with the masculine flute? It seems most plausible that the masculine flute should be symbolically equivalent to the mother's brother, as it is he who acts as initiator of the novice and is thus, on the social level, the mediator between the latter and the spirit world. He teaches the initiand to play the flutes, he gives him medicines which ensure success in adult roles, and finally he presents him with the ornament called *otohu*. The association here is clear enough, but see model 34 on p. 187.

Throughout the Orokaiva world we find the opposition of the male and female principle: between killing and nurture, bush and garden, victim and taro.

The mother and mother's brother, being the most harmonious, gentle and affectionate male/female couple known to the Orokaiva, are the most suited for the task of mediating between the fearsome spirit world and the human being. The two initiatory flutes are therefore identifed with them.

How are the *otohu* ornaments connected with (*a*) the moral qualities and (*b*) the flute of the same name? The first part of this question was answered convincingly by Williams, as we have seen. But how are *otohu* ornaments symbolically equivalent to flutes? It is relevant to recall the difference between the two identity symbols *otohu* and *hae*. Ideally, the latter is transmitted in the patriline, the former in the matriline. All other differences (e.g. that the *hae* is attached to the corporate group and the *otohu* to the exchange system) follow from the mode of transmission.

The common characteristic of initiation ceremony, sacred flutes and *otohu* ornaments is that they all ideally derive from uterine kin or, in any case, that they have no necessary connection with the clan. Initiation pries the novice loose from early over-attachment to the clan and confronts him with the more adventurous, less secure world of the exchange system (*mine*). This applies equally to girls and boys. The rigours of this new arena are very effectively dramatised by the *aguma* whose recital emphasises that it is meritorious for the *otohu embo* to kill enemies. The same message is conveyed in a different way by the mother's brother whose role includes the gift of black magic (*saruka*) to his nephew. The ornament, *saruka* and other presentations come to the nephew not of right, but in the form of *mine*, in exchange for help and obedience offered to the mother's brother and gifts made by the novice's family.

The existence of two identity symbols, *hae* and *otohu*, side by side, indicates the strong emphasis placed by Orokaiva culture upon social relationships outside the corporate group. Among the neighbouring Baruga, whose culture closely resembles the Orokaiva, but who are more strongly patrilineal, we find only one identity symbol, the *kotopo*, which serves both as *hae* (lineage emblem) and as *otohu* (honorific ornament). Initiation is here carried out by the clan, introduces the novice to full clan membership, but carries no implications for participation in a wider network.

The *otohu* flute is a voice from the spirit world, mediated through the mother's brother. This voice communicates a certain moral order. The initiand hears the flutes but at that time makes no response. If he is later presented with an *otohu* ornament, he must make pledges. The ornament, as it is thrown back and forth over his head, communicates the same message as the flute but this time the novice responds to the voice. It is thus that he makes the ornament into a symbol of his identity.

6.   Otohu *and* Hambo *Compared*

There are many resemblances between *otohu* and other *hambo*. They are made from largely the same materials. They are all, together with *di* (feathers) made accessible to men and women at the time of initiation, as soon as they have seen the *embahi*. Yet there are also many differences both in significance and in transactional custom. First of all, *otohu* may be worn on any important occasion, but *hambo* only during a dance or in other ceremonial contexts.

Hence, *otohu* might serve as symbols of high social status whereas *hambo* are less useful in this regard, being worn only intermittently and never with a purely social purpose in mind.

The usefulness of *otohu* as status symbols is further enhanced by the fact that they are transferable from generation to generation. The Member of the House of Assembly for the Northern District told me he always carried his *otohu* with him when meeting his constituents and that he would display it conspicuously attached to his betelnut bag, because a great many people would know this *otohu*: it had belonged to his *epe* who had been a famous war chief and sorcerer. He believed that people in his constituency had great respect for this *otohu*. He made it sound almost as though he was carrying the *insigne* of a hereditary chieftainship, but in fact the basis of his influence was far more complex: it was in part agnatic, in part uterine, and in large part personal. Nonetheless, the *otohu* was obviously very useful to him in establishing new social relations.

Whatever social effect a *hambo* might have would depend mostly on the beauty of its construction and the rarity of its materials. While informants might sometimes think its history and associations worthy of mention, a *hambo's* association with a particular family is usually rather loose, as the right to wear *hambo* of a particular type is never, to my knowledge, restricted to a family. The main effect and power of a *hambo* appears to be aesthetic. It is used to impress partners in a dispute, dancing partners or young women whose passions one hopes to arouse.

Unlike the *otohu,* the *hambo* does not otherwise emphasise the identity of the wearer. One the contrary, a fully decorated person, wearing a head-dress, *hambo* and face-paint, is supposed not to be recognisable as a person. One should on no account address him by name. He represents an *embahi* and, as such, is completely depersonalised. More specifically, the dancer represents a natural species – a pig, a wallaby or, in the case of women, a bird, a butterfly, a flower. The details of these identifications need to be studied more closely. The significance of the decorations is very similar to that of the masks used for dancing in other parts of New Guinea. The face and body become a medium for decorating: the individual assumes the persona of an ancestor; his private existence is covered over to display only his social function.

This total lack of personal identity inherent in the *hambo* makes the object easily transferable from one individual to another. it always belongs essentially to the ancestors and is thus alive with spirit. By transferring it to another, a man emphasises that he and the recipient share some link with the spirit world and this implies amity, the primeval absence of strife. It also probably implies in some way the message of the sacred flutes by which man's contact with the spirit world is established. Further research no doubt will enable us to be more precise about the meaning of these transactions. They occur in a great many social contexts: *hambo* are given away to settle a quarrel, to pay bridewealth, to establish and maintain an important friendship. They are frequently lent to persons about to dance at a feast, and a gift of meat is then required from the borrower. They are lent by the *kogumbari* expert for a similar consideration, and are also bartered and sold. Some people, and not always the most prominent, make large collections of them, and most people of rank have a good store of them, as they are a necessary part of the ceremonial gift exchange system. From

an economic standpoint, it is important that they represent storable wealth —
the only storable wealth of the Orokaiva. Nearly every family today keeps
hambo and feathers in a locked suitcase, thus elevating the suitcase into one of
the most ubiquitous introduced elements of Orokaiva material culture.

The distinctive characteristic of the *hambo,* as compared with other objects
of mediation considered here, lies in the type of social exchange that is mediated
by means of *hambo* gifts. One might say that the partners are exchanging spirit
participation. No doubt cultures vary in the extent to which individuals lend and
give each other their private religious paraphernalia, i.e. the objects they use to
achieve communion with their deities. In a society as exchange-oriented as the
Orokaiva, where virtually everything is exchanged, there is clearly some special
satisfaction in wearing someone else's *hambo.* Furthermore, a 'total presentation' such as bridewealth, which is intended to create a social relationship on a
great many levels, must always include the sacral level represented by *hambo.*

7.   The Nature of Mediation

In the last five chapters exchange has been discussed largely on the assumption
that it occurs on two levels. First, it occurs on the mythico-religious level where
exchange relations are stated in the form of binary oppositions or possibly also
some other more complex structures. Among the examples discussed have been
coconut/betelnut and the pair of initiatory flutes. Secondly, exchange occurs on
the social level where each exchange partner subjectively views the other as
transcendent and reachable only with the aid of some form of mediation. The
belief in the magical efficacy of any given object of exchange is validated by
notions deriving from the mythico-religious level. If A and B stand for exchange
partners/objects of exchange, M and N for objects of mediation, and P and Q for
relevant binary oppositions present on the mythico-religious level, we may
represent our model of exchange as follows:

MODEL 33

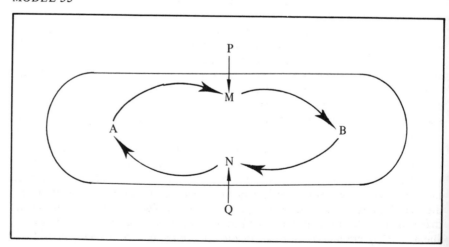

As an example of the operation of this model, we may summarise the discussion concerning the sacred flutes and the *otohu*. On the mythical level there is a binary opposition between a male and a female principle. On the social level there is a relation between mother's brother and sister's son, which is mediated (*a*) by the mother; (*b*) by the gift of an *otohu*. On the technological level, there is opposition between a male and female initiation flute (respectively *otohu* and e = mother). These complex interrelations are shown with great economy in the following diagram:

MODEL 34

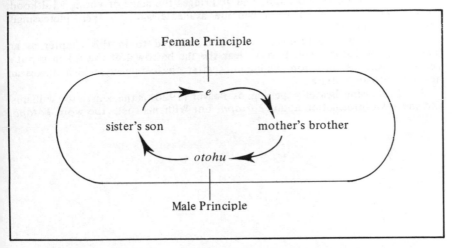

The objects of mediation under discussion in the preceding chapters have been mostly material objects, but the model is by no means confined to these. It is equally applicable to social objects of mediation. Indeed, in model 34, the word *e* appears in a double sense: as one of the two initiatory flutes, i.e. a material object, but simultaneously as 'mother', a social object. In the taro sociogram, we introduced a series of human mediators between a set of distant but equal exchange partners (model 20). In discussing the *aguma,* we found the same pattern between a set of distant but unequal exchange partners (model 31). Similarly, we may regard the mother's brother as mediator between initiand and the spirit world.

Some of the most important social exchanges are those which are mediated by a woman who is a sister of one of the partners and the wife of the other. We have already looked briefly at this type of exchange when discussing the coconut and betelnut myth (model 29). In thus equating woman with an 'object of mediation' we are not thereby postulating any essential inequality between men and women except in as far as the Orokaiva happen to be patrilocal and patrilineal, so that it is the women, not the men, whose sexual role places them in a position of mediation. We are merely suggesting that two persons standing in a relation of *dambo* mediate their social relationship through a woman with which each, in a different way, is identified, one sexually and the other non-sexually. The asymmetry is balanced out by a counter-prestation on the part of the 'husband' who either gives a woman in exchange (direct marriage exchange) or else makes some kind of reparation for having deprived his exchange partner (generalised marriage exchange).

REFERENCES

1.   Erikson, describing 'the beginnings of identity' in the adolescent, comes rather close to what I have in mind in this chapter: 'The emerging identity bridges the stages of childhood when the bodily self and the parental images are given their cultural connotation: and it bridges the stage of young adulthood, when a variety of social roles become available and, in fact, increasingly coercive.' (1963: 235).

2.   A person who receives a token is referred to in this chapter as an 'initiate', as Williams makes it very clear the the bestowal of the token is not a necessary part of initiation, and comes after the ceremony which makes an 'inistion' into an 'initiate'.

3.   I am using Beaver's spelling, as Beaver (1920) is the source for Williams' and my own information about *kortopo*, but Williams spells the word *kotopo*.

PART III
EXCHANGE AND SOCIAL STRUCTURE

CHAPTER X
MARRIAGE

1. *Introduction*

In analysing a system of exchange, our first task is to find the rules governing the objects of mediation. I have not dealt with all objects used by Orokaiva for the mediation of social exchange, but I have given enough examples to show both a method and a pattern. The effect of the rules is to place constraints upon the exchange partners. Examples of such constraints may be found in each of the five preceding chapters. In making land transfers a man is constrained, in the main, by the love for his sister who wants his land for her children. In the daily ritual of taro gifts, householders are constrained by their quasi-commensal neighbours. Gifts of pig meat are constrained even more severely by a taboo on eating pork reared by oneself or a close relative. The constraint in coconut and betelnut gifts is mainly felt after a death, with affines as preferential recipients. The *otohu* sets up constraints through the moral pledges made at the time of its transfer to the owner.

Each of these constraints compels the individual to make commitments outside the narrow confines of the small agnatic group. Land transfers to the sister, if hereditary, place the sister's son in a position of dual allegiance to the agnatic and uterine group. The taro gift network involves a majority of non-agnates and establishes a chain of non-agnates who become vicariously quasi-commensal. The obligation to keep pigs for mediating critical social relationships ensures that means are available for setting in motion new cycles of positive reciprocity, either with strangers or with former enemies. My analysis of the coconut-betelnut myth shows a commitment on the philosophical plane: it shows that Orokaiva do not view exchange merely as a social and economic expediency, but as expressing, in symbolic thought, the interdependence of the sexes. Finally, the existence of two basic identity symbols (*hae* and *otohu*) implies a profound psychological commitment to the exchange system commensurate in Orokaiva society with the commitment to the corporate group.

I have spoken, in each case, of constraints because there has been a tendency, in the study of New Guinea societies, to overemphasise the degree of freedom. A man does not give his land, his taro, his pigs, or his *otohu* to just anyone. There are very strong pulls in the direction of the corporate group and these are balanced by very strong pulls in the direction of the exchange system. Nor is it correct to assume that the former are determined by structural rules whereas the latter are determined by economic interest. A study of the objects of mediation has already shown that there are rules which make commitment to the exchange system either obligatory or preferential. Yet all the evidence brought forward so far has presented this exchange system as a set of individual, though interconnected, networks.

If our analysis cannot go beyond the identification and description of these networks, we shall clearly have failed to establish exchange as an explanatory principle for the ethnography of the Orokaiva. The success of our enterprise therefore depends on the discovery of some constraints, existing within the exchange system, which are placed upon individuals in virtue of their membership of some corporate group. If such rules exist at all, one may assume that they are most likely to be found in the marriage system.

Here we enter somewhat controversial ground. In the introduction to a symposium on marriage in the New Guinea Highlands, Meggitt has recently (1969) asserted that, in that area at least, positive marriage rules do not exist but only what he calls 'contingent preferential arrangements'. If his arguments are accepted, there would be no positive marriage rules among the Orokaiva nor, as far as I can see, anywhere else in the world. His arguments hinge on his use of the terms 'preferential' and 'prescriptive', but even if we revert to the definitions given for these terms by Lévi-Strauss (1967: xvii–xxiii) a very careful and detailed investigation is required in order to determine whether or not the Orokaiva have any preferential rules of marriage and exogamy.

It may be best to start with Lévi-Strauss' own discussions regarding the problems of Melanesian marriage rules. When he wrote *Les structures élémentaires de la parenté* (1949), the ethnographic data from which a general model for the Melanesian area could have been securely constructed were lacking. Nonetheless Lévi-Strauss wrote a brief passage on this subject and ventured a bold hypothesis. The hypothesis seemed especially bold because at that time there was only one ethnography that could be quoted to support it, a description by F. E. Williams of the apparently aberrant kinship system of the Koriari (1932). I think nonetheless that his hypothesis is a most useful starting point for the analysis of Melanesian systems:

> *La Nouvelle-Guinée, et les régions avoisinantes, présentent, à un degré exceptionnel, un phénomène que Williams a decrit sous le nom d' "affiliation sexuelle", c'est-à-dire une différentiation de statut entre le frère et la sœur, l'un suivant la ligne paternelle et l'autre la ligne maternelle. Il est impossible d'interpréter ce phénomène en fonction de l'échange restreint: mais il devient très clair quand on l'envisage sous l'échange généralisé, puisqu'en mariage matrilatéral comme en mariage patrilatéral, le frère et la sœur suivent des destins différents. L'étude des phénomènes d'affiliation sexuelle . . . permet donc de définir, à travers tout le monde mélanésien, une sorte de faille de l'échange généralisé . . . Toute l'aire orientale, "océano-américaine", comme on peut le nommer, forme donc une sorte de théâtre, où se rencontrent échange restreint et échange généralisé, tantôt pour s'opposer, et tantôt pour se combiner* (1949: reprinted 1967: 534–5).

Since 1949, Lévi-Strauss has made several further contributions to the analysis of Melanesian societies. In the second edition of *Les structures élémentaires de la parenté* he suggested that *la ligne de partage entre les sociétés traditionellement appelées "primitives" et les sociétés dites "civilisées" ne coincide pas avec celle entre "structures élémentaires" et "structures com-*

plexes" (1967: 123). In particular, he stated the opinion that many Melanesian structures '*ne relévent pas des structures élémentaires' (ibid.*: 122). We learn the precise meaning of this statement in another essay, *The Future of Kinship Studies,* published in the English language in 1966. Whereas elementary structures operate ideally within a fixed number of marriage classes, the rules of complex structures are so framed that the system requires a perpetual supply of new affinal groups for its continued operation. They produce a probabilistic alliance network. Rules of this kind are found in the Crow and Omaha systems, but also in many other culture areas, including Melanesia (1966: 21).

Since these hypotheses were published, a number of anthropologists have begun to test them empirically. To mention only two examples, Guiart (1968) has shown the presence of restricted exchange rules in New Caledonia and Kelly (1968) has shown the presence of generalised exchange on Dobu. It seems, however, that a crucial implication of the Lévi-Straussian hypotheses remains to be explored. It is suggested that restricted and generalised exchange (or perhaps restricted and complex exchange) *encounter* one another in the Melanesian culture area. This would imply the possibility of the simultaneous existence in the same society of both forms and some interaction between the two. If such a society could be found, the hypothesis implies that generalised exchange attempts to establish itself there, but *fails* to find a firm foothold, while features of restricted exchange tend to reassert themselves constantly as a result of this *failure.*

The interest of the Orokaiva case lies in the coexistence of the two systems, on the level both of norms and facts. In Orokaiva social structure we may see the two systems in interaction and discover by which factors each of the systems is maintained in opposition to the other. We thus arrive at a model on a higher level of abstraction than those of Guiart and Kelly, but comprising them both. In this model moiety systems are perpetually broken up by forces built into the structure itself: yet the model also predicts their perpetual reinstatement. The model consists, in fact, of a cyclical movement between the two patterns. The reality of Melanesian structure is not exhausted by either of the two patterns taken in isolation, but includes their necessary alternation over time and in space. The dynamic whereby this alternation is produced is the main subject of this chapter.

2. *Patrilineal Groups*

The Orokaiva are patrilocal and have dispersed patriclans. They make many statements which demonstrate their patrilineal ideology: agnates are expected to support each other in war and all other vicissitudes of life, irrespective of their place of residence. The basic inheritance rule is patrilineal. Clans and clan segments have distinctive emblems which are passed on in the patriline and identified with a common agnatic ancestor. One may even hear claims that the dispersed clan is an exogamous unit. All analytically-minded investigators, however, have been aware that this agnatic ideology covered up a very different reality. Williams remarked: 'The Orokaiva organisation very nearly approaches a bilateral system, though in theory it is patrilineal' (1925: 407). Williams was especially struck by the 'laxity' of the marriage regulations and by cases where men showed loyalty to their affines rather than their clansmen. He also noted a widespread tendency for individuals to identify with the maternal rather than the paternal clan. Evidence on land tenure, presented by Crocombe, Hogbin and Rimboldi, provides an impressive list of exceptions to the supposed rule of patrilineal inheritance and points, in addition, to the feebleness of links between the local groups making up a dispersed clan.

At the time of Williams' study, most Orokaiva villages were composed of a single clan and comprised little more than six households. The Australian authorities used a good deal of pressure to make the Orokaiva consolidate their hamlets into larger villages which could be more easily patrolled, but by 1951 Belshaw reported that most Orokaiva still lived in hamlets. In 1966 I found a good number of one-clan villages, with populations of around fifty, but the majority of the people were concentrated in larger settlements in which at least two local clan groups were residing together.

The local clan group was traditionally the smallest viable military unit, whose duty it was to defend the hamlet territory against outsiders. It had its own military leader, feasting leader, technical and magical experts. In the modern multi-clan village, the corporate scope of the local clan group has declined, as its functions have been taken over by the village. Village feasts, village boundaries, village leadership tend to take the place of the earlier local clan group institutions. Due to these changes, the unity of the local clan group has become more difficult to establish and maintain.

Crocombe, Hogbin and Rimoldi have provided full data showing that local clan groups are often divided into a number of exclusive segments they call 'lineages', which are characterised by putative common patrilineal descent from an ancestor who could often not be named. It is certainly true that we find important units intermediate between the extended family and the local clan group. First, it is possible to list four names of such major units within the Jegase local clan group and the same number within Seho. But the term 'lineage' might be deceptive unless we define it more closely.

If we look at the clan segments in Sivepe (it will soon be clear why I prefer not to call them 'lineages'), their real distinctive feature is that they either came to Sivepe as migrants from the same village or as members of the same clan. There is no evidence whatever that, in their village of origin, they would necessarily have been regarded as close kin. Their feeling of being closely related arose only subsequent to migration. The study of Orokaiva migrant groups, even comprising just a few families, easily reveals that they tend to consist of one core family to which others will rally, not because they are related by kinship but because they want to leave, are good friends of the migrating family and, most probably, have some kin or friendship links in the village where the group intends to settle. It is only after arrival there that they may, for ideological and political reasons, create the fiction of being close patrikin. A number of such groups fuse with earlier arrivals into larger units bearing a clan name adopted by all. Hence, for most purposes these smaller units are best described as 'clan segments', though it may be useful to refer to them as lineages when discussing informants' statements concerning the patrilineal ideology by which such groupings are held together.

TABLE X/1

VILLAGE POPULATIONS AND CLAN ORGANISATION
Number of villages investigated: 15

Name	Population				

(a) One-Clan Villages:

Ajoro	50	Tandai'undi
Inonda	42	Andiriha
Irihambo	30	Oripa
Sombou	70	Pangaripa
Kakita	24	Hatopa

(b) Two-Clan Villages:

Binduta	100	Jegase	Usohu
Garombi	132	Sorovi	Betu
Hamburata	91	Ehirari	Ohuru
Kongohambo	96	Pugege	Ameti
Sivepe	137	Jegase	Seho
Torogota	65	Jeipa	Jaumbi

(c) Four-Clan Villages		ve/ih	ih/av	av/so	so/ve[1]
Hohorita	348	Oripa	Besupa	Sehopa	Horeppa
Sasembata	162	Garoha	Pekuma	Ato	Takone[2]
Soroputa	200	Seraopa	Jaja	Java	Timumu

(d) Multi-Clan Villages

Kiorota	429	12 clans[3]

Notes

[1] ve/ih etc. are made up of abridgements of the Orokaiva terms *veari, ihane, avunu, sose.* for which see Chapter X, 5.

[2] No marriages between Seraopa and Jaja are permissible today, but both clans marry preferentially into the Hamburata clans.

[3] This village was settled in 1958 by refugees from the Mount Lamington eruption who previously occupied a number of smaller villages, according to the following pattern:

Homumuta	1	Haripa	2	Penonupa		
Isivita	3	Jegase	4	Berekipa		
Bosisepa	3	Jegase	4	Berekipa	11	Seraopa
Tambore	5	Oetopa	6	Ahungata		
Taremuturu	5	Oetopa	7	Pusaripa		
Pinda	8	Isivupa	9	Juvaripa		
Kandata	10	Jepuripa				
?	12	Omborapa				

Similarly, the fact that these groupings together call themselves a clan (*javo wahai*) does not imply the actual existence of agnatic connection. The term means 'one name', and that is all they share, except for uterine links which buttress the social relations between them. The clan name is important as a symbol of political identification. The close bonds between the clan segments are evident in residence patterns, in daily intercourse and mutual assistance in practical matters, though not in ritual or other formal organisation.

The second principle of grouping is the plant emblem (*hae*), already recognised by Williams (1925, 1930) as important in the Orokaiva social system. Williams describes it as 'a distinctive emblem or associate' of a clan, though he recognised it could belong merely to a segment of a clan. Most of them are vegetable species, though almost any natural or cultural object may be designated as *hae*. Williams lists three main uses: as an identity token (to mark a visit by the owner), as a mark of individual abstinence (a self-inflicted taboo, usually shown to indicate a grievance) and as a village taboo post (prohibiting access). The *hae* is regarded as an ancestor, which does not signify, as Williams carefully pointed out, that men believe themselves to be physically descendants of plants, but that the ancestor was a man bearing the name of that plant. Clan and personal names are commonly plant names and often the *hae* of a clan and its name are identical. On the question whether the *hae* is a totem, he remarked that, whatever we call it, 'it will be obvious that it is very much like one.' He noted some forms of religious respect toward *hae*, notably eating and naming taboos.

To this information we may add that in our experience the term *hae* is frequently used to describe a social group made up of persons sharing a *hae*, and that the group to which it is applied is not the clan (*javo wahai*) but a smaller formation often about the same size as a 'clan segment' or 'lineage'. As such, they are probably the basic larger unit of Orokaiva social structure.

Every individual respects a number of paternal and a number of maternal *hae*. Theoretically, a person passes on his father's but not his mother's *hae* to the next generation so that the *hae* would form an agnatic group. Most individuals have about five *hae* in regular use. I recorded forty-two *hae* names in a population of 135.

There would normally be one *hae* common to a *javo wahai*. Less wide-ranging and more distinctive *hae* would often be of more social importance. Those who were related to the same distinctive *hae* would co-operate in marriage and mortuary payments and maintain a strict exogamy rule. Though they claimed their group to be composed wholly of agnates and children of agnates, there were in fact several cases of uterine transmission for more than one generation, especially where marriages were uxorilocal. Some *hae* became unusually popular, like *topu*, a tree name which became a *hae* after a Sivepe woman died by falling off a *topu* tree. She was given the necronym Topugoru, after which all her lineal descendants adopted *topu* as a *hae*, In other instances again, persons sharing the same *hae* were quite plainly unrelated in a physical sense. In fact the membership of none of the eleven most numerous plant emblem groups was drawn from a single clan segment or even a single local clan group.

It follows that the social group called *hae* never has a membership identical with that of a lineage, if we use that term in the sense of Crocombe, Hogbin or

Rimoldi. I witnessed marriage and mortuary payments where an entire *hae* (including non-consanguines) were present, but where clansmen of different *hae* had no business to be present.

Orokaiva genealogies hardly ever extended further than two generations beyond the oldest living member of a family. Thus, I was able to draw up a sizeable list of people who lived in Sivepe and other villages around 1915, but could get no genealogical information showing how these people were related to one another. However, informants were able to tell me the *hae* of these ancestors, and these *hae* proved to be the only evidence for statements that A and B 'must have been closely related' or 'cannot have been closely related'. In contrast to the clan and clan segment (which I shall later show to be military and political units — whole or fragmentary), the plant emblem group alone has the nature of a true kinship group. Therefore we should not be surprised that the *hae* occurs prominently in the Orokaiva marriage rules with regard to incest and exogamy.

3. Williams' Theory of Orokaiva Marriage

Being a most careful ethnographer, Williams frankly admitted he was unable to understand the Orokaiva rules of exogamy. He quotes three conflicting sets of rules, given to him by informants, and was unable to discern any clear system. According to some informants the clan was the exogamous group. According to others, marriage within the clan was sometimes permissible, but marriage was prohibited between persons sharing a plant emblem. A third rule quoted to Williams was that marriage was prohibited between *du* (i.e. real and classificatory siblings) but permitted and common between cross-cousins. One task of the present essay is to resolve these contradictions.

Williams, furthermore, confessed himself unable to find any positive marriage regulations, i.e. 'any prescribed classes into which a man is obliged to marry' (1930:132). Here he was being too modest: in a subsequent discussion of 'the four forms of marriage' of the Orokaiva, he actually provided the key to the system, though he was unable to carry its analysis as far as he managed to do in some of his later ethnographies, such as those of the Koiari and the *Papuans of the Trans-Fly*.

The 'four forms' were: purchase, exchange, elopement, and capture. Marriage by capture used to be very frequent and a regular aftermath of cannibal raids. Williams reports that, under this form of marriage, relations between affines often remained hostile — which is not surprising. In many cases the hostile groups later established peace or at least a truce. One feature of such a truce used to be the payment of bridewealth for captured women. The truce was often negotiated at least partly through the influence of the captive. Though Williams has little information on the compensation paid one gathers that the usual pattern of Orokaiva bridewealth payments was followed: pigs, valuables, bark-cloth, pots, taro, etc. My own data confirm that it was not uncommon for ordinary affinal relations to be established once the captors had paid bridewealth. Children of the marriage would then set up the customary relationship with their mother's brother and even receive permanent rights in hunting lands and the like.

Elopement marriage likewise used to be very frequent. Williams reports that it led to serious quarrels, especially if the girl had been kept by her parents or brother for an exchange marriage. Usually, these quarrels were settled in due course upon payment of a suitable bridewealth and sometimes by a subsequent marriage for which the abductor's family provided the bride. Williams comments:

> The remarkable gestures of hostility against the husband's people which sometimes characterise Orokaiva marriage, i.e. the attempted dragging away of the bride by her people, the humiliation of the bridegroom, the damaging of his village and the bellicose demonstrations at the taking over of the *dorobu* (= bridewealth), all properly belong to the irregular methods of capture and elopement; they are the aftermath, the retaliation (1930:149).

The third and fourth marriage forms distinguished by Williams are purchase (i.e. obtaining a wife in exchange for *dorobu*) and exchange (*mine*, i.e. an arrangement whereby two men each make a true or classificatory sister available to the other). It seems that Williams did not differentiate clearly between modes of obtaining a wife and modes of making a valid marriage contract. One might obtain a wife in a number of ways. Certainly, capture and abduction seem to have been the most frequent at one time, but there were also child betrothals; long-standing preferential arrangements between villages; romances leading to sister exchange and marriages to seal political alliances. There was the whole gamut between choices made by lovers without parental approval and choices (probably relatively less frequent) made by parental fiat. But there were only two ways of making a valid marriage contract, namely *dorobu* and *mine*. Williams himself comes very close to this view towards the end of his chapter on 'Marriage' (1930: Ch. IX). He also maintains, no doubt correctly, that in Orokaiva thought *mine* appears as the 'ideal', i.e. preferential, mode of contracting a marriage:

> It appears that marriage by exchange is preferable to marriage by purchase — at least in the eyes of the marriageable man, and probably also in the eyes of his elders who sympathise with his desires. We may perhaps go so far as to say that the actual buying of a wife only takes place when circumstances make present or future exchange impossible (1930: 149).

This seems to place Williams' theory firmly on the side of Guiart's theory of marriage in New Caledonia: exchange marriage becomes the preferential mode, the 'model', whereas marriage 'by purchase' is demoted to the status of an ecologically caused departure from the 'model'. In this chapter I shall argue that Williams' Orokaiva theory reifies the folk model and conceals some of the complexity of Orokaiva social structure.

4.   *Elements of Restricted Exchange*

Marriage rules related to the principle of restricted exchange are actually more numerous than Williams supposed. They must be briefly reviewed before we can argue cogently that the principle of restricted exchange does not suffice to account for the rules governing the total Orokaiva marriage system. Williams was entirely right in supposing that the Orokaiva have preferential sister exchange marriage, even though actual cases recorded in the three village investigated are only 5 per cent of the total for true siblings and the proportion is declining. Sister exchange marriages were considered best because relations between affines were apt to be the most harmonious and also because no bride price was necessary. As any trouble that occurs in family life is apt to be ascribed to sorcery by affines, it was thought that families founded on sister exchange marriage would be the most likely to prosper in respect of health, stability and economic success.

Furthermore, there is an explicit rule of preferential bilateral cross-cousin marriage. All informants were agreed that the most proper marriage partner is one who is addressed as *simbo* before marriage; Williams defines *simbo* as 'child of the father's sister; children of all *tata*; child of the mother's brother; children of all *nobo*, i.e. cross-cousins' (1930: 109). Out of twenty-two married couples resident in Sivepe, fourteen actually called each other *simbo* before marriage. Williams notes that *simbo* marriages were extremely common in the communities he studies (1930:132), but does not seem to have been told of the preferential rule.

The existence of such a rule can be inferred not only from direct statements, but also from investigation of the primary meaning of the term *simbo* itself. The primary meaning is not cross-cousin and we shall later see that the two terms do not entirely share the same field of reference. *Simbo* is an arrangement of marriage. A *simbo* may be established when a boy's parents bring part of a bridewealth to the parents of a girl they want their son to marry. If the arrangement is acceptable, the parents help in the garden of their son's future affines and continue to send food. Such an arrangement is usually made immediately after the rituals following the girl's first menstruation. If the *simbo* is broken, the girl's parents must pay back the gifts. In a secondary sense, the word *simbo* also refers to that category of consanguines with which betrothals of the kind just described can be properly made. All members of that category are either cross-cousins in the strict sense, or consanguines with whom kinship can be traced neither wholly in the patriline, nor wholly in the matriline.

There are also rules establishing preferential marriage between specific villages. Though Williams did not notice the presence of this rule among the Orokaiva, he described a very similar rule obtaining among the Koiari, where he spoke of 'reciprocating pairs of groups' (1932). Under this arrangement, two local clan groups or exogamous lineages give wives to each other from generation to generation, each side supplying as near as possible an equal number. A group that has received a wife is expected to send one back in the same or the next generation. If the return prestation occurs in the same generation one may speak of sister exchange; if it occurs in the next generation, the rule is expressed by the Orokaiva as *eta data jimbari*, i.e. marrying in the mother's village.

This rule applies especially to girls who are expecting to go to the village from which their mother has been taken, thus balancing accounts between reciprocating pairs of groups. Such a rule cannot properly be described as a prescription for patrilateral cross-cousin marriage, as there is at the same time a preference for sister exchange, so that the total pattern of marriages between reciprocating pairs of groups is ideally (and in fact commonly) bilateral. I found that 35 per cent of Orokaiva marriages now in force were contracted in accordance with the rule of *eta data jimbari,* for a period not less than two generations.

Forms of dual organisation between pairs of reciprocating groups have always been of limited scope as the groups tended to reside apart from each other, and each group tended to have marriage exchange relations with several other groups at the same time. Even the short genealogies of Sivepe show evidence that the families of this village have been participating in no less than twenty-five reciprocating pairs of groups, the exchange sometimes consisting of no more than one recorded exchange of women between two villages. Interestingly enough, it was Australian pressure towards village consolidation that emphasised the tendency to dual organisation.

First of all, co-residence tends to increase the number of marriages between local clan groups which are thus thrown together. Usually, such local clan groups are already reciprocating pairs, but when co-residence is established, they begin to reciprocate at a greater rate. For instance, the Seho and Jegase local clan groups in Sivepe, comprising together sixteen households, are linked by seven current Seho-Jegase marriages. This was sufficient to define the seven Seho households and the nine Jegase households as standing in an affinal relation to one another.

In such a village the other households tend to be classified as adhering to one of the two dominant local clan groups. A few years before I came to Sivepe, Rimoldi and Waddel had both visited the village and recorded the presence of a third local clan group, called Timumu. On my arrival I found that this group, consisting of three households, had adopted the Jegase clan name, thus establishing a tidy dualist pattern between one group defined as agnates and a second group defined as affines. A few months before I settled in Sivepe, six households migrated there from Garombi. All the men were members of the Sorovi clan, though of different lineages. A year after they migrated, five of the householders were classified as part of the Jegase clan (by the use of sibling terms of address) while the sixth was classified as part of the Seho clan.

I found a similar pattern in eleven other multi-clan villages I visited. When I first inquired, I was mostly told that they were two-clan villages, the names of the clans being given in each case. Two of the villages were said to have four clans, two pairs of two. Whenever I sought detailed data, I found male householders belonging to additional clans. In Hohorita I was told that the front half was inhabited by two clans, and the back half by two further clans. In fact twelve clans were represented; when this came to light, my informants explained to me that the clan names I had been given at first were those of the 'main' clans. There seemed to be a strong ideological notion that a multi-clan village (or village section) should consist of two local clan groups. Furthermore, this arrangement affects the marriage rules: once Timumu became joined with Jegase under the same clan name, marriages between the two fused local clan, groups became prohibited.

5.   *Complementary Opposition in Village Topography*

If the reduction of multi-clan to two-clan villages had occurred only in Sivepe and a few other villages, it could easily be explained solely by processes of clan fusion which are prevalent throughout the area and which will be discussed further below. But I found it to be a regular feature of the consolidated Orokaiva villages I visited. Yet historical evidence of earlier settlements precludes the supposition that co-residence of reciprocating marriage groups was ever a regular practice or a preferential rule. Such co-residence can be explained only by Australian pressure towards village consolidation. Far from being congenial to the Orokaiva, it may better be regarded as a major potential cause of strain. When the Australian administration planned to intensify this consolidation policy after the Mount Lamington eruption in 1951, Belshaw rightly warned the authorities in a published paper (1951) that the enforced co-residence of affines would create serious social strains which might impede the administration's social development objectives. The Orokaiva response to these social strains appears to have been to restructure the multi-clan villages and give them an organisational form they are more easily able to handle. Under this arrangement agnates, uterine kin and affines live together in the same village but are sorted into two groups of real or fictional agnates. These two groups have affinal relations with one another and stand in complementary opposition in social and political affairs.

In some villages this complementary opposition is further expressed in the position of the two groups in village topography. Nearly all Orokaiva villages are built in two facing rows separated by a fairly wide grassed area known as the *araha*. For cosmological reasons that do not concern us here, these rows tend to run in the direction of the top of Mount Lamington – from downhill (*veari*) to uphill (*avunu*). The two rows are known as *mende* or *bende*, a word which may mean 'nose' or 'hillock' or 'side of a village'. The two sides are designated as *ihane* and *sose*, *ihane* being to the right of a person facing the mountain, *sose* on the left. In 1965, when Sivepe was rebuilt on a new site, all Seho men built their houses on the *ihane* side while all Jegase men built on the *sose* side.

Outwardly, the topography of this new Sivepe does not differ significantly from the earliest descriptions we have of Orokaiva villages in the early post-contact period. These villages also had two sides. They had the same short connecting lines of houses at the *avunu* and *veari* ends of the village. Williams reports that these connecting lines prevent spirits from coming into the *araha*. The only differences are in size and in the style of the houses. The basic innovation in New Sivepe lies in the arrangement of social groups on the village site. Real or assumed agnatic links now exist between all the householders on each side, whereas affinal relations exist between all the householders of one side and the other. The door openings of the affines face each other, but they are separated by the wide field of the *araha*. When people sit down to smoke and chew betelnut in front of their houses, there is easy movement between residents who live on the same side. They frequently visit each other's fires without any ceremony. But one does not cross the *araha* to sit on the other side without a serious purpose. One watches what happens on the other side; one does not always hear it. There is frequent and friendly contact between the sides but it is clear to the observer that the physical distance between them symbolises an equally real social distance.

This residential arrangement between affines is not traditional. If affines happened to live in a traditional hamlet there were no formal patterns for keeping them at a physical distance. When multi-clan villages were first established, households of the various clans were placed next to each other in a

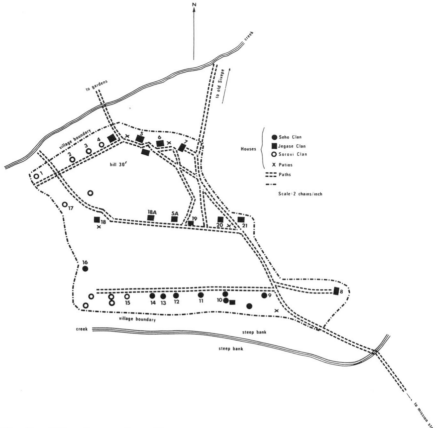

Fig. 9.   Village layout of new Sivepe.

rather irregular pattern. Village plans of Sivepe drawn by Rimoldi and Waddell in 1963 and 1964 show no formal separation between the clans. Some neighbouring villages, such as Garombi, however, did allocate one side to each of their two clans. The fact that Sivepe introduced this pattern in 1965 has no particular explanation except that it appealed to the Seho clan leader who supplied the land for the village site. One might describe his innovation as an idiosyncrasy or a fashion but at the same time it is significant that the pattern of residence he introduced resembles that familiar to anthropologists in the many parts of the world where exogamous moieties are found.

I have now shown most of the evidence for direct marriage exchange and forms of dual organisation. The question that remains to be answered is why this system was so fitfully practised. Are the discrepant cases to be explained merely by organisational factors such as lack of choice, the vicissitudes of war, the need for alliances? Or are there present in the culture a further set of rules related to marriage which we have not yet considered and which are irreconcilable with the principle of direct marriage exchange?

It is obvious, first of all, that the Orokaiva rules concerning bilateral cross-cousin marriage and reciprocating pairs of groups are not free from ambiguity. The term *simbo* is not synonymous with the term 'cross-cousin'. Not all societies which have reciprocating pairs of groups have direct marriage exchange, as Lévi-Strauss showed in respect of the Koiari. The fact that the Sivepe people were partners in no less than twenty-five reciprocating pairs of groups in two generations poses the question whether this apparent instability corresponds to a structural regularity such as the 'sex affiliation' of the Koiari. Furthermore, in view of Lévi-Strauss' analysis of the African *lobola,* we need to investigate whether the Orokaiva institution of bridewealth (*dorobu*) is consistent with the principle of direct marriage exchange. Such inquiries would not serve to deny the reality of this principle in Orokaiva culture but rather to raise the possibility of the combined presence of direct and generalised exchange.

6. Kinship Terminology

Though Williams' description of Orokaiva kinship terminology is generally very accurate, it is deficient in two respects: his definition of the term *simbo* (quoted in section 4 above) is inconsistent with Orokaiva usage and he gives no terms for female speakers. Yet it is in these two areas that we find the key to Orokaiva marriage. We have seen that a *simbo* is — always and exclusively — a marriageable consanguine. If Williams were right in saying that a *simbo* is also — always and exclusively — a cross-cousin, then a rule of bilateral *simbo* marriage would be unambiguously equivalent to a rule of bilateral cross-cousin marriage. If the term *simbo* could be positively defined as a bilateral category of cross-cousins (as the Aranda do), then again we would have a rule of bilateral cross-cousin marriage. In the absence of a positive rule, however, the Orokaiva kinship system could not be regarded as 'elementary' in Lévi-Strauss' sense of the term, and thus it would not contain a true rule of bilateral cross-cousin marriage.

Again where such a rule prevails consistently, there would seem to be no need of special affinal terms. Williams, entirely correctly, gives a set of distinct affinal terms for male speakers which would suggest that the whole system is based on generalised rather than restricted exchange. Williams' explanation of this apparent discrepancy appears to be an evolutionary one: *dorobu* came first (and established the terminology) while *mine* developed later. As we shall see, the reality is more complex, as the Orokaiva use two types of affinal terminology: one type which is consistent with generalised exchange and another which is consistent with direct exchange. The former of these two types of terminology is in regular use by men and the latter by women. This fact is consistent with the theory that the Orokaiva marriage system is a combination of generalised and restricted exchange.

For the purpose of a componential analysis of terms we shall consider only terms used in face-to-face interaction by *ego* to address an *alter* when no other relative is present. The following dimensions of contrast apply:

Consanguine(C): *Ego* traces relationship to *alter* through a chain of linkages based on filiation, or a shared clan name, or common birth in a distant village.

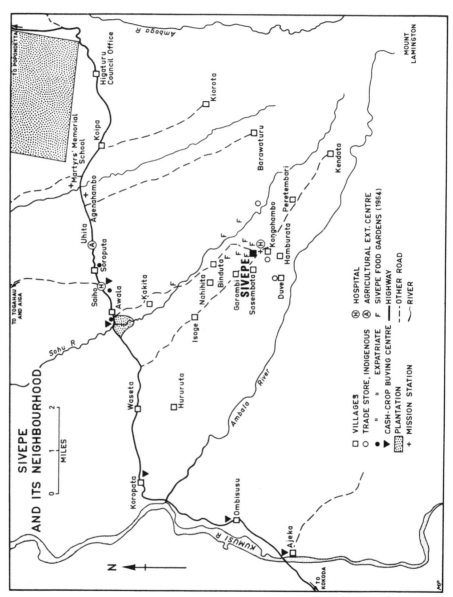

Fig. 10. Sivepe and its neighbourhood.

Affine (A): Spouses of consanguines of own and junior generation; co-eval and senior consanguines of those spouses.
Generational Removal: G–O: Same generation as *ego*. G1: One generation removed. G2: Two or more generations removed.
Sex of alter: M: Male; F: Female.
Sex of ego: Em: Male *ego* Ef: Female *ego*
Relative sex of ego and alter: SS: Same sex. OS: opposite sex.
Relative sex in consanguineal linkages; / /: Relationship is either wholly agnatic or wholly uterine. X: relationship is neither wholly agnatic nor wholly uterine. It passes through at least one opposite-sex linkage.
Marriageability (same generation only): Ma: Relationship belongs to marriageable category. NMa: Relationship belongs to non-marriageable category.
Relative age of alter: Sr: Older. Yr: Younger.

Using this code, we may define in the following way the kinship terms used in addressing consanguines. The bracketed terms are in the dialects from which Williams' information is drawn.[1]

epe:	M	Sr	G2			C	(Williams: *ahije*)
	M	Sr	G1	X		C	(Williams: *nobo*)
jape:	F	Sr	G2			C	(Williams: *ahije*)
mama:	M	Sr	G1	/ /		C	
aja:	F	Sr	G1	/ /		C	
tata:	F	Sr	G1	X		C	
apa:	SS	Sr	G–O	/ /		C	(Williams: *bitepemi*)
	SS	Sr	G–O	X	NMa	C	(Williams: *simbo*)
eambo:	SS	Jr	G–O	/ /		C	(Williams: *biteambo*)
	SS	Jr	G–O	X	NMa	C	(Williams: *simbo*)
du:	OS		G–O	/ /		C	
	OS		G–O	X	NMa	C	
simbo:			G–O	X	Ma	C	
meni:	M	Jr	G1	/ /		C	(Williams: *mei*)
iai:	F	Jr	G1	/ /		C	
ahije:		Jr	G1	X		C	
		Jr	G2			C	

This componential analysis, prepared from Orokaiva ideological statements, contains all the ambiguities characteristic of the system itself. Different local clan groups are supposed to use sibling terms in addressing each other. But this is above all a strategic device to emphasise the obligation of mutual political and military support. Extension of the exogamy rule to distant clansmen would logically follow from their classification as siblings, but serve no useful purpose. On the contrary, if local clan groups live at some distance from one another, the bonds between them will wear rather thin unless intermarriage between them actually does occur. In practice, distant local clan groups are not infrequently used as partners in reciprocating pairs of groups. They are then regarded as not 'really' agnates, and terms of address such as *simbo epe, tata* are used. Once intermarriage has been instituted such terms are regularly transmitted from one generation to the next.

Within the village, two different principles prevail according to the presence or absence of a generation difference. Where a generation difference exists, opposite sex linkages are always expressed in terms of address. A mother's brother is always called *epe*. The *epe/ahije* bond is based on mutual affection and voluntary support, whereas the *mama/meni* bond is based on strong mutual obligations and an authority/obedience relationship. On the other hand, collaterals of the same local clan group will never call each other *simbo* even though biologically they may be cross-cousins. They use sibling terms and are strictly bound by exogamy rules. In a multi-clan village, collaterals of different clans will sometimes use sibling, sometimes cross-cousin terminology. Here the criterion is whether the persons concerned shared a plant emblem (*hae*).

A rule that was expressed to me often and forcibly was that people should not marry if they share a paternal or maternal *hae*. The relationship of a person with his *hae* is one of complete identification. If a man says that his *hae* is *sasaha* grass, he means that *sasaha* grass is his 'ancestor' and that he himself *is sasaha* grass; i.e. he is completely identified with it. If two people are identified with the same plant in this way they are siblings; they cannot possibly be anything else.

In general therefore a *simbo* is someone with whom one does not share a *hae*. This rule obtains whether or not *ego* and *alter* live in the same village. A study of actual kin relationships between *simbo* in different villages bore this out. A typical *simbo* relationship would be between *fafasiso* children/*famobrososo*. The *fafasi's hae* would be transmitted to her son, but not to her son's children. The latter would therefore share no *hae* with the grandmother's natal family. Some *simbo* relationships are far more distant than the one quoted here. A typical example is the following:

Here the *simbo* relationship links families of two villages, Sivepe and Binduta. The genealogical pattern may be accounted for by extremely strong attachment between siblings of opposite sex (*du*), and for the tendency for this strong attachment to be reproduced in the next generation. The genealogical connection between *simbo* often passes between two or more of these *du* linkages. A person thus tends to have numerous *simbo* scattered in many villages with some of which has own village may never have intermarried. Even a limited amount of intermarriage between villages may set up a good number of *simbo* links between them, as the links of filiation and siblingship to which the genealogies refer are often merely classificatory. For instance, the individuals numbered (3) and (4) in the above diagram were not true but classificatory siblings.

It will be noticed that the *simbo* category can be defined only by a series of negative rules. It is a set of distant kinsmen which remains when positively defined sets of consanguines have been excluded. Marriage with the *simbo* cannot therefore be regarded as following the principles of an 'elementary' system of kinship. In practice it does not take many generations before the intermarrying groups forming a 'reciprocating pair' are married out, i.e. unable to supply any further partners to each other. In Sivepe, Jegase and Seho, even with only seven current intermarriages out of sixteen households and a reciprocating relationship of less than three generations, seemed to have nearly exhausted all marital possibilities. The difficulties of my interpreter, a bachelor belonging to the Jegase clan, will serve as an example. He was not allowed to marry the girl he loved (Seho clan) because she was a classificatory mother's sister's daughter. But there would have been equally grave obstacles if he had wished to marry into four of the remaining six Seho households, as the girls of these households shared either his father's or his mother's *hae*. The rule prohibiting marriage with a person sharing a paternal or maternal *hae* has an interesting randomising effect that should be briefly discussed. At least forty-two *hae* were used in Sivepe. The persons sharing these *hae* were by no means always close relatives. They might be wives of Sivepe men, and born in a quite different village. Again, some people had many *hae*, four or five was quite common. In these circumstances the Orokaiva rule could never produce a stable system of four or more sections, as any section might at any time adopt a *hae* which would prevent marriage with another section. Furthermore, any portentous event, such as a woman falling to her death from a certain species of tree, would lead to the introduction of a new *hae* which might be adopted by several persons for reasons of sentiment or religious awe rather than the regulation of future marriages. Finally, individuals not infrequently transmitted maternal *hae* to their children, especially if they resided matrilocally or uxorilocally.

We conclude therefore that the rule of marriage with the *simbo* resembles a game of chance in which the odds become progressively more unfavourable, though the rate at which they become worse is itself determined by chance. In practice, therefore, every village played at many tables at once, not only because of ecological circumstances, vicissitudes of war and the need for alliances, but also because the rules of marriage themselves make no other strategy possible.

7. *Sex Affiliation*

It is an understood principle that under a system of restricted exchange the matrimonial destiny of brother and sister lies in the same kinship group whereas under generalised exchange it is different. Williams' data on the Koiari, as analysed by Lévi-Strauss, show that this tribe strongly emphasises difference of matrimonial destiny by the device of giving the brother a paternal and the sister a maternal clan name. Among the Orokaiva the principle of sex affiliation is likewise utilised, though far more feebly, to convey a simple message. The firmest evidence is found in kinship terminology and in the theory of paternity.

For the purpose of componential analysis of terms used in addressing affines, one dimension of contrast must be added to those given in the previous section. We shall distinguish sister exchange and *dorobu* marriages by the following code:

Min: Sister exchange marriage. *Dor*: Marriage 'by purchase'. Under this code, we may define the following terms:

1. *Terms principally used for addressing consanguines*:

epe:	Ef	M	Sr	Gl	A
	M	Sr	Gl	A	Min
tata:	Ef	F	Sr	Gl	A
	F	Sr	Gl	A	Min
ahije:	F	Jr	Gl	A	
	Jr	Gl	A	Min	

2. *Exclusively affinal terms*

atovo:	Em	M	Sr	Gl //	A	Dor	
imbohi:	Em	F	Sr	Gl	A	Dor	(Williams: *imboti*)
behere:	Em	SS	Gl	X	A	Dor	(Williams: *betere*)
dambo:	Em	SS	G–O //		A		(Williams: *nabori*)
	Em	SS	G–O	X	A		(Williams: *betere*)
hovatu:	OS	G–O	A				
bi:	Ef	SS	G–O	A			
imi:	M	Jr	Gl	A	Dor		

The fact that a brother and sister, upon marriage, use different types of affinal kinship terms corresponds to a fundamental difference in their social position in relation to their affinal family. The brother, under a *dorobu* marriage contract, remains a perpetual debtor to his affines. He has deprived them of their most precious possession, a nubile daughter, without giving a woman in exchange. Even though he has given bridewealth and done bride service, and continued making prestations of many kinds, these propitiatory offerings do not wipe out the debt. The *imi* must therefore always act with humility and feel shame when he meets his *atovo* and even more, his *imbohi*. His sister, however, is under no such burden in her relations with her own affines. Her position is precisely the same, whether the marriage has been established by *mine* or *dorobu*. Her use of consanguineal terminology expresses her far greater familiarity and identification.

It might be argued that such familiarity and identification is the direct consequence of patrilocal virilocal residence, but such residence arrangements do not always lead to the terminological differences I have described. These differences, however, are consistent with an ideology which emphasises the detachment of women from their natal clans and their close attachment to their mother's village to which they are supposed to move upon marriage.

Such an ideology is further emphasised by the Orokaiva notions about paternity. Orokaiva believe that a male child is formed in the womb as the result of sexual congress between father and mother, but that a female child is formed by 'the mother sleeping alone'. The male child therefore carries the 'blood' of the father, enabling the child to carry on the father's lineage, but the female child does not. She is still a member of the paternal clan but the connection is evidently viewed as social rather than physiological. Accordingly all females are named by their mother's consanguines, in contrast to males who may be named by a consanguine of either side, the proper side being determined by a medicine man (See Schwimmer 1969). The effect of this theory is that a woman belongs to her clan in a less absolute sense than a man.

This theory of paternity may be explained teleologically as serving to emphasise the rights and identity of the patriclan in a social system which 'very nearly approaches' bilaterality. In Orokaiva society women very often receive a portion of patrimony land. Their indulgent brothers frequently give lands to their sister's children and such land may well pass into the hands of those children's heirs. Currently, over 50 per cent of cultivated land is owned by persons other than the cultivators, and very often the cultivator's useholds became perpetuated. Such perpetuation proceeds in spite of an explicit rule denying women hereditary rights to their patrimony useholds. The physiological reasoning by which Orokaiva women are denied full clan membership should therefore be interpreted as a symbolic statement insisting on the limits that should be placed upon uterine intrusion on clan property.

When Orokaiva informants are asked why women should not have hereditary rights over land, they usually give as the reason that a woman will marry into a strange clan and village so that it would be dangerous to give her children any rights. Such reasoning goes back to a time when the most frequent marriage forms were abduction and elopement. In practice, the fate of a woman's patrimony rights depends on where she marries: if she does marry in a friendly neighbouring village or by sister exchange, her children will probably keep her property. This is therefore the preferred feminine pattern. But if she is taken by a man from a strange village, her clan rights become precarious. We have already seen that this latter pattern of marriage is forced upon men not only by ecological contingencies but by the marriage rules themselves. Ideological devices to deny women full clan membership are consistent with this pattern. Such devices are inconsistent with restricted marriage exchange, because the latter system depends on the return of a woman's offspring to her natal clan as marriage partners in a later generation. In the Orokaiva system this is envisaged as only one of several structurally recognised possibilities.

8.   The Nature of Orokaiva Bridewealth

The most convenient way of explaining the nature of Orokaiva bridewealth payments (*dorobu*) is by contrasting them with certain types of African bridewealth (*lobola*), as analysed by Lévi-Strauss.[2] Here the recipient applies the gifts, wholly or in large part, to the immediate purchase of wives for himself or his family. *Lobola 'n'est recu que pour commencer, aussitôt, un nouveau circuit . . . Il ne sera jamais consommé, sauf, occasionellement et partiellement, à des fins sacrificielles. A peine reçu, il fera l'objet d'un remploi, sous la forme d'une épouse pour le frère ou le cousin de la jeune marié* (1967:536). Under such a system it could rightly be said that *'la femme fournie en contrepartie est remplacée par une valeur symbolique'* and that the wife-giving families received in return *'la garantie, sous forme de biens privilégiés, de trouver elles-mêmes des épouses '* (*ibid.* 540).

Papuan bridewealth objects, however, cannot generally be applied to the same ends, or are not in practice generally so applied. The most important Orokaiva *dorobu* items are: pigs, taro, pots, bark cloth, feathers and bone and shell ornaments. To this we may add, for modern marriages, money. The pigs are sacrificed and not used for breeding. The pots and bark cloths are kept by the bride or distributed in her family but are not, as a rule, applied towards a future *dorobu.* Feathers and ornaments are kept by the various recipients who use them, may give them away or trade them at their convenience, but there is no fixed practice of applying them especially for *dorobu.* There is no circuit in which wives move in one direction, and *dorobu* in the opposite direction. When a *dorobu* marriage is afoot the prospective bridegroom, the members of his paternal and maternal *hae* and, to a minor extent, other members of his clan, will amass the goods that are necessary. Pigs are specially bred, taro may be specially grown. Birds are hunted for feathers. Trade goods are assembled for the acquisition of ornaments. In modern times, the prospective bridegroom seeks employment to obtain money. If the bride's brother happens to be collecting bridewealth at the time of the wedding, his own task may be facilitated, but he is still expected to show his prowess by going through the same operations as his brother-in-law.

The difference between African and Papuan practice is basically that *lobola* cattle are preserved whereas *dorobu* pigs are sacrificed. Though we are right in supposing *dorobu* to be a set of gift exchange objects, it would be misleading to say that *dorobu* is exchanged for a woman. I have collected detailed information (as yet unpublished) about the symbolic meaning of the transfer of the objects included in *dorobu*. This formation is inconsistent with the theory that these objects are regarded as equivalent to a bride. Also, the especially aggressive behaviour of the bride's parents towards their new *imi* is hard to explain on the assumption that *dorobu* is in any way a symbolic equivalent of the bride.

The main recurrent theme of all informant's statements about *dorobu* marriage is the anger of the bride's parents. This anger is more than a mere psychological state: it is a basic part of the institution. The degree of anger may vary from one case to the next according to the amount of animosity that is felt towards the *imi's* village, family and person. If there is any hint of a breach of the exogamy rules it will be very great; if the *imi's* local clan group has a claim on a wife from the bride's village, the anger may be much less. But some degree of anger is expected in any *dorobu* marriage.

Dorobu is fundamentally a payment for anger.[3] When my interpreter wished to marry a classificatory *mosida* her father, after first refusing outright, finally set a brideprice at a rate more than four times as high as had ever been paid in the village. This was out of the question and my interpreter left the village soon afterwards. People told me this price showed the measure of the man's anger. A similar line of explanation was followed when I asked informants the meaning of the strict rules of avoidance practised towards affines. I asked: 'Why do you behave in this way? Don't you like your *imbohi*?' The reply was: 'I love her very much because it was she who gave me my wife. But I feel ashamed because I shall never be able to repay her.'

It is possible, from the evidence of rites and myths, to reconstruct the significance of the various gifts that compose *dorobu.* Summarising the results of such a reconstruction, I suggest that the gifts of taro and pig both re-enact a sacrifice in primal time where a man, identified respectively with taro and pig, is killed and eaten and is remembered as the demigod who made these gifts to mankind. When such gifts are made today it would seem that the donor is symbolically sacrificing himself to the recipients. The custom of giving clothes and cooking pots goes back to a myth where a woman is described as living alone and naked and without fire, so that she had to prepare her food by letting the sun burn it. Two men came, gave her a skirt, brought her fire and thus acted as her deliverers. These gifts, far from being 'equivalent' to a woman, are male gifts *for* a woman, and emphasise the blessings of the cultural institution of marriage. On the significance of ornaments as part of a wedding gift I am less certain, but the evidence suggests that they are pledges. They are objects of great magical power, the mere possession of which is thought to demonstrate that their owner adheres to moral principles. The gift of such objects to another party demonstrates that the donor possesses such moral objects, pledges that he will show propriety in his behaviour towards the recipient and enjoins the recipient to do the same for him.

In combination, the *dorobu* gifts convey a clear and appropriate message: the wife-taker acknowledges his indebtedness, emphasises that by taking a woman in marriage he conveys a great blessing upon her and makes pledges which ideally are binding on both parties. Acceptance of these gifts need imply no more than that the wife-givers acquiesce in the *status quo* (which has been established by abduction or elopement). Until the affines make counter gifts, *dorobu* does not even establish social relations between the two sides. This does not happen until the bridegroom's sister has bred and given a pig to him and until the bride's mother has bred and given a pig to her son-in-law. It is only then that a limited commensality between the two sides is established: they have a meal together at which the *imbohi* pretends to eat.

The continuing avoidances and dangers characteristic of Orokaiva affinal relations are all of a kind very familiar in other parts of the world, but the less usual feature is that joking relations, coldness and deliberate social distance can be terminated by the cancellation of the debt through exchange marriage. The strife of 'ordinary' affinal relations is seen as part of a longer cycle which stretches from the sister exchange marriage established as ideal by the ancestors to exchange marriages that remain present as a constant possibility.

9. *Application of the Model to Clan Formation*

The model of marriage exchange as presented here envisages the permanent cyclical recurrence, in the history of any given social group, of restricted and generalised exchange, or — as one might say — of a state of matrimonial amity and strife, unity and division. This model is given additional credibility if we consider some Orokaiva theories about social relations and if we consider the processes of clan formation.

On social philosophy only a very brief reference is appropriate here. The Orokaiva believe that due to actions of their primal ancestors, men are in permanent strife with one another and for that reason dwell apart in separate villages. They express this belief quite explicitly when explaining some of their own myths. I have described above (Chapter III) an Orokaiva myth on the origin of feasts, explaining why there is a rule that feasts may be held only when it is ritually established that food will be plentiful.

Discussion of this myth made it clear that the feast is regarded as a purely temporary interruption of the state of strife, but that it can restore a temporary harmony if ritual is properly observed. The feast-givers must have an abundance of food; they must give everything they have to their guests. Their ancestors will then bless them; their enemies will remove evil spells from their lands, and their gardens will greatly prosper afterwards.

At a feast the Orokaiva became ritually and spiritually identified with their primal ancestors and re-enact the peace and harmony that existed in original time before strife began. It was, however, the traditional belief that such a state could not be expected to last; that after the feast strife would re-assert itself. The myth instructed man to hold feasts 'from time to time', the interval between one feast and another being characterised by food shortage and warfare. Peace was not considered to be a possible permanent state, though my informants remarked that since the coming of the white man it had become so.

We find a similar cyclical pattern in the marriage practices of social groups. Let us take as the commencement of the cycle a crisis such as a military defeat or serious quarrel which leads a fragment of a social group to separate, move some distance away and establish a new settlement. Such a group will usually begin to intermarry with new groups using devices such as abduction and elopement. Gradually, they will set up a number of reciprocal arrangements with groups in the vicinity. When relations with reciprocating groups become very close, the time will come, usually after two or three generations, when marriages between these groups become impossible under the rules. At this point the former affines have all been turned into notional consanguines. Unless the two sides quarrel (which is not infrequent), the stage is now set for clan fusion.

, It could be demonstrated, from a detailed analysis of Sivepe marriages, that the composition of both the Seho and the Jegase local clan groups may be explained by this process. Three of the four 'lineages' of which the Jegase group is composed have migrated to Sivepe since the beginning of the century. One of the waves of migrants already bore the clan name Jegase when they lived at Kiorota, their village of origin. The other two groups assumed it quite recently, after more than two generations of residence and intermarriage. Seho was welded together a good deal earlier than Jegase, so that the lineages are no longer commonly distinguished by name, and the ideology of common agnatic origin is far more firmly established. Seho must, however, have had four lineages at one time and I was able to establish the village of origin of three of them, as well as numerous intermarriages with the Seho of Sivepe after arrival. Intermarriage seems to have become more difficult between these Seho lineages about fifty years ago, and fusion must have been complete by 1925. A marriage between two Seho lineages arranged around 1935 was the last, and caused much annoyance though there was no common *hae*.

I am not suggesting that the process described here explains all Orokaiva clan fusions, but only that the marriage system does in fact turn groups of affines into consanguines and that these consanguines if they live close together tend to assume a common clan name. The importance of this process for the study of kinship structure lies in the fact that it is explicable neither by rules of restricted exchange alone, nor by rules of complex generalised exchange alone. If the Orokaiva had only restricted exchange, they would not be periodically forced to look for new groups with whom to intermarry. If the Orokaiva had only complex exchange (as Meggitt seems to believe is the case for all people of the New Guinea Highlands, viz. the Introduction to Glasse and Meggitt, 1969), then there would be no explanation for the various forms of preferential marriage that are still practised and the tendency to establish forms of dual organisation.

From one viewpoint we may say that the Orokaiva system is *'une sorte de faille de l'échange restreint'*, because the Orokaiva are forever trying to re-establish such a system. From another viewpoint it is true that, having entered into new alliances and thus moved in the direction of a system of generalised exchange, they always attempt as soon as possible to convert the new alliance into a moiety system. The fear of setting up alliances with new groups is still very strong today, in spite of wide experience with travel among foreign tribes when men take up wage employment outside their own district. They still marry wives preferably from their own village, or one of the villages with which reciprocal arrangements exist. There was not a single current Sivepe marriage that fell outside this pattern.

It is certainly curious that the chief effect of white contact upon the marriage system was to emphasise the tendency to the formation of moieties through enforced village consolidation. One would have expected that greater physical security, greater mobility and the contacts brought about through labour migration would have widened rather than narrowed the men's matrimonial universe. One imagines that processes of social and economic development must ultimately make an ideology of restricted exchange obsolete. Meanwhile, however, we observe mainly a movement in the opposite direction. Not only has government pressure unintentionally increased the opportunities for village endogamy, and moiety formation, but the combined teaching of government and mission has deprecated elopement marriages, and penalised the showing of hostility between affines. The war expeditions which led indirectly to so many marriages were stopped. The concern with pacification on the part of the authorities led to an even greater preference than previously for 'safe' marriages and therefore a narrowing of the marriage universe. My records show more marriages with partners from distant villages prior to 1915 than can be found over the last generation. It is therefore complex generalised rather than restricted exchange that was (unintentionally) discouraged.

10 Conclusions

This examination of the Orokaiva marriage system indicates that membership in corporate groups (the *hae,* the local clan group and the village) all have a significant influence on marriage choice, not only negatively, by prohibiting certain partners under a rule of exogamy, but also positively, by pursuing from time to time the establishment of forms of dual organisation. Certainly every individual is more or less free to choose between the two existing systems — direct exchange and complex generalised exchange. There is, however, a constant feature on the level of group relationships, namely the existence of reciprocating pairs of groups. Another constant feature is the temporary nature of these reciprocal relationships which must collapse, due to the operation of the rules, after a few generations. This collapse may either take the form of a separation between the two groups or of a fusion into one local clan group. I have shown that the genesis of many Orokaiva local clan groups may be found in this process.

In the terms used in previous chapters one may categorise sister exchange and the women exchanges in reciprocating pairs of groups as phases of cycles of positive reciprocity. On the other hand, marriage by capture and elopement is a phase of a cycle of negative reciprocity. The long series of prestations offered by the bridegroom and the humiliations suffered by him have the effect of shifting the social relationship with the affinal group into a cycle of positive reciprocity. We therefore do not need to suppose that the bride is regarded as symbolically equivalent to *dorobu* as some African analogies might suggest. *Dorobu* is sufficiently explained as a magical device whereby a reversal in the mode of reciprocity (from negative to positive) is effected. The full range of gifts symbolises the wide scope of the resulting social relationship.

The theory assumes a profound dependence upon the affinal group. This dependence is in fact emphasised in many social, economic, political and religious situations. Ideally, an affinal relationship leads to the establishment of a pair of reciprocating groups. In the light of this understanding, it becomes clear that the exchanges analysed in the preceding chapters are consequences of the group relations set up by the marriage system. In chapter V, I showed the prevalence of a principle of dual allegiance resulting from the inheritance of land originally belonging to the mother's brother. I showed that a critical situation arises in the third generation when the uterine family does not renounce its residual rights but the social relations which give reality to these residual rights, viz. dual allegiance, becomes problematical.

The system would appear, indeed, to be so automatically productive of crises that one might wonder how it could ever have been maintained. It becomes much easier to understand if we recognise that the daughter of the marriage is expected to marry in the mother's brother's village. The land can thus revert to the people of the original village by a series of two uterine transfers. The system looks a little like the 'rope' of the Mundugumor (Mead 1935), and the latter may well have a similar explanation. It has a clear political utility as the dual allegiance pattern forms the basis of Orokaiva political alliances. It is buttressed by religious beliefs, as the spirit of a male child may be derived from either an agnatic or a uterine ancestor, by the process of reincarnation to which I have already referred.

Ultimately there would appear to be two possible outcomes of such hereditary land gifts: fusion of the reciprocating pairs of groups into one local clan group and separation on more or less hostile terms. These two outcomes correspond to the two modalities of the marriage system. The hostile modality is not a *failure* of the system but a natural and accepted part of it. Thus, the frequent migration of groups, as evidenced in Sivepe and many parts of New Guinea, should not be regarded as purely adventitious, but is structurally determined as part of a system which, as we have seen, could not work over a long period with a static population.[4]

The frequent exchanges of cooked taro reported in Chapter VI tend to keep reciprocating pairs of groups in a state of pseudo-commensality. They share not only the land but also its products. The symbolic significance of taro, as set out in that chapter, accords with this theory. Symbolically, taro are children of the marriage of the donors; they are constantly being given away both inside and outside the *simbo* relationship.

On the other hand, the pig belongs essentially to the sphere of *dorobu* marriage, not only because pigs are always sacrificed on such occasions, but because they are the institutionalised means whereby a negative cycle of reciprocity can be made positive.

Again, the coconut-betelnut myth has not merely to do with marriage as the union of two partners or even families, but is a charter for the offering of these nuts on the graves of affines by a large group of survivors who gathered for a mortuary ceremony — a ceremony which often brought together a number of entire villages. The ritual celebrates (as the myth also indicates) the ideal of sister exchange marriage.

This brief summary shows the relationship of objects of mediation to social structure. Social structure, in the sense in which I am using the term, is most clearly articulated in the marriage system, though other systems (e.g. institutionalised hereditary friendship) may also provide important clues to the structure. If the study of objects of mediation provides no more than a manual of some Orokaiva magic, the social structure provides the ultimate rationale of this magic. The structure, as analysed in this chapter, has the objectivity of a mathematical formula. The living fabric of the society has a beauty which we can never ignore and which perhaps forms the *raison d'être* of much of our study. We find this living actuality in the magical processes whereby social relationships are established, maintained and broken. We find it in the pattern of alternation of friendship and enmity, in the unpredictability of the duration of any positive or negative cycle. Barnes (1962) came very close to recognising this pattern when he suggested that the difference between African and New Guinean models may be explained by the New Guinean preoccupation with *killing*. Certainly the Orokaiva world view is greatly preoccupied with killing.

Perhaps this is a price one pays for the orientation towards exchange: one must always be prepared to see a positive cycle of reciprocity break down and a negative one begin, often in a most violent manner. Clearly, the corporate group is not a concept which leads to a full understanding of the basic operation of such a culture. It is for this reason that I have attempted an analysis in which the marriage system is the key to the structure and the institutions arise out of the operation of exchange, structured according to magical formulae which are themselves moulded by the marriage system.

REFERENCES

1. Some discrepancies between Williams' terms and mine may be due to local differences or to cultural changes. It is possible that the modern prevalence of the multi-clan village has led to reduced use of the *simbo* category and to the dropping of the term *behere* between members of the same generation. Culture change may also account for the reduced use of self-reciprocal terms between alternate generations.

2.   E. G. and J. D. Krige describe a particularly clear example (1943: Ch. IX; 1939) among the Lovedu.

3.   I discussed in Chapter VII the Orokaiva device of using anger for the mediation of social relations. Monica Wilson has described a somewhat similar mechanism for the Nyakusa (1952: 99–112; 1959: 161, 165, 217). Among the Orokaiva, however, two opposite tendencies are at work: the obligation to express at once the anger one feels and the offender's obligation to assuage that anger (whether justified or not). Much Orokaiva exchange involves prestations made by one party to compensate for anger felt by the other.

While 'anger in the heart' is disapproved by Orokaiva, most actual misfortunes are explained by anger existing in someone else's heart. The guilty person is deemed to be he who, though aware of his anger, does nothing to remove it. It is most often the victim of the angry person's retribution who is expected to feel guilty. One may show anger by harming one*self*. Such action, while overtly non-aggressive, is in fact a threatening signal to the causer of the anger.

4.   A similar discovery was made by Watson (1970) in a paper based on New Guinea Highlands data, entitled 'Society as Organised Flow'.

CHAPTER XI
EPILOGUE

I have not presented in this work all the empirical facts that may be elucidated with the proposed model of Orokaiva society. I have had space to discuss only a small minority of the myths which are at my disposal but there are a number of others that are more readily understood in the light of my analysis of social structure. The description I have given of corporate activities in patrilineal descent groups has been rather summary, even though much additional evidence could have been marshalled presenting them as competitive segments of a wider non-agnatic collectivity. The rather interesting institution of hereditary friendship, between both men and women, has not been described although this forms a not unimportant part of the total exchange network. Indeed, I have not reported the exchange network in much detail at all, largely because this has already been done in my earlier work entitled *Cultural Consequences of a Volcanic Eruption Experienced by the Mount Lamington Orokaiva* (1969).

Many of the facts reported in this earlier work can be more adequately explained in the light of the analysis offered in the present one. Orokaiva reactions to the eruption, for instance, are not easy to account for unless we can explain the powerful driving force of the *iji eha* ideology discussed in Chapter IV above. The earlier work also did not elucidate the relationship between Orokaiva and the white man. It was made clear that this relationship is an ambivalent one, positive when the Orokaiva leader plays the roles of councillor, village constable or 'committee', but negative when he plays the role of organiser of a co-operative or of transmitter of messages with a millenarian import. Although these roles were described in detail, I perhaps did not make it clear enough that they are often played by the same individuals at different times, or at the same time, and that even if they are played by different individuals, these are not necessarily thereby placed in a position of conflict between one another.

We can, however, easily account for this ambivalence if we remember that social exchange between Orokaiva and white authorities is subject to the laws of the exchange system: there is an alternation between positive and negative cycles. Some members of an Orokaiva group may be in a positive cycle of reciprocity with white authority while others are in a negative one. This does not necessarily mean that the members of the Orokaiva group are in conflict with each other. The same members of a community may support both a co-operative to which the administration objects, and a councillor who acts as an administrative mouthpiece.

The facts are that the administration provides valuable benefits (and the mission likewise) so that there is a sound basis for cycles of positive reciprocity.

On the other hand grievances inevitably arise and these are hard to resolve as the Orokaiva and the white man rarely reside in the same village, rarely eat together and very rarely intermarry. Thus the resolution of conflict is never easy as none of the traditional mechanisms is available for shifting a social relationship into a cycle of positive reciprocity. In these circumstances the Orokaiva requires channels for expressing both positive and negative reciprocity. He therefore has both. The importance he attaches to the one or to the other will necessarily fluctuate according to the changing course of events: the relative weight given to benefits received and grievances experienced at a given time.

It is a mistake to assume, as a European is easily inclined to do, that an Orokaiva is either 'friendly' or hostile to him. It would be more accurate to say that an Orokaiva is, at a given time, involved in a positive or negative exchange cycle with many *alters,* both European and Orokaiva. He usually does not have a commitment to these *alters* that goes beyond the history of the social exchange conducted with them. He assumes that if a European values the continuation of a positive cycle, he will provide sufficient benefits to maintain it. If an Orokaiva is unsatisfied with the balance of exchanges he will usually make no secret of his feelings. If a European ignores these feelings one may expect a negative cycle to begin.

My method may thus have some relevance for applied anthropology. It is unwise, in a situation such as the Orokaiva one, to ignore either the millennial-type leadership or the supporters of the administration. Councillors and similar functionaries act as bond-friends of the Europeans. Their role is non-charismatic but they can be influential as mediators in positive social exchange with the authorities. Millennial leaders tend to stand aloof from the authorities, and this, in terms of the Orokaiva system, is an expression of negative reciprocity. They are charismatic mediators in the relationship between their followers and the *dema* figure whose blessings they are endeavouring to obtain.

Now it would be wrong to suppose that the administrative Orokaiva mediators are concerned with socio-economic development whereas the supporters of a millenial movement or crypto-millennial co-operative[1] are not. I have shown in Chapter IV that the ideology of the *iji eha,* under which we may classify all development ideology of the Orokaiva, whether government-sponsored or not, is based on the assumption that the blessings of the modern age derive from a *dema*-like conceptualisation of Jesus Christ. The two types of leaders differ only in the channel of mediation between the people and the *dema*. For the councillor, the blessings are channeled through the government or mission authorities; for the messianic leader they are channelled differently.

P. Lawrence (1963) takes the view that millennial movements are a 'hindrance' rather than a 'help' to economic development in Papua and New Guinea. If the argument I put forward in the preceding paragraph is correct, the Orokaiva view all economic development as ultimately religious, whether it is channelled through a millennarian leader or the government. Lawrence's question then reduces itself to a narrower one: whether a millennarian leader is a 'help or a hindrance' in mediating the ideology of the new age. This question, however, may not be relevant to Orokaiva realities: to the extent that negative reciprocity between Papuan and white is prevalent, the millennarian leader will be valuable as mediator with the *dema* of the *iji eha*. In 1966–7, millennarian leadership among the Orokaiva was relatively unimportant and thus may be ascribed to a relatively high degree of positive reciprocity between Orokaiva and the white authorities. Among the more important benefits received by the Orokaiva were: the success of cash cropping, especially in coffee, the rapid extension of education, health and other valued services, and the rising influence of the Higaturu Local Government Council which was viewed as a gift from the government to the Orokaiva.

A significant growth of millenarianism would therefore indicate a growing emphasis on negative reciprocity. How should it be dealt with? According to the Orokaiva ethos, the authorities should make gifts or concessions to expiate their unsatisfactory performance. Repression of the movement would only perpetuate the negative cycle. Far from regarding the movements as a hindrance to development, I would regard them as a political process: consciously or unconsciously, they are means of bringing pressure to bear upon the authorities. The ultimate pressure is obtaining the benefits of development.

Knowledge of the rules of Orokaiva social exchange may help us to understand not only social but also political and religious patterns because exchange, in the sense in which I have used the term, represents a world view and penetrates a wide range of institutions and situations. If my method is applied to the analysis of millenarian phenomena, those phenomena would need to be described as essentially a mode of pursuing *ivo*. Now I have shown (Chapter VII) that *ivo*, whether under its aspect of expiation or communion, is fundamentally a magical device for the mediation of social relationships. It would follow from this argument that millenarianism has as its ultimate aim the management of social relations with white power bearers. This manipulative aspect of millenarianism is brought out clearly by Burridge (1960) who presents each new phase of the movements in Tangu as an attempt to establish more effective social relations with white powers. I cannot attempt here to prove with any finality that millennial movements are objects of mediation in a negative exchange cycle and that this would explain all their social, economic, political and religous characteristics. My only purpose is to suggest that the method proposed in this work can generate fresh and perhaps interesting hypotheses in many subjects of current interest in Melanesian ethnography.

Throughout this work, I have been concerned to demonstrate a method rather than to expound a theory. If, in conclusion, I shall now make a few theoretical remarks, this is to acknowledge debts rather than to develop new propositions. My debt to Lévi-Strauss is so obvious that little needs to be said about it. I have utilised the methods advocated in virtually all his major works. My use of the concepts of exchange and reciprocity as the basic principles of my analysis is due to the inspiration of Lévi-Struass.

Yet Lévi-Strauss' work has less to say about the methods of ethnography than about the structural analysis that must follow after the ethnography is completed. The profound implications of his thought for the practice of ethnography remain to be elaborated. Here a number of his followers have made valuable contributions which I have found very helpful. I shall confine myself here to mentioning a few examples. Dumont has shown, by practical demonstration, that in societies where positive marriage rules exist, affinity is transmitted from one generation to the next as are consanguineal ties (1957*a*, 1957*b*). Marriage thus acquires a diachronic dimension, a principle I have utilised in analysing Orokaiva social structure on the basis of the marriage rules.

Dutch scholars such as van der Leeden (1960), Pouwer (1955) and Serpenti (1965) attempted to apply Lévi-Straussian methods to the study of New Guinean societies and at once met with a new difficulty: where unilineality is weak or non-existent, an ethnographer using alliance theory is no more able to find rules[2] which unambiguously determine the membership of marriage classes than a descent theorist can determine the membership of corporate groups. In order to overcome the difficulty, Pouwer has developed what he calls the 'configurational approach', a concept I found very useful. He starts from the supposition, derived from Lévi-Strauss, that there are 'universal mental structures' upon which the social structures found throughout the world are based. The diversity of cultures is explained by ecological and historical contingencies. Lévi-Strauss, however, has actually proposed only very few of these universal mental structures: the requirement of a rule that shall be binding, the notion of reciprocity and the synthetic nature of the gift. Pouwer argues that an ethnographer needs to assume a good number of further universal mental structures if he is to make sense of actual societies (Pouwer 1965). For the analysis of New Guinean societies, he adds to Lévi-Strauss' short list: the vertical ordering principle (descent), the horizontal ordering principle (siblingship), the spatial ordering principle (association with land) (Pouwer 1966). Societies vary according to the relative weight they give to each of these structuring principles. If one principle is clearly dominant, the society will have a well-developed system of clear rules governing social behaviour.[3] On the other hand, if several principles are of somewhat similar weight, rules will often tend to be ambiguous or contradictory. Pouwer would not agree that societies of the latter type (under which he classifies New Guinea societies) are 'loosely structured'.[4] He argues instead that the structure has the form of a configuration in which the structuring principles appear as parameters limiting an otherwise free field of action.[5] In order to explain decisions taken within this free field, Pouwer appeals to Firth's principles of social organisation.[6]

I have used the 'configurational approach' by explaining Orokaiva society as the resultant of the interaction between structural principles: agnation and reciprocity. Pouwer's other two ordering principles (spatial and horizontal) have not entered my analysis as I did not wish to complicate it unduly. The spatial ordering principle probably becomes important only if land is in shorter supply than is usual among Orokaiva.[7] The 'horizontal principle' (especially the brother-sister bond) is highly important but I preferred to treat it as the pivot of the exchange system. Burridge (1959) treated siblingship as a basic structural principle among the Tangu[8] but also demonstrated the symbolic equivalence between the brother-sister and husband-wife relationships. I would therefore suggest, at least provisionally, that Pouwer's 'horizontal ordering principle' is more conveniently dissected into (*a*) bonds between siblings of the same sex, where the principle of seniority is usually emphasised, and which may therefore be accounted for by the vertical ordering principle; and (*b*) cross-sexual sibling bonds which may be accounted for by the principle of reciprocity in the same way as conjugal bonds.

As I constructed my configuration of Orokaiva society, on the basis of the principles of agnation and reciprocity, it became obvious that the principle of reciprocity is the stronger one in all social relationships except those within rather small corporate groups. This discovery was by no means novel in the study of Melanesian societies. It was made and elaborately documented by Malinowski in his study of the Trobriand Islands. Malinowski perhaps carried his theoretical reflections upon reciprocity furthest in his book on *Crime and Custom in Savage Society* (1926) where he called reciprocity 'the basis of social structure', and explained it by 'the inner symmetry of all social transactions' and 'the inner symmetry of structure (which) will be found in every savage society'. When Schapera (1957: 147) called the use of this phrase 'extremely rash', he was justified because Malinowski seemed to ignore the vertical ordering principle which is dominant in many societies (including those in which Schapera had the greatest interest) and for which Malinowski's generalisation, of course, does not hold.

Nonetheless, we must recognise that for societies where the principle of reciprocity is dominant Malinowski's work is still highly authoritative. He was certainly right in objecting to the overemphasis placed on corporate group relations by some of his immediate predecessors such as Hartland and Rivers. He was also, in my opinion, extremely wise in his choice of the elements of culture which he singled out for special consideration. His first major work on the Trobriand Islands was, in effect, a full analysis of two objects used for the mediation of social exchange: the necklaces called *soulava* and the armshells called *mwali* (*Argonauts of the Western Pacific*, 1922). This was followed by the work already referred to in which it was shown that conflict resolution does not occur primarily by the application of a system of norms but by transactional processes where moral codes appear as rhetorical devices. Malinowski's book on *The Sexual Life of Savages* (1929) was a continuation of this theme in the area where enduring structured patterns of reciprocity, buttressed by elaborate, clearly formulated codes, are most prevalent, namely the area of affinal relations. He concurrently (1965) turned his attention to mythology and magic, treating mythology as the charter of codes of exchange and magic as an unconnected set of acts for the efficacy of which the myths were the charter.

Malinowski treated magic as determined by the structural principle of reciprocity and subordinated to the dynamics of social exchange. He wrote:

> There is not one single magical act which is not firmly believed to possess a counter-act which, when stronger, can completely annihilate its effects. In certain types of magic . . . the formulas actually go in couples. A sorcerer who learns a performance by which to cause a definite disease will at the same time learn a formula and the rite which can annul completely the effects of his evil magic. (1952, reprinted 1954: 86)

Unfortunately, after developing this insight, Malinowski proceeded to treat magic as a pseudo-science without recognising its implications for the theory of reciprocity.

Perhaps more by accident than by design I have in the present work indulged preoccupations very close to those of Malinowski. I do not even have any fundamental quarrel with my predecessor's description of magic as a 'pseudo-science' as long as I may add the qualification that this 'pseudo-science', at least among Orokaiva, is mainly concerned with the manipulation of social relations. As all misfortunes are explained by Orokaiva as sorcery, and all sorcery serves to mediate negative reciprocity, i.e. enmity either on the part of the living or the dead, therefore all counter-magic is similarly part of a cycle of negative or positive reciprocity. If the counter-magic is made by the victim of sorcery, it mediates a continuing negative cycle. If the counter-magic is made by the same person who made the original black magic or *saruka,* this is done in response to conciliating gestures by the victim and signifies that the exchange has shifted into a positive cycle. Sorcery is not considered good or evil in itself nor does Orokaiva society have clearly defined norms to govern behaviour in most of the situations where it occurs.[9] It is easier to assume that the sorcerer (or his principal) has one idea of what the norms are and the victim has a different idea, and that the society will continue to have conflicting sets of norms irrespective of how the particular conflict is resolved. In some circumstances it is advantageous to shift the social relationship into a positive cycle, whereas in other circumstances it is more advantageous to fight magic with magic.

Having thus acknowledged Malinowski as one of the ancestors of the present work, I should also acknowledge the theoretical work in both sociology and anthropology which helped me to reanalyse Malinowski's data in the manner instanced above. Neither Lévi-Strauss nor his immediate followers were much help in this respect as they have not, until very recently, given detailed attention to questions of process. The study of exchange cycles, as developed in the present work, would be of little value if they were nothing but consequences of enduring structural regularities.[10] In that case there would be no difference between my exchange cycles and the 'situational analysis'[11] developed by Gluckman, Turner and van Velsen (1964). 'Situational analysis' provides meticulous data concerning conflicts involving individuals but it is always assumed that the resolution of the conflicts reasserts rather than changes the existing corporate norms.

We have seen, however, that the corporate norms of Orokaiva society are constantly changing. Clans fuse and split, relations with uterine kin go through positive and negative cycles, moiety systems arise and disintegrate, enemies become partners in alliance systems while the only enduring corporate group, the entended family, where 'situational analysis' would yield satisfactory results, is too narrow a unit for the student of the dynamics of society. Within the extended family, conflicts may actually reassert and strengthen group values. But even in a four-generation agnatic group splitting up of the group after a quarrel is normal and far from being a failure of solidarity. It is part of an atomising process which causes no crisis in the overall exchange network.

In these circumstances the prevailing pattern of social relations can be accounted for most easily by reference to a past sequence of positive and negative exchange cycles. When I speak of structure I am not referring to this ephemeral pattern of social relations but to the laws underlying the generation of the positive and negative cycles. In my discussion of the marriage system, I presented the structure as cyclical alternation of direct and complex generalised marriage exchange. One may call this the law of the operation of the marriage system. On the other hand, when I described the prevailing social organisation of

Sivepe and emphasised its resemblance to a moiety system, I explained this form of organisation by a succession of exchange cycles through which it evolved from an earlier situation when Jegase and Seho were not moieties in any sense but enemies.

This approach to the study of process derives from the anthropologists Barth (1959, 1966) and Belshaw (1967, 1970) and the sociologists Homans (1961) and Blau (1964). The relationship between the two disciplines has been complex one as Homans and Blau tend to use anthropological models in the development of their theories and Barth and Belshaw have been significantly influenced by the sociological clarification of these anthropological models. I shall discuss briefly these theories, taking Blau as my starting point. Blau writes: 'Human beings tend to be governed in their association with one another by the desire to obtain social rewards of various sorts, and the resulting exchanges of benefits shape the structure of social relations' (1964: 18). Blau distinguishes two types of benefits: 'extrinsic' and 'intrinsic'. Benefits of the former type are, in principle, detachable from the association itself, whereas a benefit is 'intrinsic' when the association itself is an intrinsically rewarding experience. In intimate relations of intrinsic significance 'individuals often do favours for one another not in the expectation of receiving explicit repayments but to express their commitment to the interpersonal relation and sustain it by encouraging an increasing commitment on the part of the other' (*ibid.*, 6). Explicit repayment is more important when extrinsic benefits are being exchanged. In my work on the Orokaiva I have dealt mainly with relations where intrinsic benefits were included in the exchange.[12]

Blau would not argue that intrinsic exchange is more 'disinterested' or 'altruistic' than extrinsic exchange. Rather, he would say that in the former case partners are more interested in the association itself than in specific benefits. The latter, Blau says, 'are sometimes primarily valued as symbols of the supportiveness and friendliness they express, and it is the exchange of the underlying mutual support that is the main concern of the participants' (*ibid.*, 95). Even in this case, however, one may speak of an exchange of benefits, as each partner offers 'support' to the other.

Blau uses this theory of social exchange to explain various forms of stratification and inequality. Inequality arises when one person needs something another has to offer but has no resources needed by the other, or needed to the same degree. What can a person do when he is unable to reciprocate? 'First, he may force the other to give him help. Second, he may obtain the help from another source. Third, he may find ways to get along without such help.' If none of these possibilities is open, the person has only one course of action left: 'He must subordinate himself to the other and comply with his wishes, thereby rewarding the other with power over himself as an inducement for furnishing the needed help' (*ibid.*, 21–2). In this way Blau explains how persons may become invested with social power, authority, influence, respect and prestige. In unequal relationships there is an imbalance in the benefits the two persons are able to offer each other; at the same time there is a compensatory power imbalance. The total association may nonetheless be said to be in equilibrium as it is gratifying to both parties. The weaker party offers such benefits as compliance, deference and respect. Unequal relationships of this kind are what Blau calls 'unilateral', as one of the partners always offers one type of benefit (e.g. compliance) whereas the other partner always supplies a different type (e.g. protection). A great many exchanges discussed in this book are 'unilateral' in this sense.

Gouldner, who calls exchanges of this sort 'heteromorphic', rightly points out (1960: 172) that their equivalence cannot be determined objectively but only by actors in the situation. All we may objectively discover is whether they are both satisfied with their deal. If they are very dissatisfied they may break off the relationship or respond by negative sanctions such as sorcery, rebellion or suicide. Often such negative responses will be discontinued if the dissatisfied party is compensated and the 'balance' restored. Actors determine questions of equivalence by the principle of distributive justice, fundamental in my analysis of the Orokaiva data and stated thus by Homans:

> A man in an exchange relation with another will expect that the rewards of each man be proportional to his costs — the greater the rewards and profits of each man be proportional to his investments — the greater the investment, the greater the profit. (1961: 75)

Sociologists have carried out many empirical tests, described by Homans and Blau, to show that social relations follow economic principles of this kind. Although the tests were done with individuals from Western cultures, usually in the environment of a small groups laboratory or an industrial enterprise, Homans and Blau have both argued that the principles are of universal validity. I doubt whether anthropologists would dispute this. On the other hand there has been a tendency for anthropologists not to become absorbed in such invariant social phenomena as it is not immediately obvious how their study could help to explain differences between cultures; in most anthropological theory, culture is treated as a variable.

Yet virtually all anthropological work makes assumptions at one point or another about the universality of some underlying mechanisms of human behaviour. In particular, implicit assumptions are constantly being made in anthropological works about what men find rewarding, not just as members of a particular society but as members of a species (Homans, *ibid.*, 383).

Several schools of anthropology have recently attempted to make such assumptions explicit. The ethnoscientists seek to do this by demonstrating their applicability in every single culture they study. Lévi-Strauss seeks to isolate a set of universal mental structures through his present mythological studies. Firth has postulated a number of universal principles of social organisation. Barth and Belshaw have adopted the social exchange theory of Homans and Blau as the basis for an anthropological theory which treats social behaviour as basically economic and which aims to explain social forms by social process (Barth) and to measure the performance of social systems (Belshaw). While this anthropological theory does not significantly diverge from Homans and Blau, it develops in more detail an explanation of the genesis of value systems. It exposes as questionable a traditional assumption made by anthropologists that the value systems with which they are dealing are in a state of perfect integration. Barth showed the co-existence of several 'paradigms' (i.e. value systems) in the same culture and argued that the relative priority of these paradigms depends on transactional contingencies.

We are thus able to understand Pouwer's 'configurational approach' from a wider perspective. At any one time, a number of paradigms are present in a culture. There is no reason why they should be integrated. After a given time, a number of transactions take place and if conditions change one paradigm may acquire relatively greater weight than the other. In our study of the Orokaiva we found that this was happening with respect to the paradigms of direct and complex generalised exchange. We found two types of changes: a cyclical movement between the two paradigms caused by the internal dynamic of the system and an irreversible change under the impact of an external force. Both types of change were predictable from the model: a cyclical change was determined by the forces within the model itself whereas the irreversible change was predictable from our knowledge of the external force (Australian intervention).

Barth rightly argues that such predictions are possible only if our model of the society in question is economical and reduced to very few basic elements. ('We should not attempt to elaborate a list of all the empirical data on observed relations.') The only weakness in his theory seems to me to lie in his method of arriving at the model. In his essay *Models of Social Organization* he describes his procedure in two different ways which seem contradictory. Taking the example of descent groups and unilineal descent in the Middle East, he first derives his model from a rather familiar discussion by Radcliffe-Brown (Barth 1966: 23). He implies that this theoretical knowledge suffices for the construction of the model. After demonstrating how this simple model can be used to explain why the structure of one Middle East society changed while another rather similar one did not, Barth shyly admits that the Radcliffe-Brown proposition was perhaps not as obvious a basis for his model as he suggested at the outset:

The form of descent groups and political corporations may be shown to vary according to the clear and definable — and perhaps superficially seemingly insignificant — differences with regard to the specific character of descent rights' (*ibid.*, 31).

If the differences were 'superficially seemingly insignificant', how then did Barth find out about their 'real' significance? It would seem that Radcliffe-Brown's essay on 'Patrilineal and Matrilineal Succession' was not the sole genitor of this model but that Barth (*a*) had to collect vast and precise field data; and (*b*) had to reduce the data to a rather abstract model, which reveals the basic elements underlying the social system. The 'minimum of specifications' to which Barth reduced the empirical data of Middle Eastern society do not differ in essence from abstract models such as might have been constructed by Leach or Lévi-Strauss. Transactionalism and structuralism are complementary rather than mutually exclusive as any structure may be regarded simultaneously and without contradiction from the viewpoint of its genesis and the viewpoint of its fundamental laws.[13]

This ends the catalogue of my principal theoretical debts. The exchange cycle model which I used as my principal tool of analysis closely resembles Barth's and Belshaw's concept 'transaction'. It is more elaborate as it makes explicit the distinction between social benefits (in the sense of Homans and Blau) and objects of mediation by which the recipient is induced to participate in social exchange. Although I hope to have shown, in the present work, the practical utility of my model, I readily admit that this is no more than a first step. If intrinsic exchange gifts are 'primarily valued as symbols', as Blau plausibly maintains, then the study of the underlying symbolic systems appears to be a fundamental task for anthropologists. I have not attempted in this book to formulate rules for the construction of exchange cycles. Such rules undoubtedly exist: while the meanings given to the symbols are basically arbitrary, there are still regularities in the manner in which objects of mediation are chosen.

I visualise these regularities as rules of grammar in Chomsky's sense, i.e. an exchange cycle may be called 'grammatical' if it meets certain conditions of adequacy so as to be acceptable in the judgment of a member of the native culture[14] (Chomsky 1957, 1964, 1966). An inquiry into the nature of these conditions of adequacy appears to me a useful next step in the development of a method for the study of exchange.

REFERENCES

1   The fact that Melanesian co-operatives often have millenarian overtones has long been known to both anthropologists and administrators. (See, for instance, Burridge 1960 *passim*; Lawrence 1964: 209.) In the Northern District such somewhat millenarian co-operatives flourished especially shortly after the Second World War. They have been described briefly by Dakeyne (1966), and by myself (Schwimmer 1969: 85–9).

2   Barnes demonstrated this point, I think convincingly, in his well-known essay 'African Models in the New Guinea Highlands' (1962), and in his subsequent rebuttal of Meggitt's counter-claims based on the Mae Enga case (Meggitt 1965, Barnes 1967).

3   Though I do not believe that Orokaiva society can be usefully analysed in this way, I ought to mention that it was done in recent years in the study of Mae Enga (Meggitt 1965), Matupit (Epstein 1964), and Huli (Glasse 1959, 1962).

4   For this concept see also: Brown (1962), Cook (1966), Langness (1964), Newman (1964), Ryan (1959), Vayda and Cook (1964). Barnes (1962) likewise holds that 'apparently arbitrary processes' determine the organisational arrangements of New Guinea peoples. I am more inclined to think that we find an excess of rules and an inherent ambiguity of the rules, as Pouwer also believes. Groves (1963) gives a good example of this tendency among Motu descent groups. Scheffler's analysis of Choiseul society (1964) is also illuminating in this respect.

5   Pouwer provides an enlightening example of his configurational method in his analysis of a Star Mountains tribe (1964). Scheffler's approach (1965) is also configurational. Burridge's studies of Tangu social structure were also in effect following the same viewpoint, though he considered siblingship the dominant principle (Burridge 1957a, 1957b, 1957c, 1957d, 1958).

6   'What the concept of social organisation does is to focus on those aspects of dynamics or process in which *choice* is exercised in a field of available alternatives, resources are mobilised and decisions are taken in the light of probable social costs and benefits.' (Firth 1964: 17)

7   For an example of this approach see Salisbury 1956, 1962: 83–4. The theoretical implications of such cases have been clearly demonstrated by Leach in *Pul Eliya* (1961).

8   See also Goodenough (1962), Langness (1964), and van der Leeden (1960) for discussions of Melanesian societies where siblingship rather than descent tends to determine the membership of corporate groups. The fullest description of a social structure based on the principles of siblingship is probably still Pehrson (1957) on the Lapps.

9   The view of sorcery presented here is close to Marwick's (see especially Marwick 1952, 1963). There are many situations among the Orokaiva, as among the Cewa, where social structure does not eliminate or regulate the competition for valued goals. Regulation (at least among the Orokaiva) occurs through the exchange system and sorcery becomes a competitive device. If A is injured, B can gain transactional advantage if it is believed B is the sorcerer. On the other hand, A may profit if he accuses B of sorcery while knowing B's powers are small.

10   A number of followers of Radcliffe-Brown have remarked on the importance of exchange in New Guinea societies. (See, for instance, Reay 1959, Berndt 1962, Kaberry 1967.) While advocating and practising careful study of the transactional aspects of New Guinea societies, they are hampered by a theory which accords the principle of reciprocity no structural significance. When Kaberry (1967) discusses normative systems, she seems to regard these systems as relying for their coherence solely on the principle of unilineal descent.

11   Situational analysis is always explicitly based on an equilibrium theory. Gluckman especially has often expressed the strongest objections to exchange theory even though he and his school have made a remarkable contribution to the study of the manipulative, bargaining, transactional approach to life (see Gluckman, 1955, 1968 and Paine 1968; Turner 1957 and Stanner 1959; Van Veisen 1964).

12   Although in this discussion I have dealt almost entirely with intrinsic exchange (which is by far the most common among the Orokaiva), I am well aware of the importance of extrinsic exchange in New Guinea (see for instance Pospisil 1964).

13   This point is argued in more detail and very convincingly by Jean Pouillon in 'Sartre et Lévi-Strauss, Analyse Dialectique d'une relation dialectique/analytique' (1966). It also emerges clearly in Godelier's discussion on the object and methods of economic anthropology (1965) where he distinguishes three levels: the transactional, the conscious model and 'unconscious rationality' which represents deeper structural laws.

14   Pierre Boudon (1967, 1968) has begun the development of a theoretical model for this purpose thus foreshadowing some of the ideas presented in the present work. The method I propose here for the application of Chomsky's generative grammar to the study of exchange systems is, however, by no means the same as Boudon's.

BIBLIOGRAPHY

Barnes, J. A., 1962: 'African Models in the New Guinea Highlands', *Man*, LXII, No. 2.

——, 1967: 'Agnation Among the Mae Enga: A Review Article', *Oceania*, XXXVIII: 33–43.

Barnett, Homer G., n.d.: 'A Comparative Study of Culture Change and Stability in Displaced Communities in the Pacific', University of Oregon, mimeo.

Barrau, Jacques, 1965: 'L'humide et le sec', *Journal of the Polynesian Society*, Vol. 74: 329–46.

Barth, Fredrik, 1966: *Models of Social Organization*, London, R.A.I. Occasional Paper No. 23.

Bateson, Gregory, 1958: *Naven* (2nd ed.), Stanford University Press.

Beaver, Winifred N., 1916: 'Kumusi Division', in: Commonwealth of Australia, *Papua Annual Report for the Year 1914–15*, pp. 48–55, Melbourne, Government of the Commonwealth of Australia.

——, 1920: 'The Use of Emblems or Insignia of Man-Killing among the "Orokaiva" Tribes of the Kumusi Division', in: Commonwealth of Australia, *Papua Annual Report for the Year 1918–19*, pp. 97–9, Melbourne, Government of Commonwealth of Australia.

Belshaw, C. S., 1951a: 'Resettlement in the Mount Lamington Area', MS filed New Guinea Research Unit, Port Moresby.

——, 1951b: 'Social Consequences of the Mount Lamington Eruption', *Oceania*, XXI: 241–52.

——, 1965: *Traditional Exchange and Modern Markets*, Englewood Cliffs, N.J.: Prentice-Hall.

——, 1967: 'The Conditions of Social Performance', Vancouver, mimeo.

——, 1967: 'Theoretical Problems in Economic Anthropology' in: *Social Organisation, Essays Presented to Raymond Firth*, ed: Maurice Freedman, pp. 25–42.

Benson, Canon James, 1955: 'The Bapa Saga and the Brothers Ambo', The Anglican (Melbourne), 4 March, p. 6.

——, 1955: 'Kikiri and Gatara', *The Anglican* (Melbourne), 18 March, p. 6.

Berndt, R. M., 1962: *Excess and Restraint*, Social Control among a New Guinea Mountain People, University of Chicago Press.

Blau, Peter, 1964: *Exchange and Power in Social Life*, New York, Wiley.

Bohannan, Paul, 1955a: 'Some Principles of Exchange and Investment Among the Tiv', *American Anthropologist*, 57: 60–70.

——, 1955b: 'The Impact of Money on an African Subsistence Economy', *Journal of Economic History*, XIX, No. 4.

Boudon, Pierre, 1967: 'Essai sur l'interprétation de la notion d'échange', *L'Homme* VII (2): 64–84.

——, 1968: in 'À propos de la notion d'échange et de la grammaire générative, Discussion, par Dan Sperber et Pierre Boudon', *L'Homme* VIII (2): 104–19.

Brookfield, H. C., 1966: 'An Assessment of Natural Resources', in: *New Guinea on the Threshold*, (ed. E. K. Fisk), pp. 44–79, Canberra, Australian National University Press.

—— and Paula Brown, 1963: *Struggle for Land*, Melbourne.

Brown, Paula, 1962: 'Non-Agnates among the Patrilineal Chimbu', *Journal of the Polynesian Society*, 71:57–69.

Bulmer, R., 1960: 'Political Aspects of the Moka Ceremonial Exchange System among the Kyaka People of the Western Highlands of New Guinea', *Oceania* 31.

Burridge, K. O. L., 1957*a*: 'Disputing in Tangu', *American Anthropologist*, 59: 763–80.

———, 1957*b*: 'Friendship in Tangu', *Oceania* XXVII: 177–89.

———, 1957*c*: 'The Gagai in Tangu', *Oceania* XXVIII: 56–72.

———, 1957*d*: 'Descent in Tangu', *Oceania* XXVIII: 85–99.

———, 1958: 'Marriage in Tangu', *Oceania* XXIX: 44–61.

———, 1959: 'Siblings in Tangu', *Oceania* XXX, 128–54.

———, 1960: *Mambu (A Melanesian Millennium)*, London, Methuen.

———, 1965–6: 'Tangu Political Relations', *Anthropological Forum*, I: 393–411.

———, 1969*a*: *New Heaven, New Earth*, Oxford, Basil Blackwell.

———, 1969*b*: *Tangu Traditions*, Oxford, Clarendon Press.

Capell, A, n.d.: Unpublished manuscripts concerning the Binandere group of languages.

Chignell, Arthur Kent, 1911: *An Outpost in Papua*, London, Smith, Elder.

Chinnery, E. W. P. and W. N. Beaver, 1915: 'Notes on the Initiation Ceremonies of the Koko, Papua', *Journal of the R.A.I.*, XLV: 69–78.

———, 1916: 'The Movements of the Tribes of the Mambare, Division of Northern Papua', and a Language chart of the Northern Districts of Papua, being Appendices 2 and 3 of *Commonwealth of Australia: Papua Annual Report for the Year 1914–15*, pp. 158–70, Melbourne, Government of Commonwealth of Australia.

Chinnery, E. W. P. and A. C. Haddon, 1917: 'Five New Religious Cults in British New Guinea', *Hibbert Journal*, vol. 15: 448–63.

Chomsky, Noam, 1957: *Syntactic Structures*, The Hague, Mouton.

———, 1964: 'On the notion "rule of grammar"', and 'A transformational approach to syntax', in J. Fodor and J. Katz, eds., *Structure of Language: readings in the philosophy of language*, Englewood Cliffs, N.J., Prentice-Hall.

———, 1966: *Topics in the Theory of Generative Grammar*, The Hague, Mouton.

Commonwealth of Australia, 1966: *Annual Report to Parliament on the Territory of Papua* for the Year ending 30 June 1965, Canberra.

Cook, Edwin A., 1966: 'Cultural Flexibility: Myth and Reality', *Anthropos* 61: 831–8.

Craig, Ruth, 1969: 'Marriage Among the Telefolmin', in: *Pigs, Pearlshells and Women* (eds. R. M. Glasse and M. J. Meggitt), pp. 176–97, Englewood Cliffs, N.J., Prentice-Hall.

Crocombe, R. G., 1964: *Communal cash Cropping among the Orokaiva, New Guinea Research Unit Bulletin* No. 4.

———, 1966: 'A Modern Orokaiva Feast', in *Orokaiva Papers, New Guinea Research Bulletin*, No. 13, pp. 69–78.

———, 1967: 'Four Orokaiva Cash Croppers', *New Guinea Research Bulletin* 16: 3–22.

——— and G. R. Hogbin, 1963: *Land, Work and Productivity at Inonda, New Guinea Research Unit Bulletin*, No. 2.

CSIRO 1964: 'General Report on lands of the Buna-Kokoda Area, Territory of Papua and New Guinea', *CSIRO Land Research Series*, No. 10.

Cunnison, Ian, 1954: (translator): *The Gift* by Marcel Mauss, London, Cohen and West.

Dakeyne, R. B., 1966: 'Co-operatives at Yega', in *Orokaiva Papers*, pp. 53–68, *New Guinea Research Bulletin*, No. 13.

Dumont, Louis, 1957a: *Hierarchy and Marriage Alliance in South Indian Kinship*, Occasional Papers of the R.A.I., No. 12.

——, 1957b: *Une Sous-Caste de L'Inde du Sud*, Paris – The Hague, Mouton.

Dupeyrat, André, 1965: 'Essai de classification des peuplades de la Papouasie', Ch. III, 'Les peuplades du littoral septentrional de la péninsule papoue', *Journal de la Société des Océanistes*, XXI 79–104.

Durkheim, Emile, 1961: *The Elementary Forms of Religious Life*, New York, Collier.

Epstein, A. L., 1964: 'Variation and Social Structure: Local Organisation on the Island of Matupit, New Britain', *Oceania*, XXXV: 1–25.

Erikson, Erik H., 1963: *Childhood and Society* (2nd. ed.), New York, W. W. Norton.

Evans-Pritchard, E. E., 1939: 'Nuer Time Reckoning', *Africa*, Vol. 12, No. 2.

——, 1956: *Nuer Religion*, Oxford University Press.

Firth, R., 1939: *Primitive Polynesian Economy*, London.

——, 1951: *Elements of Social Organisation*, London, Watts.

——, 1959: *Economics of the New Zealand Maori*, Wellington, Government Printer.

——, 1964: *Essays in Social Organisation and Values*, London School of Economics, Monographs in Social Anthropology, No. 28.

——, 1967: 'Themes in Economic Anthropology: A General Comment', in: *Themes in Social Anthropology*, (ed. R. Firth), London, A.S.A. Monographs 6.

Geertz, Clifford, 1966: *Agricultural Involution*, University of California Press.

Gentzen, Gerhard, 1934: 'Untersuchungen ueber das logische Schliessen', *Mathematische Zeitschrift*, 39: 176–210, 405–431. Translated with commentary as: *Recherches sur la déduction logique*, Presses Universitaires de France, 1955.

Glasse, R. M., 1959: 'Revenge and Redress among the Huli: a Preliminary Account', *Mankind* V: 277–89.

——, 1962: *The Cognatic Descent System of the Huli of Papua*, Canberra, Australian National University.

Gluckman, Max: 1955: *Custom and Conflict in Africa*, Oxford, Basil Blackwell.

——, 1965: Politics, *Law and Ritual in Tribal Society*, Oxford, Basil Blackwell.

——, 1968: 'Psychological, Sociological and Anthropological Explanations of Witchcraft and Gossip', *Man* 3: 305–8.

Godelier, Maurice, 1965: 'Objet et méthodes de l'anthropologie économique', *L'Homme* V: 32–91.

Goodenough, Ward E., 1962: 'Kindred and Hamlet in Lalkai, New Guinea', *Ethnology* I: 5–12.

Gouldner, Alvin W., 1960: 'The Norm of Reciprocity: A Preliminary Statement', *American Sociological Review*, 25: 161–78.

Grace, George W., 1968: 'Classification of the Languages of the Pacific', in: *Peoples and Cultures of the Pacific* (ed. A. P. Vayda), pp. 63–79, New York, Natural History Press.

Groves, Murray, 1963: 'Western Motu Descent Groups', *Ethnology* II: 15–30.

Hobbes, Thomas, 1965: *Leviathan*, London, Everyman.

Hogbin, G. R., 1966: 'An Orokaiva Marriage', *Orokaiva Papers*, New Guinea Research Bulletin, No. 13, pp. 79–101.

Hogbin, Ian, 1967: 'Land Tenure in Wogeo', in: *Studies in New Guinea Land Tenure*, pp. 1–44, Sydney University Press.

Homans, George C., 1961: *Social Behaviour: Its Elementary Forms*, London, Routledge and Kegan Paul.

Howlett, Diana R., 1965: *The European Land Settlement Scheme at Popondetta*, New Guinea Research Unit Bulletin No. 6.

Hubert, Henri and Marcel Mauss, 1964: *Sacrifice: Its Nature and Function*, London, Cohen and West.

Jarvie, I., 1964: *The Revolution in Anthropology*, London, Routledge and Kegan Paul.

Jensen, Ad. E., 1960: *Mythos und Kult bei Naturvoelkern*, (2nd. ed.) Wiesbaden, Steiner.

Kaberry, Phyllis M., 1967: 'The Plasticity of New Guinea Kinship', in *Social Organisation*, Essays Presented to Raymond Firth, London, Cass.

Keesing, Felix M., 1952: 'The Papuan Orokaiva Vs Mount Lamington: Cultural Shock and its Aftermath', *Human Organisation*, 11, #1.

Kelman, Herbert C., 1962: 'Processes of Opinion Change' in *The Planning of Social Change* (eds. W. G. Bennis, K. B. Benne, R. Chin), New York, Holt, Rinehart and Winston, pp. 509–27.

King, the Rev. Copland, 1927: *Grammar and Dictionary of the Binandere Language*, Sydney, D. S. Ford.

Klingebiel, A. A. and P. H. Montgomery, 1961: *Land capability and classification*, Agricultural Handbook 210, Soil Conservation Service, U.S. Department of Agriculture.

Krige, E. G. and J. D., 1939: 'The Significance of cattle exchange in Lovedu Social Structure', *Africa*, Vol. XII.

——, 1943,: *The Realm of the Rain Queen*, London, Oxford University Press for International African Institute.

Landtman, Gunnar, 1927: *The Kiwai Papuans of British New Guinea*, London, Macmillan.

Lane, R. B., 1965: 'The Melanesians of South Pentecost, New Hebrides', in: *Gods, Ghosts and Men in Melanesia*, (eds. P. Lawrence and M. J. Meggitt), Melbourne, Oxford University Press.

Langness, L. L., 1964: 'Some Problems in the Conceptualisation of Highlands Social Structure', *American Anthropologist*, #4, Pt. 2: 162–82.

Lawrence, Peter, 1963: 'Religion: Help or Hindrance to Economic Development in Papua and New Guinea?', *Mankind*, Vol. 6, No. 1: 3–11.

——, 1964: *Road Belong Cargo*, Manchester University Press.

——, 1967: 'Land Tenure Among the Garia', in *Studies in New Guinea Land Tenure*, pp. 91–148, Sydney University Press.

Lawrence, P. and M. J. Meggitt, 1965: 'Introduction' in *Gods, Ghosts and Men in Melanesia* (ed. P. Lawrence and M. J. Meggitt), Melbourne, Oxford University Press, pp. 1–26.

Leach, E. R., 1954: *Political Systems of Highland Burma*, London, Bell.

——, 1961a: *Rethinking Anthropology*, London School of Economics Monographs on Social Anthropology, No. 22.

——, 1961b: *Pul Eliya, A Village in Ceylon*, London, Cambridge University Press.

Leeden, A. C. van der, 1960: 'Social Structure in New Guinea', *Bijdragen tot de Taal-, Land- en Volkenkunde* 116: 119–49.

Lévi-Strauss, Claude, 1949: *Les structures élémentaires de la parenté*, Paris, Presses Universitaires de France.

——, 1958: *Anthropologie structurale*, Paris, Plon.

——, 1961: 'Le geste d'Asdiwal', *Les Temps Modernes*, no. 179.

——, 1962: *La pensée sauvage*, Paris, Plon.

——, 1962T: *Le totémisme aujourd'hui*, Paris, Presses Universitaires de France.

——, 1964: *Mythologiques I: Le cru et le cuit*, Paris, Plon.

Lévi-Strauss, Claude, 1966: *Mythologiques II: Du miel aux cendres*, Paris, Plon.
——, 1966: 'Introduction à l'oeuvre de Marcel Mauss', in Marcel Mauss, *Sociologie et anthropologie*: ix–lii, 3rd. ed., Paris, Presses Universitaires de France.
——, 1967: *Les structures élémentaires de la parenté*, 2nd. ed., The Hague, Mouton.
——, 1968: *Mythologiques III: L'origine des manières de table*, Paris, Plon.
Mair, Lucy P., 1948: *Australia in New Guinea*, London, Christopher.
Malinowski, Bronislaw, 1920: 'Kula; the Circulating Exchange of Valuables in the Archipelagoes of Eastern New Guinea', *Man*, No. 51.
——, 1922: *Argonauts of the Western Pacific*, London, Routledge and Kegan Paul.
——, 1925: 'Magic, Science and Religion', in *Science, Religion and Reality*, ed. J. A. Needham, London, (reprinted Malinowski 1954).
——, 1926: *Crime and Custom in Savage Society*, International Library of Psychology, Philosophy and Scientific Method, London and New York.
——, 1926M: *Myth in Primitive Psychology*, Psyche Miniatures, gen. ser. No. 6, London (reprinted Malinowski 1954).
——, 1929: *The Sexual Life of Savages in North-Western Melanesia*, London.
——, 1954: *Magic, Science and Religion and Other Essays*, New York, Doubleday.
Marwick, M., 1952: 'The Social context of Cêwa witch beliefs', *Africa*, 22: 120–135 and 215–33.
——, 1963: 'The Sociology of Sorcery in a Central African Tribe', *African Studies* 22 (1): 1–21.
Mauss, Marcel, 1966: *Sociologie et anthropologie*, Paris, Presses Universitaires de France, 3rd ed. (expanded).
——, 1967: *Manuel d'ethnographie* (2nd. ed.) Paris, Payot.
——, 1968: Oeuvres 1: *Les fonctions sociales du sacré*, Paris, Les éditions de Minuit.
Mead, Margaret, 1935: *Sex and Temperament in Three Primitive Societies*, London, Routledge.
Meggitt, M. J., 1965(*a*): *The Lineage System of the Mae-Enga of New Guinea*, Edinburgh, Oliver and Boyd.
——, 1965*b*: 'The Mae Enga of the Western Highlands', in *Gods, Ghosts and Men in Melanesia* (eds. P. Lawrence and M. J. Meggitt), pp. 105–31, Melbourne, Oxford University Press.
Meggitt, J. J., 1969: 'Introduction' in *Pigs, Pearlshell and Women* (eds. R. M. Glasse and M. J. Meggitt), pp. 1–15, Englewood Cliffs, N.J., Prentice-Hall.
Monckton, C. A. W., 1921: *Some Experiences of a New Guinea Resident Magistrate*, London, John Lane, The Bodley Head.
——, 1922: *Last Days in New Guinea*, London, John Lane, The Bodley Head.
——, 1934: *New Guinea Recollections*, London, John Lane, The Bodley Head.
Morrawetz, D., 1967: 'Land Tenure Conversion in the Northern District of Papua', *New Guinea Research Bulletin*, no. 17.
Murray, J. H. P. (Sir Hubert), 1912: *Papua or British New Guinea*, London.
Nadel, S. F., 1957: *The Theory of Social Structure*, Melbourne University Press.
Newman, Philip L., 1964: 'Religious Belief and Ritual in a New Guinea Society', *American Anthropologist*, 66: #4, Pt. 2: 257–72.
——, 1965: *Knowing the Gururumba*, New York, Holt, Rinehart and Winston.
Paine, Robert, 1968: 'Gossip and Transactions', *Man* 3: 305–8.
Panoff, M., 1968: 'The Notion of Time among the Maenge People of New Britain', Port Moresby, mimeo.

Parker, R. S., 1966: 'The Growth of Territory Administration', in: *New Guinea on the Threshold* (ed. E. K. Fisk), pp. 187–220, Canberra, Australian National University Press.

Pehrson, Robert N., 1957: *The Bilateral Network of Social Relations in Konkama Lapper District*, Bloomington, Indiana University Publications.

Plant, H. T., 1951: 'Re-establishmet of the Isivita Villages', Port Moresby, New Guinea Research Unit Library.

Pocock, David F., 1964: 'The Anthropology of Time Reckoning', *Contributions to Indian Sociology*, 7: 18–29.

Pospisil, Leopold, 1964: *The Kapauku Papuans of West New Guinea*, New York, Holt, Rinehart and Winston.

Pouillon, Jean, 1966: 'Sartre et Levi-Strauss, Analyse Dialectique d'une relation dialectique/analytique', *L'Arc* 26: 60–65.

Pouwer, Jan, 1955: *Enkele aspecten van de Mimika-cultuur*, The Hague, Staatsdrukkerij en Uitgeversbedrijf.

——, 1961: 'New Guinea as a Field for Ethnological Study', *Bijdragen tot de Taal –, land – en Volkenkunde*, 117: 1–24.

——, 1964: 'A Social System in the Star Mountains: towards a reorientation of the study of social systems', *American Anthropologist*, 66, No. 4, Pt. II, 133–62.

——, 1965: 'De structurele methode in punten', University of Amsterdam, mimeo.

——, 1966b: 'Structure and Flexibility in a New Guinea Society', *Bijdragen tot de Taal-, Land- en Volkenkunde*, 122: 158–69.

——, 1966a: 'Toward a Configurational Approach to Society and Culture in New Guinea', *Journal of the Polynesian Society*, 75: 267–86.

Radcliffe-Brown, A. R., 1951: 'The Comparative Method in Social Anthropology', in: *Journal of the R.A.I.*, Vol. 81, Parts I and II.

Raglan, Lord, 1963: 'Kinship and Inheritance', *Studies in Kinship and Marriage* (ed. I. Schapera), London, R.A.I.

Rappaport, Roy A., 1968: *Pigs for the Ancestors*, New Haven, Yale University Press.

Read, K. E., 1959: 'Leadership and Consensus in a New Guinea Society', *American Anthropologist* 61: 425–36.

Reay, Marie, 1953: 'Social Control among the Orokaiva', *Oceania*, XXIV: 110–18.

——, 1959: *The Kuma, Freedom and Conformity in the New Guinea Highlands*, Melbourne University Press.

Rimoldi, Max, 1966: *Land Tenure and Land Use among the Mount Lamington Orokaiva*, New Guinea Research Bulletin, No. 11.

Ryan, D. J., 1959: 'Clan Formation in the Mendi Valley', *Oceania*, XXIX: 259–89.

Sahlins, Marshall D., 1963: 'Poor Man, Rich Man, Big-Man, Chief', Comparative Studies in Society and History 5: 283–300.

——, 1965a: 'On the Sociology of Primitive Exchange', *A.S.A. Monographs*, No. 1: 139–236.

——, 1965b: 'Exchange Value and the Diplomacy of Primitive Trade', *Proceedings of the 1965 Spring Meeting*, American Ethnological Society, pp. 95–129.

——, 1968: 'Philosophie politique de l'"Essai sur le don" ', *L'Homme*, VIII (4): 5–17.

Salisbury, R. F., 1956: 'Unilineal Descent Groups in the New Guinea Highlands', *Man*, LVI: No. 2.

234   *Exchange in the Social Structure of the Orokaiva*

Salisbury, R. F., 1962: *From Stone to Steel*, Melbourne University Press.
Sartre, Jean-Paul, 1960: *Critique de la raison dialectique*, Paris.
Schapera, I, 1957: 'Malinowski's Theories of Law', in: *Man and Culture* (ed. Raymond Firth), London, Routledge and Kegan Paul, 139—56.
Scheffler, Harold W., 1965: *Choiseul Island Social Structure,* University of California Press.
Schutz, Alfred, 1967: *Collected Papers* I, The Hague, Nijhoff.
Schwimmer, Erik G., 1967: 'Modern Orokaiva Leadership', *Journal of the Papua New Guinea Society*, Vol. 1 (2): 52—60.
——, 1969: *Cultural Consequences of a Volcanic Eruption Experienced by the Mount Lamington Orokaiva,* Eugene, University of Oregon, Comparative Study of Cultural Change and Stability in Displaced Communities in the Pacific, Report No. 9.
——, 1969V: 'Virgin Birth', *Man* 4: 132—3.
——, 1970: 'Alternance de l'échange restreint et de l'échange généralisé dans le système matrimonial orokaiva', *L'Homme*, X, (4), 5—34.
Serpenti, L. M., 1965: *Cultivators in the Swamps*, Assen, van Gorcum.
Simonis, Yvan, 1968: *Claude Lévi-Strauss ou la 'Passion de l'Inceste'*, Paris, Aubier-Montagne.
Smith, Robertson, 1889: *The Religion of the Semites*, London.
Sperber, Dan, 1968: 'Le structuralisme en anthropologie', in: *Qu'est ce que le structuralisme?*, Paris, Editions du Seuil, pp. 167—238.
Stanner, W. E. H., 1959: 'Continuity and Schism in an African Tribe: a Review', Oceania, XXIX: 208—17.
——, 1953: *The South Seas in Transition*, Sydney, Australasian Publishing Co.
——, 1960—3: 'On Aboriginal Religion', *Oceania*, XXX, 108—27; 245—78; XXXI 100—20; 233—58; XXXII: 79—108; XXXIII 239—73.
Steiner, Franz, 1954: 'Notes on Comparative Economics', *British Journal of Sociology* V: 118—29.
Strathern, Andrew, 1966: 'Despots and Directors in the New Guinea Highlands', *Man* (n.s.) 1:356—67.
——, 1969: 'Descent and Alliance in the New Guinea Highlands', *Proceedings of the R.A.I. for 1968*, pp. 37—52.
Taylor, G. A., 1958: 'The 1951 Eruption of Mount Lamington', Canberra, Department of National Development, *Bureau of Mineral Resources Geology and Geophysics Bulletin*, No. 38.
Thurnwald, Richard, 1916: 'Banaro Society: Social Organisation and Kinship System of a Tribe in the Interior of New Guinea', *Memoirs of the American Anthropological Association*, No. 8.
Tomlin, J. W. S., 1951: *Awakening, A History of the New Guinea Mission*, London, Fulham Palace.
Turner, Victor W., 1957: *Schism and Continuity in African Society*, Manchester University Press.
Van Velsen, J., 1964: *The Politics of Kinship*, Manchester University Press.
Waddell, E. W. and P. A. Krinks, 1968: 'The Organisation of Production and Distribution among the Orokaiva', *New Guinea Research Bulletin*, No. 24.
Wagner, Roy, 1967: *The Curse of Souw*, University of Chicago Press.
Watson, J. B., 1970: 'Society as Organised Flow', *South-Western Journal of Anthropology*, Vol. 26, June.
White, Nancy, n.d.: Manuscript Collection in English and Orokaiva.
Williams, F. E., 1924: *The Natives of the Purari Delta*, Territory of Papua, Anthropology Report no. 5.

Williams, F. E., 1925: 'Plant Emblems among the Orokaiva', *Journal of the R.A.I.*, 55: 405–24.
——, 1928: *Orokaiva Magic*, London, Oxford University Press.
——, 1930: *Orokaiva Society*, London, Oxford University Press.
——, 1932: 'Sex Affiliation and its Implications', *Journal of the R.A.I.*, 62: 51–81.
——, 1932/3: 'Trading Voyages from the Gulf of Papua', *Oceania*, III (2): 139–66.
——, 1934: 'Exchange Marriage and Exogamy', *Man*, 34: No. 131.
——, 1936: *Papuans of the Trans-Fly*, London, Oxford University Press.
——, 1940: *Drama of Orokolo*, London, Oxford University Press.
——, 1940/2: 'Natives of Lake Kutubu', *Oceania Monograph*, No. 6.
Wilson, Monica, 1952: *Good Company*, London, Oxford University Press.
——, 1959: *Communal Rituals of the Nyakusa*, London, Oxford University Press.
Worsley, Peter, 1957: *The Trumpet Shall Sound*, London, McGibbon and Kee.
Wurm, S. A., 1966: 'Language and Literacy', in: *New Guinea on the Threshold* (ed. E. K. Fisk), pp. 135–48, Canberra, Australian National University Press.
Young, Michael W., 1971: *Fighting with Food*, Cambridge University Press.

INDEX

237